INNOVATIONS IN OFFICE DESIGN

INNOVATIONS IN OFFICE DESIGN

THE CRITICAL INFLUENCE APPROACH TO EFFECTIVE WORK ENVIRONMENTS

Diane Stegmeier

WILEY

JOHN WILEY & SONS, INC.

Library of Congress Cataloging-in-Publication Data:

Stegmeier, Diane, 1954–
    Innovations in office design : the critical influence approach to effective work environments / Diane Stegmeier.
        p.   cm.
    Includes bibliographical references and index.
    ISBN 978-0-471-73041-5 (cloth)
      1. Office layout.   2. Work environment.   3. Office decoration.   I. Title.
    HF5547.2.F745   2008
    658.2'3—dc22
                                                                                            2007022260

Printed in the United States of America

10   9   8   7   6   5   4   3   2   1

This book is dedicated to the two most critical influences in my life:

To Lou, my best friend, husband, and self-proclaimed cheerleader, who encourages me to pursue my goals. And to our son, Matthew, the center of my universe and an amazing individual who lives up to the meaning of his name—gift from God—every day.

CONTENTS

FOREWORD

BY GREG BENDIS

Good advice is timeless—and so are good relationships. Diane Stegmeier and I have been in pursuit of excellence, and have shared the same core business values, for many years. Those values stem from immersing ourselves in our clients' world to help make a positive difference—for me, as a commercial real estate advisor, and for Diane, as a change management consultant. So I was very interested to learn of her 10-year research initiative exploring why seemingly appropriate workplace designs had failed.

Diane's efforts in examining the cultural, operational, and environmental factors impacting behavior in the workplace are impressive, and the results, eye-opening. In the words of Dr. Prentice Knight, CEO of CoreNet Global, the 7,000-member worldwide association of corporate real estate professionals, "Diane Stegmeier's landmark findings on workplace behavior in the corporate setting will prove vital in determining workplace strategy over the next 10 years." Having had the opportunity to preview the final manuscript for this book, I'm confident you will agree with Knight's testimonial on the significance of Diane's research results.

Innovations in Office Design is a reference book written for workplace professionals unlike any one I've ever read. It does not dictate a specific design solution nor advocate the product portfolio to complete the space. The book does not suggest organizations remove business leaders from their private offices and house them in the open plan, nor does it recommend decision makers cave in to human resistance to change, allowing managers to maintain dedicated, enclosed workspaces that may be occupied less than 40 percent of the workweek. Diane takes a truly comprehensive approach to understanding the business barriers to the successful implementation of physical space design—whether the workplace strategy is focused on cost reduction, supports the blended workforce resulting from a recent merger, centers on attracting and retaining talent, or aims at accommodating the multigenerational workforce. The Critical Influence methodology identifies areas of resistance to change and addresses them, enabling architectural and design firms to do what they do best—create the appropriate workplace solution.

"Form follows function" is a modern design philosophy I learned about while pursuing my degree in architecture. It is another common theme between Diane's and my approach when advising our clients. Unfortunately, however, businesses tend to take a backward approach to the acquisition and development of their work environments. First, a building is selected; then an architect is hired to fit the requirement into the space; once the plans are complete, a contractor is hired to build it; finally, furniture is ordered. When the space is ready, employees are uprooted from their existing environment and expected to function in new ways, reflecting new workplace behaviors deemed necessary for achieving the organization's goals. When these goals are not achieved, management is at a loss as to why their good intentions failed.

Because I am typically retained by my clients when they are first considering new accommodations, I have an excellent opportunity to pave the way properly for the architects, furniture vendors, and contractors to become engaged early in the process and to participate in necessary strategic exercises. Bringing together this "intellectual capital" as the strategy unfolds ensures that form truly does follow function, and that good intentions are ultimately realized. Now, what has also made it possible to better serve my clients is engaging Diane to educate the business leaders of the client organization on the Critical Influence System, even before I begin my work. Doing so ensures that the most appropriate real estate strategy for an organization can then be developed.

Innovations in Office Design is a must-read for anyone who wants to become a value-added partner in the process of creating a new work environment, and to differentiate themselves from those arriving late in the sequence of events—thus forced to operate in a reactionary mode where creativity and abilities are stifled. The Critical Influence Design Model featured in this book, in my opinion, is the key to communicating to clients and prospective clients alike an approach that will address the increasingly complex business issues with which they struggle today, as well as prepare them for emerging challenges they may not yet have considered. For the architectural and design community and all those who help shape the physical environment of the business world, consider the new knowledge you'll gain from reading this book to be good advice—and timeless.

Greg Bendis is a commercial real estate consultant and broker based in Newport Beach, California. He has developed and implemented real estate strategies for his clients in more than 160 cities in the United States and abroad.

PREFACE

I was recently asked what I hoped to achieve with this book, *Innovations in Office Design: The Critical Influence Approach to Effective Work Environments.* Good question.

I began to reflect on my research specializing in the impact of physical space on behavior in the workplace. My thoughts then turned to my study of the role of leadership in driving organizational change. I pondered the specific lessons I had learned from my postgraduate study of innovation and organizational change at Harvard, Duke, and Case Western Reserve Universities. As these thoughts began to converge, I came to realize that what I hope to achieve with this book is best told by a story I'd like to share with you now.

In the third century BC, Greek mathematician Archimedes was asked by King Hiero of Syracuse to ensure that his gold crown, made by the local goldsmith, included every bit of the precious metal the craftsman had been supplied to create the king's headdress. In a serendipitous visit to the public baths of Syracuse, Archimedes determined the mathematical formula to measure the volume of the king's crown—an irregular-shaped object—as he observed water spilling over the edge of the too-full tub into which he stepped. In his excitement, he apparently forgot he was unclothed. He ran through the streets of Syracuse naked, shouting "Eureka, I found it!"

As an author, my goal for you, the reader of this book, is to discover—at minimum—one important concept that will result in an "aha!" moment as it relates to your involvement in the development of effective workplaces. That key learning may shed light on the perplexities surrounding seemingly sound workplace solutions that ultimately failed. Perhaps a new approach or an added insight will contribute to elevating your current level of success in your chosen field.

A word of warning, however: When you discover an idea that you realize will save you much frustration on your next workplace project, please don't make the same mistake that Archimedes made. Do remain fully clothed. You know how your coworkers hate distractions in the workplace!

TRANSFORMATION NECESSITATES EMBRACING CHANGE

Throughout *Innovations in Office Design: The Critical Influence Approach to Effective Work Environments*, you'll be introduced to findings I've drawn from my research with organizations in diverse industries, which reveal barriers that have appeared on workplace transformation projects time and again. You may recognize challenges you've faced in your own work. You may also be exposed to obstacles you have not yet experienced, but that may surface in future projects.

A consistent message I hear from professionals—whether architects, interior designers, or facilities executives and corporate real estate leaders—who regularly confront resistance to change in the physical workplace is that they wish to be engaged in strategic planning at a higher level in the organization. These professionals do not like receiving "edicts" passed down from above, to which they can only react. They want to be contributors in early discussions, before the strategies are cast in stone, to give their input and advice regarding the challenges that affect the very core of the business. With a solid business case in hand, and by effectively positioning the importance of physical space to achieving overall organizational results, they can become active members of the team determining what those changes need to be and, thus, help drive the transformation.

Innovations in Office Design started out as a message to the architectural and design communities about the challenges they face in designing workplaces. This book has been written specifically for *you*. To say this is a book on workplace design that touches on resistance to change is an understatement.

My message is *about* resistance to change—applied to the physical work environment. It focuses on the challenges inherent to developing effective workplace strategies and the resultant physical space solutions aimed at satisfying seemingly conflicting objectives. The book is about:

- Improving collaboration in the workplace to increase the organization's innovative outputs.
- Dramatic cost cutting to improve the profitability and financial strength of the enterprise.
- Branding the organization to create a beneficial difference in the eyes of both external and internal customers.
- Emphasizing attraction and retention strategies in preparation for the severe talent shortage that will plague employers.
- Facing the escalating rate of restructuring, mergers, and acquisitions.
- Coping with the complexities of the multigenerational, and increasingly diverse, workforce.
- Doing more work with fewer people, and competing for limited internal resources.
- Addressing employee demands for work-life balance.
- Understanding an increasingly distributed workforce.
- Creating competitive advantage through new products, services, and approaches to the market.

Consider the learning objectives I've set forth in the following sidebar. View them as a personal challenge that, by addressing them, will help you to arm yourself with the ammunition required to protect your workplace projects—and yourself—from

LEARNING OBJECTIVES

- Identify barriers to the successful implementation of workplace strategy, avoiding the common mistakes made in driving change.
- Serve as a strategic business partner to the organization, and join in decision making earlier in the process.
- Ensure the workplace solution does not bear 100 percent of the burden of transforming the way people work.

unreasonable expectations from the organization on changing behaviors in the workplace.

Increasingly, I am convinced that the audience for *Innovations in Office Design* includes not only architecture and design professionals, but also those in human resources and business management in general, who are faced with resistance to change and organizational inertia. I am confident that there is an "aha!" or two in this book for them as well.

ACKNOWLEDGMENTS

For their willingness to share their talents and expertise with the readers of *Innovations in Office Design: The Critical Influence Approach to Effective Work Environments*, through diverse case studies and exemplars of workplace design, I express my sincere thanks to the following architectural and design firms: BHDP Architecture, *Cincinnati, Ohio*; Callison, *Seattle, Washington*; CUH2A, *Princeton, New Jersey*; Eppstein Uhen Architects, *Milwaukee, Wisconsin*; Gensler, *Denver, Colorado, Phoenix, Arizona, San Francisco, California, and Santa Monica, California*; Hillier Architects, *Princeton, New Jersey*; Hixson, Inc., *Cincinnati, Ohio*; HOK Canada, *Toronto, Ontario*; Meyer Design, Inc., *Ardmore, Pennsylvania*; Robert Luchetti Associates, Inc., *Cambridge, Massachusetts*; Shepley Bulfinch Richardson & Abbott, *Boston, Massachusetts*; STUDIOS Architecture, *San Francisco, California and Washington, D.C.*; the Design Alliance Architects, *Pittsburgh, Pennsylvania*; and Whitney Inc., *Oak Brook, Illinois*.

This book could not have been written without the generosity of those who shared their insights and lessons they have learned from their vast experiences, and those who contributed their unique talents and skills, thereby contributing to the success of this initiative. I am forever grateful to the following individuals: Hal Adler, Greg Bendis, Kevin Beswick, Christopher Budd, Collin Burry, IIDA, LEED AP; Don Crichton, ARIDO IDC; Phil Dordai, AIA, LEED AP; Brian Ferguson, Eileen Forbes, Sandrine Fugier, Mark Golan, Beth Harmon-Vaughan, FIIDA, *Assoc.* AIA, LEED AP; Paul Harris, Judith Heerwagen, Ph.D.; Bob Johansen, Ph.D.; Kevin Kampschroer, Kevin Kelly, AIA; Brian Kowalchuk, AIA; Arnold Levin, Blake Mourer, AIA, LEED AP; Suzanne Nicholson, ASID, NCIDQ; Mike Parker, IFMA; Kevin Powell, Martin Powell, AIA, NCARB, LEED AP; Vladimir Pravotorov, Sherman Roberts, Kevin Robinson, Mike Stanczak, Erik Sueberkrop, FAIA; Lisa Velte, SPHR; Al West, and Ron Weston, AIA, LEED AP.

For their patience in working around my deadline schedule for *Innovations in Office Design*, I extend my appreciation to my family, friends, and clients, who never hesitated to accommodate me so that I could devote the time and effort necessary to ensure successful results.

I also wish to acknowledge John Czarnecki, Raheli Millman, Donna Conte, and Janice Borzendowski of John Wiley & Sons, Inc., for their advice and technical expertise in transforming more than 10 years of research, education, and experiences from a concept into the book you are holding in your hands today.

INTRODUCTION

The foundation of Critical Influence Design lies in research findings on the impact of physical space on behavior in the workplace. In 1996, I began to study example after example of office workplaces that "did not work." This exploration was not about critiquing the competencies of the architectural and design firms, or the design integrity of the failed workplace transformation projects. The investigation was centered on why appropriately designed workplace solutions failed. What barriers existed—overtly or covertly—that were not being recognized and addressed by the client organization?

What started as a quiet and personal curiosity grew to involve architects and interior designers with whom I had worked on past projects. I invited them to share their challenges and frustrations. Gathering honest feedback from trusted colleagues was a natural, easy process. I am neither an architect nor an interior designer, so I did not pose a competitive threat to their business firms. And because I do not advocate specific products, I am unbiased as to the portfolio of components selected to support the physical work environment. My work is focused on identifying and helping the client organization address the barriers to the effectiveness of the workplace design. I assist in clearing the canvas so that the architect or interior designer can paint the appropriate workplace landscape.

What started as a trickle of comments quickly began to feel as if someone had opened up the floodgates. Initial interactions led to unsolicited calls from other members of the architectural and design communities who had heard about my exploration of factors creating barriers to workplace strategy success. Contract furniture manufacturers and dealers invited me to meet with workplace transformation teams in their customer accounts, which, more often than not, resulted in a request to sit down with the organization's top executives. Now I was hearing the real story. Along with the articulation of the actual business issues these leaders felt impacted the enterprise negatively, I saw the visible signs of concern and frustration on their faces and in their body language. Direct and to the point, these executives did not attempt to frame their business issues within the context of physical space for my benefit. I could do that myself later. What I was gathering were illustrations of the barriers that were hindering the core of the enterprise from advancing in its goals. From separate dialogues, I was able to glean the type of data I needed to develop a comprehensive approach that could be applied universally to most any organization.

WHAT DEFINES THE WORKPLACE DESIGN CLIMATE?

The workplace design climate is a function of the prevailing psychological state of businesses tied to the economy. Much like the swing of a pendulum, the confidence of business leaders to invest in new workplace environments can move from one extreme to the other. During a robust economy, new office buildings and renovations of existing space are recognized as necessary to support new work patterns and activities. Budgets are more generous, and there is focus on "doing the project the right way." When the economy shows signs of slowing down, organizations are quick to put workplace projects on hold or cut the initiatives altogether. And during weak economic conditions, when a facilities project is deemed absolutely necessary, "doing things right" quickly becomes "How can we put a bandage on what we currently have?"

The corporate tightening of the belt in the early 1990s eventually relaxed as the strengthened economy resulted in the need to hire new employees in response to an increased demand for products and services. Many white-collar workers who had been downsized due to business process reengineering earlier in the decade had taken the time to invest in learning new, more advanced skills prior to reentering the workplace. Combined with their experience prior to cuts in the workforce, their newly acquired education meant these so-called knowledge workers were poised to entertain multiple job offers from companies struggling to secure the talent that was needed to support the attainment of redefined growth objectives.

During the mid- to late 1990s, when the economy was strong and venture capital was readily available, many start-up companies appeared on the business landscape. These new firms typically began operating in the black much sooner than expected, attracting additional financial investments, as well as job candidates looking for the excitement of working in a start-up—and the signing bonuses, hefty paychecks, and stock options previously only available to the executive ranks in the corporations from which they were resigning. Dollars were invested in the physical space; the start-ups spent money "because they could," and the established, larger companies as a tactic to support what was being called the War for Talent.

The pendulum changed direction again, heading toward the other extreme. With an economy already considered weak, business spending came to a screeching halt following 9/11. Wave after wave of downsizing, instituted in reaction to a paralyzed economy, impacted more than the individuals who lost their jobs. Yes, staff members who survived phase after phase of layoffs still drew weekly or biweekly paychecks, and earned vacation time and health care benefits; nevertheless, they were affected by psychological stress. Employees felt little security in the workplace. There was no guarantee they would not be targeted in the next round of "rightsizing"; they saw other talented coworkers pack up their personal belongings after receiving their termination notices; and they knew family members, friends, or others in the community who had been affected by the reduction in the workforce. To many of these individuals, the organizational attitude was "be thankful you have a job." No one dared ask for a new ergonomic chair, much less offer suggestions about how the entire physical workplace environment could be revamped to inspire innovation.

As the pendulum slowly reversed its course again, these survivors moved into the robust economy feeling little allegiance to their employers; rather, they had a personal commitment to look out for themselves at all costs. Justifiably, employers became fearful of losing key talent and so began formulating retention strategies targeted toward those employees who possessed unique skills not easily replaced or who had strong industry knowledge or competitive intelligence. During this time period, sophisticated employers focused on preparing for the future. Thus, updating the work environment was seen as an investment in attracting job candidates, to hedge against the next talent shortage.

Fast forward to today. What have business leaders learned from these extremes in economic health? Will office project budgets ever be considered generous again? It's time to reflect upon what have we learned during these two extreme conditions—and the cautious positions in between when the economy was beginning to heat up or cool off. The key learning, as observed in recent, well-thought-out investments in upgrading workplace environments, is that a conservative approach enables the organization to weather the storms during shifts in the economy. Ignoring the "power of place" by failing to provide the appropriate workplace to optimize employee performance in a period of business growth can be just as foolish as initiating an expensive workplace expansion just when the company is planning to lay off 40 percent of its staff. The key to smart investment in the workplace is to be generous with that which enables flexibility. The most adaptable components are typically not the least expensive, yet they can save money in the long run by accommodating new staff members in times of growth, or supporting more work done by fewer people in periods of economic recovery. An ever-present focus on incorporating flexibility into workplace design can help leverage limited resources regardless of the economy in general or the specific financial condition of the organization itself at any given point in time.

PREVIEW OF WHAT'S AHEAD

Throughout *Innovations in Office Design* you'll notice a strong emphasis on examples and case studies of organizational challenges architectural and design firms must meet as they create work environments that foster collaboration and leverage the interdisciplinary talents of the workforce. Chapter 1, "An Interdisciplinary Approach," sets the tone for architects and designers who are themselves adopting a project framework of diverse talents. You will read about the success of a very large interdisciplinary team—one with 125 members from a variety of architectural and design firms and related professions. You'll walk through a case study on the Sprint Nextel operational headquarters project, from initial concept to move-in. You'll also learn how that company's workplace has evolved to accommodate its workforce today.

The rigorous training that architects and interior designers undergo seldom prepares them for all they face head-on in the business world. Aligning the firm with experts in complementary areas of specialization can produce better workplace solutions that address the complex requirements of clients. Chapter 1 identifies the values—and perceived risks—of an interdisciplinary approach. For individuals committed to partnering, with a goal of better serving their clients, this chapter of the book includes a compilation of key components identified by those who have been successful in engaging in collaborative initiatives.

What Is Critical Influence Design?

Many organizations' attempts to implement new workplace strategies centered on improving collaborative human behavior have produced less than optimal results—or have failed altogether—due to influences that the company may not know are linked. The physical workplace has a strong impact on employee behavior, yet those charged with developing workplace solutions must understand the other factors that impact employee use of the workplace. Chapter 2, "The Critical Influence System,"[1] introduces an infrastructure composed of interdependent tangible and intangible factors that can enable or hinder the achievement of organizational goals.

In case you haven't already guessed, the physical workplace is a Critical Influence on employee behavior. It's actually one of 15 influences you'll be introduced to in Chapter 2. Frankly, from the pressure organizations place on workplace

professionals—architects, interior designers, facilities and corporate real estate executives, as well as the many allied fields that support office design projects—you would think that the physical workplace is intended to solve all of the enterprise's problems. And we wonder why the workplace often bears 100 percent of the burden of transforming the way people work! It should not, and it doesn't have to, if workplace professionals gain an understanding of the barriers standing in the way of full optimization of the appropriate workplace solution.

The quiet curiosity that began, in 1996, to nag me to investigate why good workplace strategies often fail has indeed grown into the passion that drives my work. I'll even admit to what some have called my obsession to help organizations better manage change. Many of the concepts I share in this book stem from lessons I learned researching 140 organizations, in 24 industries, over a 10-year time frame. Participants in the research study represent diverse business enterprises, including banking and finance, high-tech, nonprofit, manufacturing, energy, consumer products, telecommunications, professional services, pharmaceutical and healthcare, education and research, entertainment, transportation, government, and others. Headquarters locations for these entities cross diverse geographic boundaries throughout the United States, as well as in Canada and Western Europe. Strategically, the businesses targeted for this study varied in size from under 100 employees to those with tens of thousands of employees spanning the globe.

Research has revealed that developing and implementing the ideal office design does not guarantee the physical space will be used as the designer intended. Furthermore, even if the end users make an honest attempt to work in the space as the physical cues indicate, other Critical Influences may impede the type of behaviors the organization requires to achieve its goals. Archimedes may have discovered his mathematical formula in an accidental, serendipitous manner, but nothing quite so spontaneous or glamorous led to my discovery of the various elements of the Critical Influence System. For me, it was a slow process, unfolding over a decade, during which I compiled data on each individual Critical Influence I found to impact the success or failure of the physical workplace strategy. I identified recurring problems and analyzed interrelated factors with which organizations were struggling. The Critical Influence Design Model—an outcome of this research on the Critical Influence System—is a multidisciplinary approach that incorporates practical design techniques, management principles, and behavioral studies.

Importance of Critical Influence Design to Innovation Goals

A key finding of my research was that innovation is increasingly an important area of focus for business leaders today. The senior executives of 89.3 percent of the organizations in this study, initiated in 1996, said they were concerned about the lack of innovation in their enterprises and recognized collaboration as a means to improving innovative outputs. Participants in the research stated this emphasis on innovation in a number of ways, including:

- Improve speed-to-market.
- Gain competitive advantage.
- Create revenue streams through new products, services, markets, or approaches.
- Change the rules of the game in the industry.
- Attract investors and employees via image.
- Serve customers better, faster, cheaper.

The results of research conducted by the Innovation Exchange at London Business School corroborate my findings. The Exchange uncovered that 70 percent of organizations with "a positive attitude towards innovation were outperforming their competitors." An additional 17 percent of the companies studied declared performance at least on par with their competitors due to an organizational mind-set that emphasizes innovation. Quantitatively, these firms had realized an increase in profits and market share when compared with their closest industry rivals.[2]

Chapter 3, "Creativity, Innovation, and the Innovation-Friendly Workplace," will introduce a common oversight made in office design, which should be addressed as organizations come to rely on an increasing percentage of annual revenue from products or services in their first several years in the market. We'll also look at a "wave of innovation" as it coincides with the classic marketing approach of viewing a product's sales over time throughout that product's life cycle. We'll tie that concept to the need for maximum flexibility, mobility, and adaptability of the physical workplace, and the opportunity for architects and designers to translate those requirements to support the fluidity of the organization.

"It is not the strongest of the species that survive, but the one most responsive to change."
—CHARLES DARWIN

> *"The greatest danger for most of us is not that our aim is too high, and we miss it, but that it is too low and we reach it."*
>
> —MICHELANGELO

Importance of Critical Influence Design to Profit Goals

While not every organization is strategically focused on climbing to higher levels of innovative output, employee collaboration, or team dynamics, the benefits resulting from improvements related to such initiatives are hard to ignore. The examples featured in the book can also be interpreted and used as lessons learned in the overall improvement of human performance in the workplace—a sound business objective for most organizations. Achieving higher levels of profitability is on the mind of most business leaders, whether it is the number 1 priority or slightly lower on their list of objectives. It is only by elevating the enterprise to an appropriate altitude of financial strength and success that enables the most profit-centric executive to take a moment to look down and see a whole other set of possibilities of what the organization is capable of achieving.

A facilities executive from a global company recently asked me if taking the time to gain knowledge of the Critical Influence System was valuable if her only charge was to cut costs. In her words, her employer was focused entirely on the bottom line and finding ways to improve profitability—now! My first response was that, of course, a corporatewide emphasis on strengthening the financial health of the enterprise is a worthy charge, and that the goal of improving profitability is certainly understandable, and common, among maturing industries such as the one where she worked. Given that intensifying global competition had begun to reduce the company's market share and negatively impact profitability, resulting in customer perception of its products as commodities, her employer was responding very predictably to their position in a maturing industry.

But then I told her that in my interface with clients, in which profitability was *the* driving force, knowledge of the Critical Influence System could, indeed, make a difference. Those professionals charged with the development, design, and implementation of a productive work environment, who have a better understanding of what influences employee behavior, have said they are able to operate "a few steps ahead" of the workforce population. They can anticipate where resistance is likely to surface, which allows them to develop contingency plans where appropriate. Chapter 3 will explain how to reach a balance between the design of physical spaces to enable innovation and performance maximization to ensure optimal levels of productivity.

Conditions Critical Influence Design Was Developed to Address

Professionals in the fields of architecture, interior design, real estate, and facilities management are often expected to achieve seemingly conflicting objectives, such as:

- Aggressively slash costs by reducing real estate holdings, closing unprofitable facilities, consolidating locations, subletting facilities no longer needed, moving managers from private offices to an open plan, reducing square footage of workstations, and switching from dedicated to shared—or unassigned—workspaces.

- At the same time, continue to support the organization's other goals of increasing productivity through teamwork and collaboration, improving employee morale, providing employees more choices and control over the work environment, increasing innovation, and creating an environmental showcase to attract and retain talent.

Chapter 4, "Under the Influence," offers insight into which workplace transformation projects are most susceptible to the Critical Influence System. The holistic approach of Critical Influence Design was developed in response to numerous clients who struggled with implementing physical space changes in conjunction with other significant organizational challenges, such as:

- Restructuring, mergers, and acquisitions
- High-velocity environments
- Physical space as a currency
- Competitive office versus collaborative workplace
- Multigenerational workforce
- Telework
- Emphasis on work-life balance
- Attraction and retention strategies

The case studies featured in Chapter 5, "Collaborative Workplaces That Work," were selected to represent diverse organizational profiles. The workplace projects articulate the universal nature of Critical

Influences on behavior in the workplace regardless of the industry in which the enterprise operates or its size or location. These studies include the following exciting workplace initiatives: Alcoa Corporate Center, Marconi Communications, SEI Investments, GSA WorkPlace 20\20, Analytical Graphics Inc., Pfizer Global Research & Development, Cisco—the Connected Workplace, Gensler Headquarters, and De Lage Landen. Common threads running through each of these, and other successful workplace transformation projects, are highlighted to demonstrate examples related to the Critical Influence System in this chapter as well as throughout other sections of the book.

Chapter 6, "Collaborative Workplace Principles,"[3] shares the results of numerous facilitated brainstorming sessions conducted for interior designers, architects, and end users, where the focus was on identifying and analyzing factors that can enable, or create barriers to, innovation in the workplace. In some of these meetings, the exercise was tied to a client's specific goal to improve collaboration in the workplace in order to produce richer innovative results for the enterprise. In other cases, the activity was structured as a workshop for architects and designers from a variety of diverse firms, where all participants could learn from the knowledge exchange among industry peers. This chapter of the book identifies cultural, operational, and environmental elements that enable collaborative behavior, and continues the emphasis on understanding elements that impact the success of workplace design. Interior design alone will not create fertile conditions for optimal performance. Other key factors, especially those that business leaders define, influence, and control, must also be considered if the physical space is to serve as an effective guide to desired employee behaviors.

Chapter 7, "Collaborative Principle Index,"[4] puts a humorous spin on some of the demands that organizations make on the office environment—sometimes expecting it to perform nothing short of a miracle. There is an element of truth, as well as lessons to be shared, in the section titled "The Eight Myths of Workplace Collaboration."[5] Insights have been captured from diverse organizations that have struggled with changing behaviors when challenging these myths. In this section, each myth is linked to specific Collaborative Workplace Principles that were applied—or should have been applied—to meet that challenge.

Chapter 8, "Critical Influence Design Model,"[6] illustrates the interdisciplinary approach to effective workplace design. Beginning with a simplified graphic depicting a collaborative relationship between the architectural and design firm, a commercial real estate advisor and a change management consultancy, the narrative explains the graphic in terms of partner roles and the ownership of the workplace strategy by the A&D organization. The chapter also offers insight into a sample project in the form of a timeline, complete with responsibilities, phases, and milestones. The model is then expanded to include specialized expertise required by the client's unique business needs. This portion of the book also explores emerging areas of specialization that may be brought onboard to collaborative workplace design teams in the future, and shares a futuristic view of the Critical Influence Design Model.

What Critical Influence Design Is Not

Critical Influence Design differs from other approaches to developing workplace strategies and solutions in that it is not prescriptive of a particular workplace solution. Rather, it identifies and addresses barriers to the successful implementation of the architectural and design firm's workplace strategy. Thus, Critical Influence Design should not be regarded as a bandage approach, to quickly repair only the surface of an inefficient workplace. It is better described as a thorough diagnosis by a team of "surgeons," each of whom possesses a particular expertise.

The methodology also cannot be implemented in isolation by an architect, interior designer, or other workplace professional. The active participation of the organization's senior management is required.

In short, Critical Influence Design, with its integration of practical design techniques, management principles, and behavioral studies is unlike other methodologies. Chances are, the complexity of your clients' business challenges is unlike any they've faced in the past. Driving significant workplace change necessitates taking a significantly different approach. Certainly, the benefits to the client can be numerous, but the architectural or design firm stands to gain much from the process as well. The opportunity to be perceived as a strategic business partner of the client

organization may very well be the greatest end result of all.

In today's fast-paced business environment, it seems everyone is looking for a quick fix. Shouldn't a new solution for the physical workplace produce instantaneous results? The perception that there is no time to wait for the behaviors of the workforce to change is short-sighted. For when an organization insists upon just-in-time change, and is able to achieve some observable sign of change in employee actions, that change is typically driven by fear, and thus is typically only a surface-level reaction to the situation at hand rather than sustainable behavioral change. Even in consulting engagements, during which the initial dialogue with the business leaders of the client organization is heavily focused on measurable results, by the time the change management proposal is approved, a contract is written, and work is underway, often there is a reluctance to establish baseline metrics of how well the current physical workplace is supporting the desired employee behaviors. There is an ever-present sense of urgency to move forward, to create the ideal work environment solution. Fast-forward to the organization's employees happily working in the new building or space. When the time comes to measure the improvement of new versus old physical space, the executives are looking so far into the future they may have little interest in determining the degree to which their investment in the new office environment produced measurable results.

Chapter 9, "Applying the Model," makes a final business case for an interdisciplinary approach to workplace design, by highlighting client business issues that will

"It's hard to increase speed when the gas pedal is already pushed to the floor."
—AUTHOR UNKNOWN

increasingly need to be addressed as part of the workplace strategies architects and interior designers develop in the future. This chapter illustrates preconditions for success in adopting the Critical Influence Design Model on a workplace transformation project. Chapter 9 also serves as a compilation of key "takeaways" from the preceding chapters—a refresher on important concepts, lessons learned from diverse architectural and design firms and their clients, and the words of respected thought leaders.

There is no one right answer for how to transform the workplace and the behaviors of those employed to work in it. Nor does the Critical Influence Design Model attempt to serve as a paint-by-number kit for the ideal workplace design that will attract, engage, and retain talented employees, generate collaboration and knowledge exchange, as well as produce innovative outputs for the organization. If such a template were available to those planning new workplace environments, it would not be enough. We would also want a user's manual that would include a troubleshooting guide to advise us how to immediately detect, then eliminate, each factor contributing to human resistance to change.

NOTES

[1] Stegmeier, Diane, Critical Influence System, 2002.
[2] von Stamm, Bettina, "About: Innovation," www.designcouncil.org.uk.
[3] Stegmeier, Diane, Collaborative Workplace Principles, 2002, www.stegmeierconsulting.com.
[4] Rosenblatt, Paul, and Diane Stegmeier, Collaborative Principle Index, 2003.
[5] Rosenblatt, Paul, and Diane Stegmeier, The 8 Myths of Workplace Collaboration, 2003.
[6] Stegmeier, Diane, Critical Influence Design Model, 2006, www.stegmeierconsulting.com.

CHAPTER 1
AN INTERDISCIPLINARY APPROACH

"It is amazing what you can accomplish if you do not care who gets the credit."
—HARRY TRUMAN

Creative thinking that leads to innovation occurs in diverse fields of work: science, mathematics, the arts, and others. In many circumstances within these branches of knowledge, collaboration is central to the development of new ideas, procedures, products, and creations. To devise workplace environments that effectively support new ways of thinking, planners and designers can learn from parallel fields. Doing this, however, requires an open mind and an ability to translate work behaviors from other disciplines for use in the white-collar workplace. The Critical Influence Design approach will give readers new insight to help them make these translations.

In *About: Innovation,*[1] Dr. Bettina von Stamm conveys a need for a shared language between designers and managers in order to break down communication barriers, which exist due to differences in education and value systems. According to von Stamm, it is a challenge to embed an understanding of design in business education, and vice versa. To meet this challenge, the emphasis should be placed on the benefits the client will receive by taking an interdisciplinary approach, one that brings design and business professionals together, rather than viewing one skill set as more important than the other to the success of a project. As von Stamm writes, we should be building on the strengths of these two disciplines: "The idea is not to find the lowest common denominator but make the most of the differences."

VALUES AND PERCEIVED RISKS OF AN INTERDISCIPLINARY APPROACH

In 2002, I had the good fortune to meet Beth Harmon-Vaughan at the Foundation for Interior Design Education Research (FIDER) Future Vision strategic planning workshop. Harmon-Vaughan was on the board of directors of this organization, which sets the standards for interior design education and conducts the quality assurance process of accreditation. I had been invited to facilitate the strategy session and guide the organization's design leaders through a process to gain consensus on common goals and establish objectives for the future of FIDER. (Note: FIDER, founded in 1970, is now known as the Council for Interior Design Accreditation.[2])

Four years later, I interviewed Harmon-Vaughan for *Innovations in Office Design: The Critical Influence Approach to Effective Work Environments.*[3] Her insight on collaborative teams is drawn from diverse experiences, often working side by side with design firms and construction companies that, though competitors, shared a focus—the best interest of the client. In "The Case for Collaboration" featured in the *Implications Newsletter* (April, 2006) by InformeDesign, she argued the need for a new model for project leadership. In the past, the various resources could be deployed in a linear sequence, whereby one specialist's expertise could be built upon the contribution of the resource touching the process before it was handed off. A common concern about this type of approach is that it involves an extended period of time to develop the workplace design. To address that concern, Harmon-Vaughan recommends leveraging technology and adopting an iterative model, whereby the network of experts can quickly design and examine various alternatives, proceeding on a fast-track basis.[4]

The iterative approach can result in savings of both time and money. Even more important is that the workplace solution is a much better

one, comprising the synergy of multiple experts working together to contribute every step along the way.

Critical Influence Design also endorses moving away from a linear design process, and involves a holistic, integrated approach in managing the client's workplace changes, as well as other organizational changes impacting the human capital of the company. In my work as a change management consultant, I may be pulled into a project quite late in the process, for what I call the "bandage approach." The new workplace design, including numerous iterations, has already been presented to the client, but the communication strategy has not yet been developed and rumors are running rampant, resulting in an increasing level of resistance among employees. My job is to convince the workforce that they should accept the new workplace as "the right thing to do for the business," a task complicated by the fact that each employee is concentrating on what he or she is losing personally. Unfortunately, there is little fluidity at this stage of the game for negotiation. The decisions have been made, and it's really too late to do much more than help the wounds heal a bit more quickly.

What I typically uncover are numerous barriers to the newly designed workplace, preventing it ever having a chance to be successful. As people begin moving into the new office, the physical work environment becomes the perpetrator of all wrongs. Everything that is wrong with the company, its processes, and employees' behaviors is attributed to the new workplace. The openness of the new office is to blame for acoustical distractions and interruptions by coworkers. The new teaming area designed for collaboration is not being used. Inconsiderate workplace behaviors have not changed a bit and, in fact, seem magnified in the new space. All these perceptions reflect negatively on the organization's internal workplace transformation team, along with their external architectural and design partners.

Digging deeper into the client organization, I then discover a number of different initiatives or strategies being implemented simultaneously, yet independently. There may be significant departmental improvements, such as an information technology (IT) strategy focused on implementing an enterprise resource planning (ERP) system, a human resources (HR) initiative focused on increasing employee engagement, or a sales support client segmentation strategy to realign customer service and all internal support mechanisms. In each of these areas for business improvement, the workforce will be impacted by changes being driven by IT, HR, and sales support, *in addition* to the adaptations employees will be asked to make as a result of the new physical workplace solution. Ideally, the client should have implemented and managed change on an integrated basis; conversely, the introduction of a new workplace design should not have been carried out by the workplace transformation team in isolation, without the appropriate support from the enterprise.

From my research—and the resultant theory on the Critical Influence System impacting human behavior in the workplace—I share two key findings:

1. The success of workplace transformation is impacted by other influences on the organization's workforce.
2. Workplace transformation creates an opportunity to drive other changes necessary for the organization's success in the future.

Why does the development of a change management plan remain a linear step in the design process, rather than being integrated early, as part of an interdisciplinary approach? Too often, architectural and design professionals progress on the development of the workplace strategy in a linear, sequential fashion until they uncover stumbling blocks. At this point, an external change management consultant is called in to assist, to reduce human resistance to a manageable level. The linear process is then passed back to the designer. Not only does this approach waste time, it also results in a much lower level of employee acceptance of the workplace changes. Instead, parallel paths need to be established, with touchpoints along the way, to ensure barriers are identified and addressed as early in the process as possible— ideally, prior to the workplace strategy being developed.

What are the risks of not addressing workforce resistance early in the design of the workplace solution? Significant changes in the eyes of employees disrupt business processes and shift focus away from achieving the critical goals of the organization. Productivity declines as distractions increase. As mentioned above, too often, organizations are juggling the transformation of the work environment, as well as a number of other changes, in isolation, yet members of the workforce may be touched by many or all of the issues: adapting to new leadership and structures; fear of ongoing waves of downsizing; concerns over changing expectations for work behaviors; anxiety that the organizational culture will not be sustained due to mergers, acquisitions, or consolidations; concerns over greater individual accountability, or fear that functions will be outsourced. The list lengthens as complexities in the business world intensify.

The cost of helping overcome employee resistance to change through an effective change management process is typically much less than the costs of the associated risks:

- Loss of productivity prior to, during, and following the change
- Reduction of innovative outputs due to withholding of critical information by staff members
- Loss of intellectual capital due to unnecessary employee turnover
- Reduction of competitive advantage as members of the workforce join other organizations in the specific industry, or employers in the same geographic region vie for talent
- Decline in customer satisfaction and profitability due to a reduction in external focus

Workplace professionals are under intense pressure to produce physical space solutions that drive the desired organizational results. Their most innovative office design ideas may need to be compromised, hence diluted, to a less-than-optimal recommendation on how people should be working in support of the establishment's short- and long-term goals. Identifying and addressing barriers to change early in the design process is less costly than attacking those same issues later. Moreover, the design

process may have to be interrupted to combat the threat of managers resigning from the company because their private offices are being taken away. This results—at minimum—in lost productivity, and the intended project deadlines being thrown out the window, whether or not key employees do leave the company.

Quite often, there is a perceived risk of a loss of control by the designer when another workplace authority is brought in to support the project. Will the planners and designers be seen as incompetent because they need additional assistance? How should the overlap of knowledge be addressed when a new expert is placed on the project team? Is the client paying for duplicate efforts? Although each professional contributing to the workplace project has a unique area of specialization, they share some common ground, which, from the outside looking in, one could construe as redundancy or knowledge overlap.

In fact, speaking from experience, there *should* be an abundance of common ground—after all, each expert is performing in the workplace field. You want your project teammates to have full awareness of your functions; that does not mean, however, that they are providing the same services to the client. And it certainly does not require handing over control to another expert who has been pulled in to contribute a narrow area of expertise. A shared commitment to do what's best for the client's project of course may require compromise; and the clear definition of roles is imperative as part of this effort. True professionals will make these collaborative engagements work as smoothly as possible and, in the process, will benefit personally from the knowledge gained through these experiences.

To illustrate the effect of unfounded fears, I'll share a situation involving Christopher Budd, a principal of STUDIOS Architecture, and a highly talented workplace expert. Budd truly "gets it." He is a rare individual who fully understands the workplace and the impact of physical space on behavior. As the story goes, a third party, looking from the outside in, knew that change in management was an important issue for a particular customer, but was extremely hesitant to rock the boat by introducing external consultants to the architectural firm and its client. At the time, Budd was director of STUDIOS Consulting Services (SCS). The third party was open in sharing his perception that a change management consultant would be "stepping on the toes" of STUDIOS, an architectural firm with a very strong consulting practice. After much delay caused by fears of the third party that he would lose the opportunity to sell products to the client if he ruffled the feathers of the architects, I was introduced to the project team. The professionals on this team welcomed the addition of change management specialists— and, by the way, saw no risk of losing control of the design process. They understood immediately how my education, research, and experience would complement the architectural firm's expertise. The only negative was the client's frustration that the third party had not introduced me earlier in the process!

Long story short, the fears of the third party were unfounded. Those confident in their talents are typically the most generous in sharing their philosophies and expertise with other professionals, and Budd is no exception. He possesses the intellectual curiosity that opens his mind to other workplace specialists' theories and approaches; and he has the kind of passion for excellence that ignites creativity in collaborative work groups.

Convincing other industry professionals that you, as an outside consultant, present no threat to their existence can be challenging for anyone put in the position of becoming a member of interdisciplinary workplace teams and contributing unique expertise. Often, it can be difficult to get people to understand that you are working with the client to identify and address the barriers to the successful implementation of the architectural and design professionals' workplace solution. When you get the "deer in the headlights" response, it may be much easier to tell them what you *don't* do. You are neither an architect nor an interior designer; you do not endorse a particular workplace design or product solution. What you do provide is:

- *Education* to the client's leadership team on the critical influences on their workforce
- *Identification* of specific barriers that may hinder the success of the workplace strategy
- *Consultation* on reducing those barriers in preparation for the workplace transformation

INTERPRETATION BY DIVERSE DISCIPLINES

An interdisciplinary approach can also mean interpreting the client's industry-specific business issues by viewing the challenges through a different set of lenses and developing the workplace solution without assumptions about that industry or with preconceived notions about what a workplace should look like for a business operating in a particular type of commercial enterprise. To understand these concepts, consider the following practical example of a client wanting to change its internal processes from a linear sequence to a collaborative integration of efforts. You'll have the opportunity to read the entire case study on this example in Chapter 5, "Collaborative Workplaces That Work."

Brian Kowalchuk, director of Design & Architecture of CUH2A in Princeton, New Jersey, was asked by a client to create a "hierarchy of spaces." Many workplace professionals would have interpreted that request as the desire to reflect the organizational chain of command, using an increasing allocation of square footage and higher quality of finishes as employees moved up the corporate ladder. But for this client, Pfizer Global Research & Development's Drug Discovery Laboratory in Groton, Connecticut, it had nothing to do with corporate power or politics. Rather, the hierarchy of spaces was intended to reflect work process in the discovery of pharmaceutical innovations. Thus, CUH2A's workplace design had to accommodate a specific infrastructure for the total number of teams of chemists, as well as the number of chemists per team. The same approach had to be implemented to develop the physical space for the total number of teams of biologists, including the number of biologists per team (see sidebar and Figure 1-1).

To do so, they sought not only to reduce the amount of time to bring a new product to market but, perhaps more importantly, to improve the quality of the organization's innovative output. In Chapter 5, you'll learn the details of how Kowalchuk and the CUH2A team leveraged physical space to create an environment centered on discovery and innovation, and in the course of their design work, took an approach that had never been attempted on such a large scale in the pharmaceutical industry (see Figure 1-2).

Another benefit synergy brings to an organization is that it enables diverse interpretations of the same challenge by colleagues from various disciplines. Engaging peers from other departments or groups in problem solving not only can expedite resolution but may, in fact, result in a much more creative solution to the quandary. In my consulting practice, I often interact with facilities managers through my involvement with the International Facility Management Association (IFMA) and its Corporate Facilities Council (formerly known as the IFMA Corporate Headquarters Council).[5] Many professionals in this

PFIZER GLOBAL RESEARCH & DEVELOPMENT'S "HIERARCHY OF SPACES"

CUH2A created collaborative areas appropriate for the size of the group in the research community, from the smallest to the entire Pfizer Global Research & Development campus.

1. Chemistry Group: 3 people
2. Chemistry Lab: 6 people (2 teams of 3 individuals)
3. Chemistry Discipline Critical Mass: 12 people
4. Biology Discipline Critical Mass: 18 people
5. Therapeutic Zone Team: 30 to 60 people
6. Wing: 120 people
7. Floor: 270 people

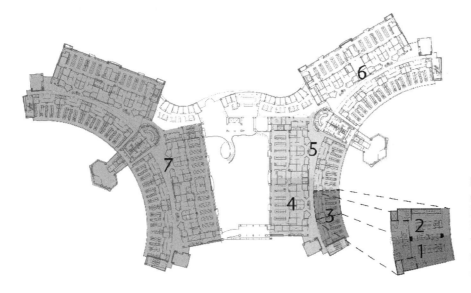

Figure 1-1: The hierarchy of spaces of Pfizer's Global Research & Development facility reflects the work process in the discovery of pharmaceutical innovations.

Courtesy CUH2A.

Figure 1-2: Architectural site plan for Pfizer's Drug Discovery Laboratory in Groton, Connecticut.

Courtesy CUH2A.

field are working diligently to elevate the role of facility manager to the level of a strategic business partner in the organizations where they are employed. When asked by IFMA members for coaching on how to operate more strategically, I frequently suggest they make the effort to better understand the human capital of their companies. A heightened awareness of human resources issues and initiatives will support their preparation for dialogues at the C-level of the enterprise.

In "Where Is Workplace Transformation Hiding?," an article written by Christopher Budd for the International Development Research Council (which, in May 2002, became CoreNet Global,[6] the corporate real estate association), he suggests that more companies ask the question, "What if the outcome of the facilities manager role was to construct physical environments as part of organizational development, supporting a profile of work patterns and attitudes that benefit the business?" Budd points out the strategic importance of the organization to ask facilities management professionals to take a more holistic view of the business, and become less involved in "the minutiae of counting and accounting for every wall and piece of furniture."[7]

COLLABORATION BETWEEN ARCHITECTURAL AND DESIGN FIRMS

Sprint Nextel Operational Headquarters Project

It's one thing for an architectural firm to be asked by a client to work with their preferred independent consultant. It's another thing for the client to have two or more architectural firms work collaboratively on a project when, in the past, these entities may have been competitors in the market.

Recall from earlier in this chapter that Beth Harmon-Vaughan emphasized her experience working on collaborative teams, including groups composed of experts who sometimes compete against each other when pursuing new business opportunities. Such was the case with her involvement on the Sprint Campus project in Overland Park, Kansas, from 1997 to 2001. The largest corporate office campus in the United States, the project involved 18 buildings (plus 3 service buildings), with a total of 4 million square feet of office space designed to support 14,500 headquarters employees (see Figures 1-3 and 1-4).

A strong driving force behind the project was the "One Sprint" philosophy, which shaped the organizational culture. The workplace being planned would need to attract the new generation of workers, who were, in the words of Faye Davis, Sprint Nextel's vice president of Corporate Real Estate, "not really satisfied with a narrow frame of a work environment."[8]

An important design criterion for the new space was to enhance "synergy among departments" dispersed among more than 60 locations throughout Kansas City. The company believed that could be accomplished by decreasing the geographic distance between work groups while increasing face-to-face interaction. Davis commented, "We wanted to construct an office environment that would foster teamwork and encourage interaction and cooperation at every level."[9]

Figure 1-3: Aerial shot of the 4-million-square-foot Sprint Nextel Operational Headquarters in Overland Park, Kansas, the largest corporate office campus in the United States.

Courtesy Sprint Nextel.

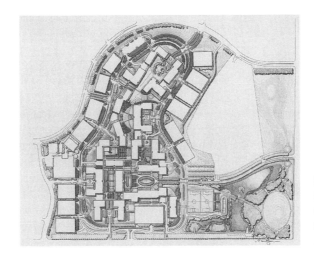

Figure 1-4: Drawing of the Sprint Campus, designed to accommodate 14,500 headquarters staff members.

Image courtesy Hillier Architecture.

Harmon-Vaughan explained that the Sprint leadership group focused on these same values—of teamwork, cooperation, and interaction—in selecting its architectural and design partners. To meet the aggressive project schedule for this high-profile endeavor of consolidating more than 60 office locations, which required highly specialized areas of expertise, Sprint created a team formed from design firms and construction companies that often competed against each other in the market. The sheer size of the project necessitated expertise many other workplace projects may never require. Harmon-Vaughan was one of 125 team members who represented design, program management, construction, technology, and numerous support functions working on the Sprint headquarters project.

For starters, urban planning principles were employed to cluster amenities around the Sprint office complex, because walking across a 225-acre campus would be too long a trek in the winter. As well, specialized knowledge was needed to design traffic patterns to reduce congestion at peak times. Further, responding to employees' requests for a "dining experience" that was a destination rather than an extension of the campus required expertise not only in the design of food service facilities but also in analyzing the process flow of serving nearly 15,000 hungry mouths each workday.

In considering the diverse specializations required for such a complex project, the *co-opetition framework*—a concept that combines the advantages of both competition and cooperation—was determined to be the best solution to ensure project success for the Sprint enterprise.

Hillier Architecture, lead architect on the initiative, served as a positive role model for flexible collaboration, based on its own culture.[10] The firm prides itself on "respecting and celebrating the extraordinary differences among the people and places on the planet." Bob Hillier, founder of the firm, walks the talk. His staff is organized in specialized studios of 25 to 30 team members each; and centers of excellence have emerged based on the development of employees' unique areas of expertise. The members of these studios connect with each other to collaborate

on large projects, then disband after they contribute their required skills. The Sprint Campus needed the same commitment to a cohesive yet fluid team approach—but on a much larger scale.

Ron Weston, AIA, principal of Hillier, shared his thoughts on developing a collaborative design process.

The owner, architect, and construction teams were colocated in an on-site office during the design and construction work. Design ideas were openly shared and discussed, with all participants buying in to solutions. The design team itself was composed of staff from five separate architecture and interior firms [Hillier Architecture, BDY Architects, Rafael Architects, BNIM Architects, and Gould Evans Goodman Architects]. Over time, the project design team developed its own focused culture, independent of the distinct design practices involved.

Design ideas were vetted as part of an open dialogue among architects, designers, owner executives, users, construction managers and other stakeholders. Traditionally, architects and designers retreat to their studios or drafting rooms to develop and document design solutions. On the Sprint Campus team, the architectural studio and design process was opened up to the owner and construction teams.

It is my belief that, on large-scale projects, the more time that the project team can spend together during the design process the better. The Sprint Campus design team spent long hours working, socializing, and re-creating as a group. Doing so helped build a unified project spirit and culture, which ultimately was reflected in the success of the campus.

To foster the building of relationships and trust critical to a group of this size, for the duration of the five-year project, the client provided the 125-member team with 30,000 square feet of office space, on-site. Sprint trained these external members more intensely than some organizations train their own employees. Harmon-Vaughan and the others were provided with everything they needed to optimize both individual and group performance—computers, a telecommunications system, and other tools, as well as comprehensive training. The project leadership also orchestrated social events to enhance personal connections integral to these new business relationships, and as a forum for recognizing team achievements.

Solution Development: The Learning Process

The approach to developing the workplace solution for Sprint involved a thorough investigation of possibilities long before the groundbreaking in 1997. A diverse group of approximately two dozen individuals set out to research the architecture and design of other large corporate campuses around the country. They visited 15 sites, including those of Compaq, Ameritech, Microsoft, Sears, Sun Microsystems, and Monsanto.

It stands to reason that on a headquarters campus large enough to justify its own zip code (if incorporated, the campus would be the twenty-seventh largest town in Kansas), small errors made during the design process would be magnified, equating to extremely expensive mistakes. To reduce this risk, Sprint provided an exploratory environment for testing possible choices for workplace interiors. A 5,000-square-foot mockup was erected, where the team could experiment with important elements

such as lighting, acoustics, and mobile furniture.

Other critical design decisions required consideration of Sprint's history of a high churn rate. Similarly, the workplace design had to accommodate nearly half of the company's employees moving annually from one location on campus to another and, in many cases, to a different building. To accomplish fluidity of the physical space, "home bases" (standardized 8 by 9.5 foot spaces, as shown in Figure 1-5) were laid out on a grid. The grid incorporated "department support spaces" that could be utilized as determined appropriate by the individual work group. For example, a support space could become a reference library for one department; six months later, it might morph into a training room for a new team occupying that departmental grid.

The emphasis on collaboration among and between departments was reflected in the design of the buildings' interiors, as follows:

- To optimize interaction and communication, the workplace strategy called for no building on campus to be more than five stories high; and wide staircases increased the opportunity of colleagues coming in contact with one another on a regular basis.
- Spaces referred to as "interaction nodes" and "solitude nooks" were scattered throughout the campus, and could be selected as an alternative to a given employee's home base, dependent on a desire for peer interaction or a need for privacy.
- Stand-alone break rooms and multipurpose rooms encouraged

Figure 1-5: With Sprint's high churn rate (nearly half of its employees move annually from one location on campus to another), the use of "home bases" (standardized 8 by 9.5 foot spaces) supports the company's requirements for fluidity in the workplace.

Courtesy Sprint.

social and business conversations (see Figures 1-6 and 1-7, and Figure 1 in the color insert).

- Meeting rooms were designed in variety of sizes to accommodate diverse team requirements.

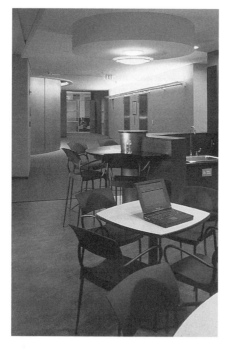

Figure 1-6: Break rooms designed for the Sprint facility incorporate a diversity of configurations to accommodate different tasks occurring in these spaces throughout the day.

Image courtesy Hillier Architecture; photography © 2002 Sam Fentress.

In addition, to reduce potential frustration caused by working within a very fluid work environment, touchscreens with phones were installed in lobbies and other places throughout the campus as a means of expediting locating colleagues for planned meetings, as well as to communicate in the days before mobile phones became ubiquitous (see Figure 1-8).

Lessons from the Sprint Project

A number of lessons can be learned about fostering a design partnership from the experiences of those involved in the Sprint project. Here's what Ronald C. Weston has to say:

The success of the Sprint Campus project was grounded in a commitment by all stakeholders to form a 'true design partnership.' The owner, architect, and construction teams worked together from the outset as a unified group.

Partnering was made an integral part of the design and construction approach from

Figure 1-7: Multipurpose rooms on the campus serve as hubs where Sprint employees can interact.

Image courtesy Hillier Architecture; photography © 2002 Sam Fentress.

start to finish. The owner (Sprint) budgeted significant funds to support the partnering and collaborative efforts of the project team. Partnering events during the five-year process included a kickoff retreat and quarterly off-site retreats; celebrations and social gatherings in recognition of team milestones and accomplishments; and bonus incentives for teamwide performance.

A successful collaborative design process requires support and leadership from the owner. From beginning to end, Faye Davis, Sprint Nextel's vice president of Corporate Real Estate, invested time and money in support of project team partnering activities.

Evolution of the Sprint Workplace

At the time *Innovations in Office Design* was being written, the Sprint organization continued to evolve. The fluid workplace solution strategically designed for change supported the merger of Sprint and Nextel on August 12, 2005, which brought together

approximately 80,000 employees from two unique cultures. In April 2007, *Fortune Magazine* ranked Sprint Nextel number 53 on the Fortune 500 List, with more than $43.5 billion in annual

Figure 1-8: Sprint building lobby.

Image courtesy Hillier Architecture; photography © 2002 Sam Fentress.

revenues in 2006 (an increase of 25.5 percent over 2005) and a total of 64,600 employees.[11]

The physical workplace has gone through an evolution of its own, in response to the changing requirements of Sprint Nextel's workforce. Eileen Forbes, portfolio strategy manager of the company's Enterprise Real Estate group, shared the details of this evolution, which occurred in three broad areas.[12]

1. Workplace Evolution: Technology Offers More Choices for When, Where, and How Sprint Nextel Employees Work

- Team members come together in virtual meetings when face-to-face opportunities are not possible.
- Many business trips are now unnecessary.
- Employees who regularly split their work time between office and home now work from a growing number of "third places," such as airports, restaurants, doctors' waiting rooms, and others.

- Thin client-server applications, the prevalence of self-service solutions, and digital documentation methods give employees access to work resources from anywhere, without relying on paper files.

Workplace Implications: Technical and Interior Architecture More Generalized and Integrated, Rather Than Customized for Single-Purpose Work Practices

- Expanding capabilities of presence-based applications facilitate impromptu collaboration in the virtual and physical environment (geolocation indication, etc.).
- Very few reasons exist to maintain an individual, dedicated workspace for access to paper, voice, or data resources.
- There is an increased need for universal access to voice and data.

Figure 1-9 illustrates this first area of evolution.

Figure 1-9: In the evolving Sprint Nextel workplace, interior architecture has become more generalized, providing spaces that accommodate the diverse tasks taking place on campus.

Courtesy Sprint Nextel.

2. Workplace Evolution: Changing Office Utilization Patterns

- Eighty percent of employees come to the Overland Park campus (Sprint Nextel's operational headquarters) every day, but peak use of individual workspace is less than 50 percent.
- Conference rooms are heavily utilized, and end-user demand for spaces where groups can meet is growing.
- Formal meeting spaces often are used for team collaboration activity, sometimes exhausting network connectivity and access to power supply for laptops.
- There is increasing demand for dedicated team collaboration spaces that restrict access to the rest of the campus population and allow work in progress to remain in place for days, weeks or months at a time.
- Many workstations are used by more than one person.

Workplace Implications: Repurposing Space Allocation

- Rigorous reevaluation of the spaces dedicated to individuals, groups and entire campus community was undertaken.
- The size of individual space was reduced in order to devote more space to group and community collaboration areas.
- Wireless LAN coverage is provided across the entire campus.
- Informal collaboration spaces were created in the open plan environment, offering sufficient power supply for laptops and smart devices.
- Flexible, dedicated "war rooms," which become the main work locations and seat assignments for weeks during extended teaming sessions or critical operations, are established.

Figure 1-10 illustrates another aspect of the project's evolution.

Figure 1-10: Meeting employee demand for more team spaces at Sprint Nextel was achieved by reducing the typical footprint for individual spaces, and shifting square footage to areas designed for group activities.

Courtesy Sprint Nextel.

3. Workplace Evolution: Heightened Aesthetic Expectations

- The common belief is that interior satisfaction, workability, and usability are critical team performance factors.
- Hierarchical status as reflected in the seating provided is less tolerated.
- Desire for color and the "cool" factor.
- Expectation of brand evidence with high-tech look and feel.

Workplace Implications: Office Space Primarily Designed for Innovation, Learning, and Gathering

- Individual focused work is supported by a smaller footprint and in a variety of ways, maximizing choice and flexibility.
- Dynamic and flexible settings encourage creativity.
- Multipurpose group and community spaces contribute to team performance.

- Uninhibited access to windows and views to the outside improve worker satisfaction.
- Free address environment and fewer hard-wall offices support employee expectations for openness as well as the facilities' need for flexibility.
- Rotating art collection, reflecting the brand and culture of the organization, improves workplace satisfaction.
- More cultural norms (cleanliness, accessibility, noise level, etc.) govern shared spaces.

Figure 1-11 illustrates the third aspect of the project's design evolution.

Eileen Forbes and other members of Sprint Nextel's Enterprise Real Estate team are, wisely, continuing to study new work practices and the implications they have on office design. As Sprint Nextel continues to evolve as an organization, the flexibility designed into the Overland Park campus project will enable future

Figure 1-11: Using fewer hard walls satisfies aesthetic expectations through openness, and enables greater flexibility to create collaborative areas within the evolving Sprint Nextel work environment.

Courtesy Sprint Nextel.

transformation of the physical and virtual workplace.

KEY COMPONENTS OF AN INTERDISCIPLINARY APPROACH

"Many ideas grow better when transplanted into another mind than in the one where they sprang up."
—OLIVER WENDELL HOLMES

The best team to contribute to an innovative workplace design is often composed of individuals representing diverse areas of expertise. Leveraging the unique skills of each team member can produce a richer output and, often, reduce the amount of time for the overall design development. Most architectural and design firms will not be selected to participate on a project the scope of that for Sprint's headquarters. Nevertheless, the key components of an interdisciplinary approach can be applied successfully to simpler collaborative endeavors of shorter duration.

A major difference between pulling together a cross-functional team within your own organization and clients pooling the experts required for their projects often has to do with the availability of resources needed, as well as the importance of the project in comparison to other activities under way. In your own firm, you draw from available talent, perhaps negotiating their involvement on your assignment against another opportunity.

Put yourself in your client's shoes. Consider that your architectural or design firm may be working on physical space projects for a dozen or more customers; but for the client, this is *the* project, the top priority—and, often, for that individual, promises the visibility needed for career advancement. In hand-picking the resources to support the project, the client will seek out, for example, the highly specialized expert on change management who understands the impact of physical space on human behavior in the office environment.

More and more often, clients are not seeking a single firm to serve as a jack-of-all-trades. Not for *the* project, and certainly not for *this* project, which will require managers to move out of their private offices to function in a totally open workplace or with no dedicated workspace assignments. Remember, their careers may be at stake! Their employers are encouraging collaborative relationships both within the company and as part of the connections with their customers, day-to-day suppliers, and highly specialized external resources when necessary. The trend is moving away from the single-source, do-it-all provider in favor of the very fluid approach of multidisciplinary teams that form and disband as client requirements dictate. The onus is on individual team members, often from competing organizations, to learn to "play well together."

SUMMARY

Critical Influence Design is an interdisciplinary approach involving diverse areas of expertise. As the core team is established, whether its members are chosen by the client organization, or a group of experts from several firms are strategically aligned according to the needs of prospective clients, it's important to understand the key components of this approach to ensure the highest level of success. A number of factors are essential to an effective interdisciplinary approach to workplace design, drawn from experience in collaborating with other professionals, both when aligned to proactively pursue new business and when assigned by a client as a member of a core team. They are:

- *Shared vision*. Each member of the core team should be committed to contribute his or her expertise in the best interest of the client's vision for the workplace transformation project.
- *Different terms of engagement*. The contract between the client and each core team member may vary greatly. Team members need to accept that each contract is highly dependent on: the expertise the specialist is hired to contribute, the phase or phases in the project during which those skills will be utilized, and the investment of time necessary to perform the activities required.
- *Role clarity*. Most likely, there will be circumstances where two or more core team members are capable of conducting a certain project activity. To eliminate the chance of conflict, roles should be defined early during team formation, and put in writing. Core team members need to be willing to hand off overlapping activities to an equally qualified associate, if appropriate, to achieve the client's vision.
- *Conceptual thinking*. Each core team member needs the ability to visualize in the abstract and to work in undefined, gray areas.

- *Strength and patience*. Each member of the core team must excel at articulating new ideas to others. He or she must also be willing to help others understand unfamiliar concepts.
- *Balance of approaches*. Each core team member must be willing to balance his or her own approach with that of others.
- *Ability to compromise*. Just as there is no one way to approach a client's project, there is no one right workplace solution. Each core team member must be prepared to make concessions.
- *Commitment to communication*. Lines of communication relate to the links between the client and individual core team members, as well as between core team professionals themselves. Ideally, the client and the entire core team agree on who receives which communications, whether there should be one point of contact between the client and the core team leader, or whether another structure should be used to share information throughout the project.
- *Touchpoints*. The client and the core team should schedule specific times to meet at critical junctures throughout the project to share updates on individual and shared activities.
- *Realistic timeframes*. Although individual core team members can estimate the amount of time needed for their own activities, they can create problems if they attempt to do this for others. Individuals should never commit to deadlines on behalf of others, especially for tasks

for which they have little or no experience.

- *Impact on others*. As core team members make recommendations regarding actions within their areas of expertise, they must be willing and able to recognize the implications of these suggestions on others' areas.

- *Shared spotlight*. Core team members should acknowledge that they are working with the best of the best, and be willing to share the spotlight. The focus should be on team performance, not on specific superstars.

In conclusion, leveraging the expertise of diverse disciplines for workplace transformation projects is of growing importance. The clients of architectural and design firms are being encouraged to establish collaborative relationships with their day-to-day service providers, as well as highly specialized external resources deployed on an as-needed basis. By keeping the goal in mind to better serve the client, professionals sharing their expertise among members of an interdisciplinary workplace team can realize time savings and, often, produce a much more innovative design solution.

NOTES

[1] von Stamm, Bettina, "About: Innovation," www.designcouncil.org.uk.

[2] Council for Interior Design Accreditation (formerly the Foundation for Interior Design Education Research, www.accredit-id.org).

[3] Harmon-Vaughan, Beth, FIIDA, Assoc. AIA, LEED AP, interview with the author, August 10, 2006.

[4] Ibid. "The Case for Collaboration," *Implications Newsletter*, InformeDesign, April 5, 2006. http://www.informedesign.umn.edu (accessed October 1, 2006).

[5] International Facility Management Association, www.ifma.org.

[6] CoreNet Global, www.corenetglobal.org.

[7] Budd, Christopher, "Where Is Workplace Transformation Hiding?," IDRC Communicator Online, August 22, 2001. http://www.idrc.org.communicator.online/co010822.htm (accessed July 11, 2006).

[8] Hedgcoth, Rachael, "Corporate Headquarters Can Strike a Balance in Kansas City: Sprint Campus Unfolds as the World Watches," *Expansion Management Online*, March 1, 1999. http://www.expansionmanagement.com/smo/articleviewer/newsdatabase_print.asp (accessed December 5, 2006).

[9] "Sprint's Massive Economies of Scale: 10 Percent-Plus Savings on $700 Million Kansas City HQ," *Site Selection*, week of January 24, 2000. http://www.siteselection.com/ssinsider/snapshot/sf000124.htm (accessed December 5, 2006).

[10] Hillier Architecture, www.hillier.com.

[11] *Fortune Magazine*, Vol. 155, No. 8, April 30, 2007, pp. F-3-4, F-70.

[12] Forbes, Eileen, Portfolio Strategy Manager, Enterprise Real Estate, Sprint Nextel, communications with the author, February 2007.

CHAPTER 2
THE CRITICAL INFLUENCE SYSTEM

KEY FACTORS ENABLING A SUSTAINABLE PLATFORM FOR CHANGE

As previewed in the Introduction, the foundation of the Critical Influence approach to effective workplace environments began slowly, almost as a curiosity, as a study of well-designed offices that failed to achieve the goals intended by the organization. Over a 10-year time frame, this workplace study came to involve 140 organizations in 24 diverse industries. Many of these firms had intended to create environments that would improve productivity, enable teamwork, and inspire collaboration; and every one of them expected better business results.

Why have so many workplaces designed for collaboration failed to live up to the organizations' expectations? Why does internal competition continue to thrive in environments developed to foster a sense of community and common goals?

Inherent in *Innovations in Office Design* is a twofold goal: first, to understand and, second, to share why many organizational attempts to implement new workplace strategies, centered on improving collaborative human behavior, have produced less than optimal results—or have failed entirely. Architects and interior designers learn early that the physical workplace has a strong impact on employee behavior. The Critical Influence System theory takes this knowledge one step further, by formally positioning the physical workplace as one of 15 Critical Influences on behavior in the workplace. In doing so, it introduces the other 14, and demonstrates the interrelatedness of this set of elements. Together, as explained in this chapter, these tangible and intangible factors operate interdependently and can enable or hinder the achievement of organizational goals.

Since its development, the concept of the Critical Influence System has been employed in the analysis of a number of very

> "Problems cannot be solved by thinking within the framework in which the problems were created."
> —ALBERT EINSTEIN

Figure 2-1: Most architectural and design professionals are so good at what they do that clients think they can operate blindfolded and with one hand tied behind their backs. What the client doesn't see is that behind their backs, fingers are crossed for good luck that the workplace strategy just developed will be met without resistance.

Courtesy PureStock.

workforce from the psychological stress that accompanies such change.

DEFINING THE CRITICAL INFLUENCE SYSTEM

Those charged with developing workplace design solutions must understand first that the physical workplace is only one factor in the holistic Critical Influence System, albeit the one of greatest concern to professionals charged with establishing and implementing a workplace strategy.

The good news for architects, interior designers, and corporate real estate and facilities management professionals is that the physical workplace is not the panacea to enabling the desired human behavior in the workplace. Why is this good news? After all, professionals in the field have invested heavily in acquiring specialized knowledge of the impact of physical space on behavior, and have painstakingly been applying this knowledge to create what they believe to be effective organizational environments that will produce specific, desired results. At minimum, the news should alleviate feelings of failure professionals might develop when one of their "properly designed" workplace solutions fails. They need to recognize that, often, the failure is due to factors out of their control.

That is why it is so important that professionals arm themselves with a deep understanding of the other key factors that influence human behavior in the workplace. With this "ammunition" they can take a more proactive approach with executive decision

diverse organizations, including banking and finance, high-tech, nonprofit, manufacturing, energy, consumer products, telecommunications, legal and other professional services, pharmaceutical and health care, education and research, entertainment, transportation, government, and others. The theory makes sense whether the business is large and expanding, or small and intends to stay that way. Common to each of these organizations is human resistance to change. Many business leaders today would agree that "incrementalism" just doesn't work in today's competitive environment. As a result, employees are forced to deal with more rapid and dramatic changes than in the past. As an organization implements a significant change initiative, the biggest risk is not the change itself; rather, it is in doing nothing to protect the makers early in the change process, with the goal of joining forces to address organizational requirements holistically. Architects, interior designers, corporate real estate and asset managers, and property and facilities management professionals then can serve more as strategic business partners to organizations, rather than as recipients of organizational edicts.

Research conducted on the impact of transformation on the human capital of the organization includes the study of the dynamic relationship between organizational goals and expectations and employee behaviors, as shown in Figure 2-2.

The analysis of the Critical Influence System explores that relationship in depth, and demonstrates that the two forces can either coexist in harmony or in great conflict. In the latter case, the result is loss of productivity, damage to morale,

and increased employee turnover. As changes to the organization are introduced, the relationship itself often changes, as a function of the magnitude of change and the level of employee resistance to that change (see Figure 2-3).

In many organizations, the changes inherent to a workplace

Figure 2-2: The relationship between an organization's goals and the expectations of its employees—and the actual behaviors of members of that workforce—is dynamic. As changes are introduced to employees, a harmonious state can quickly become one filled with opposition.

©1996 Diane Stegmeier.

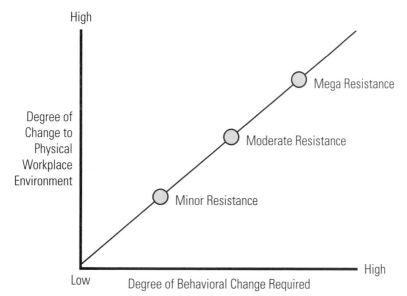

Figure 2-3: The level of employee resistance to workplace change is a function of the degree to which the physical space will be transformed, coupled with the level of behavioral change employees will be expected to make.

© 1996 Diane Stegmeier.

transformation project are planned in isolation from other initiatives being undertaken by other functional groups in the enterprise, such as human resources, information technology, marketing, or security. While these teams are managing their projects to meet their own departmental goals, which may vary greatly, typically they share one thing: any changes being designed most likely will involve adaptations the workforce will be expected to make. When this stream of changes seems unconnected to staff members, their perception may be that the company is operating under a "change du jour" or "program of the month" philosophy. Thus, their natural response often is to ignore or downplay what they're asked to do—after all, won't this current initiative soon be forgotten, only to be supplanted by the next one? That is why workplace transformation initiatives have a much greater chance of success when communicated to employees as a part of holistic organizational changes, linking the need for adaptations in the physical work environment to specific business challenges and goals faced by the enterprise.

Critical Influences, displayed in Table 2-1, are both tangible and intangible elements that impact

behavior in the workplace. Needless to say, the Physical Workplace is one of these. Architects and interior designers already understand the impact of this influence on employee behavior; what they also need to recognize is the interrelatedness of the other 14 factors on the level of success of any workplace strategy.

Refer back to Figure 2-2. To that dynamic relationship between organizational goals and expectations and employee behaviors add the 15 Critical Influences to understand the graphic depiction of the Critical Influence System shown in Figure 2-4.

Too often, whether a workplace solution is effective in supporting the desired human behavior is examined after the fact, and in isolation from the other key factors. Thus, in many cases, the results produced by the workplace design are perceived as suboptimal, due to incongruence with other critical influences that office interiors professionals may not recognize are linked.

To ensure understanding of the dynamics of the system—and why so many things can go wrong when attempting to implement a new workplace strategy—we'll explore each of the Critical Influences in turn.

TABLE 2-1 Critical Influences on Behavior in the Workplace

Vision and Mission	Core Values	Culture
Image	Leadership Behavior	Compensation
Rewards and Consequences	Technology	Knowledge Management
Organizational Structure	Autonomy and Authority	Business Processes
Communications	Performance Management	Physical Workplace

© 2002 Diane Stegmeier.

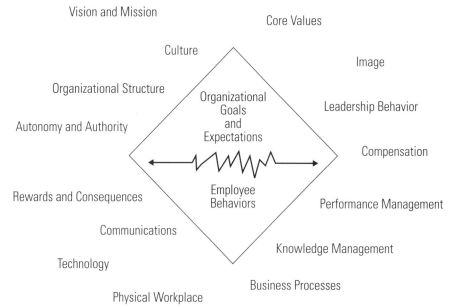

Vision and Mission

Core Values

Culture

Image

Organizational Structure

Organizational Goals and Expectations

Leadership Behavior

Autonomy and Authority

Compensation

Employee Behaviors

Rewards and Consequences

Performance Management

Communications

Knowledge Management

Technology

Business Processes

Physical Workplace

Figure 2-4: The 15 Critical Influences are those tangible and intangible elements that impact behavior in the workplace. These elements have a dramatic effect on the dynamic relationship between the organization's goals and expectations and employee behaviors. When there is incongruence, the organization will be impeded from achieving its goals.

© 2002 Diane Stegmeier.

KEY FACTORS INFLUENCING HUMAN BEHAVIOR IN THE WORKPLACE

Vision and Mission

The vision and mission statements of organizations are as diverse as the individuals who craft the words. But however much the words may differ, the two go hand in hand to lead any enterprise to its future.

- The vision statement articulates the future state the organization wishes to create.
- The mission statement describes how that vision will be achieved.

The vision statement is focused on long-term direction—where the organization is headed—whereas the mission statement deals with the present, relative to such details as what the business is today, the markets it covers, and how it serves its customers. Together, these statements should be a positive driving force that reflects why the enterprise exists. At the same time, it should guide employees in the right direction for the long term, even as it lays out the path when shorter-term adaptations are made according to annual strategic plans, quarterly goals, or the priorities of any given workday. An organization's vision or mission statements may evolve over time, in response to changes in the industry in which it operates, but, generally, there is no rewriting of the "why we exist" exercise that takes place each December as the board of directors and executive leaders look to the next calendar year. That is, the messages contained in the organization's vision and mission statements should be sustainable.

As an example of this concept, consider a firm in the financial services industry that included in its mission statement verbiage emphasizing the importance of building its reputation and success through long-term, trusting relationships with its customers. The firm was relatively small, yet operated on a national basis. The mission statement was indeed a reflection of this goal. Many of its clientele had worked with the firm for decades, and word-of-mouth referrals fueled the company's growth over the years. Its customers were always given the benefit of the doubt—sometimes to the detriment of the firm's bottom line. Nevertheless, the focus remained on maintaining trust in its business-to-business working relationships.

At the time I was called in to consult with the company, it was going through great organizational change. The executives wanted to take a more comprehensive approach to manage a number of individual change initiatives, which included an internal restructuring. But they were concerned that this restructuring would not be transparent to the external environment—that is, they feared that any processes that veered from "business as usual" would be noticed by their clientele and, perhaps, result in the loss of some longstanding accounts.

By the time I began working with this firm, it was well into the integration of a new computer system, which was proving cumbersome for even the most technologically savvy employees. Moreover, the computer system was down more than up and functional; consequently, voicemail messages went unanswered in the Customer Care Department as staff members had to be away from their desks trying to resolve customer problems by manually searching through archived files of hard-copy documents located in a large storage area adjacent to the main office building. Inevitably, frustrated customers began calling the top ranks of the company to complain about the extended response times, which led to additional stress on the organization's customer care representatives. Employee morale began to sink.

Things got worse when a very talented and dedicated customer care representative, who consistently received excellent ratings each year in customer satisfaction surveys, developed a stress-related medical condition. His physician prescribed a reduction in hours and temporary removal from the work environment, recommending that he work from home for four to six weeks. This should have been no problem due to the capabilities of the company's telephone system and the nature of the tasks this employee was expected to perform. However, rather than grant this alternative workplace option, the company chose to put this top-notch employee on short-term disability. Why? Senior management contended, "We've never allowed this type of thing before." They also showed a remarkable lack of trust: "How do we know he'll actually be working six hours each day?" And they worried that "others will want to telework."

What happened to the company's vision that centered on trusting relationships? Was it just a marketing slogan? Not only did the customer service rep in question wonder, but several top customers did, too, commenting on the lack of trust and short-term thinking the company was exhibiting. Actions speak louder than words, was what many thought at the time.

Core Values

Everyone has heard the adage "the customer is always right," yet most of us have found ourselves more than once walking away from a transaction at a restaurant, the dry cleaners, an insurance company, or a bank muttering angrily, "I'll never do business again with a company that treats me like *that!*"

Core values of organizations should serve as guidelines that all employees—including executive leaders—are expected to follow in their day-to-day activities. Developing a list of non-negotiable principles such as "We treat employees with respect" or "Ethics in everything we do" is not in itself a bad exercise. But, if they're not backed up in practice, such principles become meaningless.

This core principle of another firm was stated as: "We give the customer the benefit of the doubt." Sounds great. But when senior management at this company began getting irate phone calls from customers, it became clear that it was not being practiced. Customers complained, for instance, that "I felt I was being called a liar," when reporting missing items from orders they had placed.

It was discovered that a new middle manager, responsible for supervising the call center staff, was trying to make a name for himself by protecting company profitability. He had begun to prohibit shipping replacement products to customers without first arguing that the company could not have possibly forgotten an item or accusing them of not clearly articulating their requirements. This behavior, understandably, left consumers bewildered and angry.

In this example, there was incongruence with the critical influence of Performance Management. That particular manager was charged with maintaining a certain level of profitability for his employer. As a quantitative metric, this is common and quite easily measured. What lacked in the measurement system for that individual's job description was an emphasis on customer satisfaction, a qualitative metric more difficult, yet just as important, to address.

Too often, organizational values become quickly overlooked following the orientation of a new hire. In working with this particular firm, I arranged for the company's CEO, together with the human resources manager, to hold meetings with each office location to reintroduce the core values to employees and facilitate exercises to help employees learn how to translate each of the core values into their day-to-day activities.

How do an organization's core values relate to its physical work environment? In particular, as more and more companies consider moving managers out of private offices into open-space plans, core values can be leveraged to gain acceptance of the new workplace strategy. Managers resisting such a change may cite reasons such as needing to maintain a private office because they must deal with confidential customer statistics. But when an enterprise has established values such as "working as a team to provide customer excellence" or "all employees are respected equally," it may become more difficult for those who are losing their private workspace to argue a business case linking the new workplace design to the organization's core values. In these cases, managers will need to be reminded that the customers are being served by the entire team, and that the team approach is what is necessary in the increasingly complex business environment.

Image

An organization's image may well be the primary area of focus for a new workplace strategy. Creating a physical environment that enables a company to brand itself "forward thinking," "progressive," or "entrepreneurial" may be a tactic to support a human resources strategy to fulfill the need to hire new talent. Or a new workplace plan may be driven by the desire to attract additional stockholders, or secure customers in a newly targeted market. The office interior is essential to make a statement to potential new clients and/or job candidates the moment they step off the elevator. Whitney Inc., Oak Brook, Illinois, has done an exemplary job of articulating the desired image of each of its clients, as shown in Figures 2-5, 2-6, 2-7, and 2-8. Each design solution immediately sends a specific message to anyone entering the space.

It's important to point out, however, that individuals working within an organization may perceive its image quite differently from that portrayed in the company's annual report. Executives may honestly feel they are progressive in their approach, that they are keeping an eye on the big picture, and empowering those at lower levels to make decisions on issues they are involved in on a daily basis. In contrast, lower-level employees may feel they have only the responsibility, not the authority, to make things happen.

Figure 2-5: To create a more inviting space for clients, Mesirow Financial, in Chicago, turned to Whitney to create an executive floor plan that exudes the warmth and elegance the company envisioned for itself.

© 2007 Whitney, Inc.

Figure 2-6: When Synovate relocated from the northwest suburbs to Chicago's business district, it wanted to signify major changes in its corporate culture by designing a unique office environment using vibrant colors, unusual fabrics, and interesting carpeting patterns.

© 2007 Whitney, Inc.

Figure 2-7: With the Curiosity Wall at its hub, Synovate's New York work environment trades formal for casual in its desk units, conference rooms, and seating areas.

© 2007 Whitney, Inc.

Figure 2-8: On the Curiosity Wall at Synovate, the word "curiosity" is imprinted in languages from countries around the world, conveying the company's status as a global market research firm. Whiteboards and flat-screen TVs dot the wall, emphasizing the importance of communication and idea exchange in the office.

© 2007 Whitney, Inc.

Thus, they turn to upper management continually for approval to make even minor decisions, and often leave work at the end of the day feeling frustrated that this "progressive" company does not practice what it preaches and shows a decided lack of confidence in the staff.

The image of an organization is not solely the result of internal forces, such as its public relations department or its marketing staff. Outside influences also contribute. If, say, a company becomes the target of news media due to a highly visible lawsuit filed against it, the negative fallout generated may last much longer than the actual court case. Or, should union members be seen picketing outside a manufacturing plant when a potential customer arrives to tour the facility, an entirely different image from what the client expected or

hoped to see may be permanently cast in his or her mind.

Here's an example related to the physical workplace. As more baby boomers reach retirement age, it becomes critical for organizations to recruit new talent and build trust among younger generations of workers. Consequently, today, employee engagement is receiving as much attention as creating the customer experience. Smart organizations are actively recruiting top talent in their twenties today, in hopes of grooming their business leaders of tomorrow. If a firm's college recruitment brochure boasts of a high-energy, open, and collaborative workplace, shouldn't potential new hires actually see that when they arrive for a job interview? Assume the architectural and design firm has designed the ideal physical space solution in alignment with the organization's future vision. Collaborative vignettes, each with its own personality, are scattered throughout the facility to encourage team interface. State-of-the-art technologies are in place. The corporate café is equipped not only with food and beverages but also with whiteboards and work tools to capture the next spontaneous great idea.

But what if interviewees observe instead a sad underutilization of the spaces designed to enable interaction and knowledge sharing? What if the presence of human beings in the office is sensed primarily by hearing voices behind the closed doors of private offices and conference rooms throughout the building? And what if the café is void of any activity, and the team spaces are empty? The result may be that the really "cool" spots in the workplace look as if they've been put there "for show." The enthusiasm of any new college graduate seeking his or her first career position is bound to be deflated after touring such an office environment. What he or she is seeing will be a far cry from the image in the brochure, which reflected a buzz of diverse and exciting activities taking place at the same time. Instead, the candidate may see the type of place he or she wants to avoid.

Is a strategically created organizational image sustainable? Or is there a "subimage" inherent in the organization that can undermine the image executive leaders want to present to potential stockholders, targeted customers, key job candidates, and other critical individuals in the external environment? As you delve into the interrelatedness of Critical

Influences, begin to look for ways you can leverage factors that enable a sustainable image. Likewise, take note of factors that can erect barriers to achieving the desired image in the eyes of those internal and external to the organization.

Culture

The culture of an organization is often illusive and hard to describe accurately—especially by those at the top of the firm. That does not stop new hires, vendors, customers, and others external to the firm from forming first impressions—often that are quite accurate. Consider what happens when customers call an organization with a simple question, only to be bounced from department to department before getting an answer. They may accurately characterize the company as having a complex structure, as being difficult to work with, or having employees who lack proper training. Similarly, vendors who have proposed new and much-needed technology, but have been unsuccessful in convincing their client to adopt the suggested product, may describe the organization as risk-averse or slow to make decisions. Yet the companies themselves may see their culture as entrepreneurial and employee empowered.

When clients understand the impact organizational culture can have on employee behavior and, subsequently, on the productivity of the firm, but feel stuck when attempting to identify what that culture actually is, most likely it is time that business leaders take a very different approach. Such was the case with a well-known, global Fortune 500 company considered a leader in its industry, progressive in its product development initiatives, and with a world-class sophisticated distribution system. The company had an excellent reputation for being one of the best places to work, for employing top talent, and for never being content to rest on its laurels. The business leaders wanted to better understand the positive aspects of their corporate culture, in order to leverage those factors while undergoing companywide changes. They were also committed to identifying and addressing any negative elements to more effectively manage the changes being driven.

The following excerpts are drawn from an interactive session—an organizational metaphor exercise—I facilitated for the executives. I asked the leadership team to compare their company to an unrelated object, in this case, a finely tuned car. After overcoming some initial resistance, ideas began to flow. Several of the positive descriptions follow:

The company's set of core values is the steering wheel of the car. This set of values guides all employees and keeps each individual from running off the road.

Training initiatives offered to employees are the spark plugs of the vehicle. The company's philosophy of preventative car maintenance as a means of survival results in the spark plugs being changed regularly to ensure the car operates at an optimum level of performance.

Peers are the windshield wipers of the automobile. If there is a complex problem to solve, your peers within the organization are willing to help clear away the mist of confusion, even if only intermittently.

The company's strong focus on team recognition is the sun visor of the car. To prevent a single individual from basking in the bright light, the culture emphasizes team

spirit and encourages the individual to recognize his or her peers for their contribution to that individual's success.

Conversely, the organizational metaphor exercise conducted for the same client also identified barriers as perceived by the participants:

While the field sales force is the accelerator of the automobile, ready to move full-speed ahead, the company's independently owned distributors are the brakes, often working against the sales representatives employed by the organization. The brakes and the accelerator need to work together more closely than any other components of the car. When they work in harmony, the drive is smooth and pleasant. When they do not work in sync, the ride is filled with jolts and false starts and stops.

The vehicle lost two options when the company recently went public: door locks and tinted windows. In the past, the organization measured its performance for internal purposes only. With the company no longer being privately held, Wall Street is the police officer shining a flashlight into the car, hoping to find something you are trying to hide.

Notably, participants in this exercise ask to continue after the facilitator calls an end to it. Also, many clients want to repeat the exercise with different levels of management, or in different departments or divisions, to take a pulse on perceptions. The results of such an activity reveal how well a culture can enable the achievement of organizational goals.

The metaphor of a car mirrors many of the key cultural elements of any client organization—the relationship between a company's numerous interrelated parts, its interactions with employees, and its external environment. As a result of this exercise, gaps will appear between where an organization currently stands and where its executives feel the firm needs to be, acting as fuel for further discussion.

Workplace design professionals seeking to reflect the organizational culture in the development of the physical space may indeed face numerous barriers and widespread incongruence. Attempting to drive organizational change by establishing a new collaborative workspace geared for teamwork without having a heightened awareness of the impact of other elements on the success of the design will result in unnecessary frustration. Increasingly, professionals in architecture, interior design, corporate real estate, and facilities management are expected to be well versed in human resources issues such as generational issues, attraction and retention challenges, and flexible work schedules. Investing time to learn about the various elements of the Critical Influence System can greatly enhance the understanding of the human resources challenges of any organization and aid in the development of more successful workplace strategies.

Likewise, human resources professionals are being encouraged to become educated in the fundamental principles of the physical workplace. Consequently, some are beginning to discover the power of place. In the article "Space: Another HR Frontier," which appeared in the Society for Human Resource Management's *HR Magazine*, author Robert Grossman, an attorney, highlighted the workplace transformation of the Thomson Legal and Regulatory Group headquartered in St. Paul, Minnesota. The Thomson organization sought a

workplace design that would articulate the firm's collaborative culture and speak to job candidates of its energetic, fast-paced environment.

To begin, Brian Hall, Thomson's CEO, selected specific individuals to serve as members of a cross-functional workplace project team to ensure all key issues would be addressed from different perspectives. Included on the team for this important initiative was Tim Blank, vice president of Human Resources-Technology. Thomson Legal and Regulatory Group's six floors were transformed from a "vast sea of gray-color cubes" to a diverse workplace community. The Thomson community includes open team areas that are balanced with workstations to offer more privacy. Senior leaders were removed from corner offices on the top floor and strategically positioned in glass offices near the circulation paths, for increased interface with all levels of employees. Spontaneous knowledge sharing is encouraged by the placement of comfortable venues throughout the space, including a café in the community's "downtown," where one can select from private nooks or the open area to conduct activities.[2]

But what happens when the physical workplace does not reflect the desired culture of the enterprise? Incongruence between how a company describes its culture and what individuals internal and external to that organization perceive it to be can have damaging effects. A good example of this dilemma involves the office environment of a distributor of healthcare instrumentation and consumable products that promoted itself as "world class," touting its environmentally friendly packaging

"While space is the structural control system, culture is the social control system."[1]

——DIANE STEGMEIER

and its best practices that supported just-in-time delivery to hospitals throughout the United States. Its distribution center was pristine; great pride was evident in the care given to its state-of-the-art conveyor system that transported materials from sparkling-clean shelves to the spotless packaging area.

This enterprise liked to invite prospective customers to visit the distribution center, to see for themselves the superior care and handling of each and every product. The tour even included a stop at the company's efficiently organized truck garage, where customers could watch an employee polish the corporate logo on the side of the brand-new vehicles being loaded with materials and readied for shipment. On one tour, however, a potential customer accidentally wandered into the front offices adjacent to the distribution center. The term "world class" most certainly did not describe the dismal workplace where office staff took care of customers' requests. Furniture was mismatched and in ill repair, and the office equipment looked like it had not been updated since the 1960s. Employees attempted to add lumbar support to their old chairs by strapping small pillows onto the backs with duct tape. Even sadder was the impact this work environment had on the morale of the company's front-office employees. The visitor could go home and forget about what he saw, but for the employees relying on a paycheck, the next morning they were scheduled to work would arrive all too quickly.

Organizational Structure

Business structures have changed over time in response to shifting social influences and organizational theory. Frederick Taylor, the "father of scientific management," offered sound advice for businesses operating in the Industrial Age. Focused on the principles of task specialization and production efficiency, he recommended a "unity of command," whereby each employee reported to only one individual within the overall chain of authority. The findings of Harvard University's Elton Mayo, in the 1920s and early 1930s, from the Hawthorne studies conducted at Western Electric in Chicago, launched new thinking about the physical work environment, human motivation, and worker productivity. These research results are said to have launched the human relations movement in organizational theory. Reinforced in the 1940s by the introduction of Abraham Maslow's hierarchy of needs, the importance of applying principles of sociology and psychology in the workplace increased among business leaders. In the 1950s and 1960s, the thought leadership of Peter Drucker, Rensis Likert, Laurence Peter, Kurt Lewin, Douglas McGregor, Warren Bennis, and others became required reading for those charged with advancing their organizations to future success. Vanderbilt University's Richard L. Daft suggested that "organizational form and design are the ultimate expression of strategy and implementation."[3] The classic structural framework proposed in 1979 by Henry Mintzberg, the Cleghorn Professor of Management Studies at McGill University in Montreal and a professor of organization at INSEAD in Fontainebleau, France, began serving companies that were aggressively pursuing innovation as a strategic intent. The specific organizational design envisioned by Mintzberg, an *adhocracy*, is a matrix structure developed for survival in a complex, dynamic environment. High-performance teamwork is enabled through numerous horizontal linkages and empowerment. In an adhocracy, professionalism is emphasized, cultural values are strong, and decision making is encouraged at all levels of the organization.

As the Industrial Age gave way to the Information Age, the heightened complexity of work necessitated a more holistic approach to organizational analysis. The typical business structure needed to incorporate growing uncertainty and the interdependency of subsets of the whole system. The principles of systems thinking, contingency planning, adaptation, and change readiness became the guidelines for business leaders in developing organizational structures.

The more recent work of Henry Mintzberg, developed in the late 1990s, in conjunction with Ludo Van der Heyden, the Solvay Chair for Technical Innovation at INSEAD, echoes the need for organizational preparedness in order to tap competitive opportunities and to understand how innovative ideas flow throughout the structure via a system of hubs and webs. The visual depiction of the structure, in the form of an *organigraph*, helps business leaders prepare structurally for innovative outputs. American physicist Joseph Henry perhaps said it best: "The seeds of great discoveries are constantly floating around us, but they only take root in minds well prepared to receive them." Executives are learning that innovation favors a combination of prepared minds and strategically crafted

organizational structures. These same leaders, however, often fail to recognize the impact of the physical work environment on the innovative outputs critically needed for survival in the competitive global economy.

Only a few organizational structures, which have been adopted in the business world at different points in time, have been highlighted here. As architects and interior designers create workplace environments for their clients today, against which model of organizational structure will a solution be judged for its effectiveness? What will change? What will remain the same? If there's one thing we can count on, it's that the only constant is change. The need for an enterprise, its structure, workforce, and physical and virtual workplace environments to be flexible and adaptable, to respond to whatever changes are on the business horizon, cannot be overstated. But you might well ask: Does an organizational structure exist that is agile enough for today's unpredictable business landscape as well as for the unpredictable future?

If you ask any number of individuals in the business world to visualize a corporate hierarchy, the typical description will be of a pyramid. A pyramid maintains the precise, hard-edged structural shape, incapable of flexing. It does not morph according to changes in the external environment. Robert Johansen and Rob Swigart challenged our thinking about organizational flexibility and adaptability in their book *Upsizing the Individual in the Downsized Organization: Managing in the Wake of Reengineering, Globalization, and Overwhelming Technological Change.*[4] In it they introduced the concept of the "Fishnet Organization," shown in Figure 2-9.

If you think about the concept of the Fishnet Organization as it applies to how things actually get done in today's workplace, you'll see this flexible, yet incredibly strong structure makes perfect sense. In the words of Robert Johansen, "Economies of scale (where bigger is almost always better) are giving way to economies of organization, where you are what you organize, inside—and especially outside—your organizational boundaries.[5] The creation of numerous teams is driven by changing demands being made from within and outside of the enterprise. An individual is often a member of multiple groups. Collaborative, task-driven units form, achieve what they are charged to do, then disband. With each new temporary hierarchy that forms around a project or initiative comes new connections within that node, as well as relationships between the ever-changing collection of nodes. In the

Fishnet Organization, the structure of each temporary team is as large as it needs to be to incorporate the diverse talents required to accomplish the given initiative. That's not to say that permanent hierarchies do not exist in this structure. On the contrary, the formal authority in the organization acts to support the various temporary hierarchies that form and dissolve over time.

While conducting research for this book, I discussed with Bob Johansen my plan to apply the concept of the Fishnet Organization to the design of the physical workplace. Johansen has spent more than three decades as a forecaster, and until 2004 served as president and CEO of the Institute for the Future, the independent, non-profit research group focusing on discontinuities and emerging dilemmas that will challenge how we approach complex issues three to ten years into the future. I was excited to learn that his new book, *Get There Early: Sensing the Future to Compete in the*

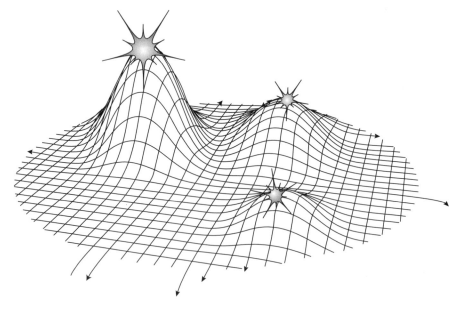

Figure 2-9: The concept of the Fishnet Organization articulates the importance of an organizational structure that is both strong and flexible, enabling it to adapt to change.

Bob Johansen, Get There Early: Sensing the Future to Compete in the Present, *San Francisco: Berrett-Koehler, 2007.*

Present, includes his thought leadership on the role of the office and other physical places where "real work" gets done. He said, "Gradually, organizations are coming to think of the office as a flexible array of activities—not necessarily a fixed place." Johansen advises us to "learn to be comfortable being uncomfortable. Offices as we know them are part of our current comforts, but the ground is shifting beneath the office."[6]

In Chapter 3, we'll discuss the flexibility of the physical workplace, which enables it to morph and adapt to "waves of innovation" as teams form, work, and disband, to coincide with the classic stages of the product life cycle.

Leadership Behavior

Many organizations attempting to improve teamwork and collaboration employ workplace solutions such as cybercafés and other types of comfortable, lounges and breakout areas designed to motivate employees to interact with each other spontaneously. Unfortunately, in these same organizations, too often the leaders stay tucked away in private offices, conducting structured meetings in formal settings. The workplace integration team members within these companies are left to scratch their heads, wondering why the front-line staff avoids the collaborative spaces.

It is human nature to want to be seen in a positive light by senior management. Staff members typically will mirror the actions of their organizational leaders—in this case, by avoiding being seen in the spontaneous interaction spots. Leaders planning to institute these types of social-work environments need to be educated on the impact their actions have among the workforce, that they cannot expect one thing of their employees and another of themselves. They, too, must commit to embracing the new workplace. To that end, for a 21-workday period (the time it takes before an activity become a habit), I ask senior managers, when scheduling meetings, to arrange with their peers to use these collaborative venues. Doing so sends a clear and positive message to their direct reports that it is not just acceptable to be seen working in a more relaxed and enjoyable environment, but it is desirable.

An interesting example involves a recent workplace transformation project undertaken with an architectural and interior design firm. Based on the client's evolving business objectives, it was determined that a much more open office environment was necessary to improve the exchange of information at all levels of the rapidly growing company. The interiors group recommended to the CEO that rather than providing private offices for each member of the senior leadership team in the new building being planned, they would design an open leadership community. The proposed leadership work environment would solve an issue they had been struggling with for years—being unable to quickly determine whether executives were in the office or traveling, in the middle of a conversation, or available to assist in sharing guidance with a peer, and so on. An open ecosystem would visually signal the presence of colleagues to accelerate decision making at the top level of the enterprise. This, in turn, would trickle down to expedite work flows throughout the entire organization.

The drawings of the interiors team conceptualized a well-thought-out leadership environment that would be sufficiently distant from casual internal traffic and visitors in the building, to mitigate the risk of inappropriate exposure of confidential information. A rich color palette and top-grade finishes would be used to create an executive aesthetic, which was sophisticated, and much improved over the current private offices and support area.

One of the vice presidents on the senior leadership team was vehemently opposed to taking the executives out of their private offices and moving them into an open leadership space. He was struggling with a psychological loss of status he feared would result if he was uprooted from his executive suite. Despite the fact that his boss, the CEO, supported the transition, and was willing to reside in a space identical to his direct reports, the vice president's resistance went unabated. One afternoon, the CEO told me that this vice president had stormed into his office that morning carrying a large stack of articles he had printed from his Internet search supposedly proving that removing managers from their private offices would fail. Fortunately, the CEO knew his colleague all too well, and told him to "come back once you've read all of the articles." Long story short, soon after that incident, the VP became one of our staunchest advocates for transitioning to an open leadership space.

Perhaps one of the articles the VP read was Gensler's "Well-Designed Office Key to Improving Employee Performance: New Survey,"[7] which introduced the latest results on the impact of design on business performance. The 2006 version of this annual U.S. workplace survey focused on eight industries: accounting, banking, legal, financial services and insurance, energy and telecommunications, entertainment and media technology, product manufacturing, and retail. The participants in the survey mirror the average manager in the America: 42 years old, in a mid-level management position or higher, working in an office of 209 employees, employed by an organization with 3,711 employees and an annual revenue of $354 million. Among the survey findings was the statistic that 62 percent of office workers in the United States "have great respect for leaders who work in an open plan environment with their teams, rather than in private offices."

Autonomy and Authority

The current business climate is characterized by organizations focusing on simultaneously addressing increasing revenue while reducing costs. Ongoing downsizing has created the need to do more work with fewer people. There are not enough hours in the day for executives to micromanage their direct reports. This situation results in the condition I call "autonomy out of necessity," which is quite different from autonomy as a strategic intent.

Organizations have historically concentrated power in the uppermost layers of the management structure. However, in the past two decades, many of the most successful of these entities have strategically driven change in their governance systems. With autonomy as a strategic intent, organizations attempt to bring decision making to the front line and put it in the hands of those staff members closest to the situation. This shift in control has benefited organizations in a number of ways:

- Lower-level employees became better prepared to advance in their careers within the company.
- The delegation of power, however small, to the lower levels of departments helped retain talent in the organization.
- A more positive culture was created, necessary for attracting new, more highly trained staff during the War for Talent.
- Executives had more time to focus on strategic, forward-thinking activities that could create sustainable growth for the organization.

An increasing number of organizations are emphasizing client centricity and are giving staff members greater levels of autonomy, with the goal of providing improved customer service. To meet these objectives, workplace designs are becoming more complex; for example, including spaces dedicated to gathering customer data that can aid in understanding client preferences and anticipating specific requirements. In Figure 2-10 Robert Luchetti Associates, Cambridge, Massachusetts, designed an attractive solution for the Fidelity Wall Street Investors Center in New York. The inviting space integrates interactive kiosks for online and telephone customer support.

Granting staff members at lower levels of an enterprise the autonomy and authority to make decisions is the easy part of the equation, however. It is much more challenging to truly understand the risks of moving from centralized control to

Figure 2-10: A focus on client centricity is reflected in these interactive kiosks offering online and telephone assistance to Fidelity Wall Street Investors Center's customers, New York City. Robert Luchetti Associates designed this welcoming environment, which balances openness with a sense of privacy for customers handling their financial matters.

Planning and Design: Robert Luchetti Associates; photographer and photo copyright 2001, Paul Warchol.

decentralization. Employees may be given autonomy and authority beyond their capabilities to enact; and the organizational culture may be one that makes staff members uncomfortable in approaching management to admit they are unprepared for their new roles. A new governance system may also run head to head with outdated business processes that erect barriers to smoothly executing more flexible decision-making processes.

As noted previously, many workplace strategies include moving managers out of private offices and into the open plan, among their subordinates. The theory behind this physical space change is that the leader shifts from a role of manager or controller to one of a coach or guiding resource, to support front-line staff with their increased responsibilities in making decisions for the organization. Despite a properly designed physical space where the manager and his or her direct reports are colocated in alignment with a new governance system, this workplace strategy can fail due to an incongruence in the culture or business processes.

Even where the architectural and design firm's client is renovating its existing facility or building a new one, and makes a conscious decision to maintain private offices for its managers, Critical Influences can come into active play and serve to undermine the success of the workplace strategy. For example, at one manufacturing company, the new workplace strategy was failing due to negative pressures not obvious to the leaders of the enterprise. A client I had begun consulting had just kicked off a significant organizationwide strategy to differentiate itself from its competitors by leveraging its strong

reputation for customer service. To that end, the firm escalated the importance of response time to and resolution of customer complaints to grow market share as a means of attracting and retaining distributors purchasing its products. My role was to collaborate with the independent interior designer to "reinvent" the physical work environment for the customer service department. By analyzing the client's aggregate customer base, demographic mix, and purchasing trends, I recommended restructuring the existing approach to client support based on the varying degrees of profitability, loyalty, and future revenue potential of both existing and targeted customers. Interdisciplinary teams were put into place, pulling the appropriate levels of talent and skills from the engineering, special applications, and pricing groups to join customer service representatives in better supporting customer centricity. Members of the interdisciplinary teams were colocated in "neighborhoods" designed to meet, and exceed, the unique requirements of the manufacturing company's distinct customer value groups. Each neighborhood workspace was positioned to provide just-in-time customer support, featuring an updated computer system with instantaneous access to data at the front line. The openness of the physical work environment allowed team members to hear when a customer service rep was struggling to solve a customer's problem, and to offer advice based on their own experiences. The theory behind the design of the space sounded logical; however, a barrier existed that, if left unaddressed, would undermine this new workplace concept.

My client was alerted to two red flags raised in the organizational diagnosis of its Critical Influence System.

- Customer service representatives reported to operations, which was intent on protecting every penny of profitability in the manufacturing and shipping processes.
- The CSRs were given absolutely no authority. Throughout the day a parade of customer service staff members, beginning at the new interdisciplinary team space, snaked down the long corridor toward the private office of the vice president of operations, who insisted on being informed of every detail of customers' claims, and deliberated her approval of each concession that would count against the operational budget.

It eventually became clear that a great number of the sign-offs needed by the service representatives were caused by factory personnel failing to include a small container of touch-up paint with customer orders. This forced CSRs to be away from their phones on average for 17 minutes while waiting to get approval on an item costing the company $1.29. It was not until the reporting structure was changed that the new workplace design became effective.

The customer service representative began reporting to the vice president of sales, who understood client centricity. Together, we immediately established an appropriate sign-off authority for each CSR experience level. Less experienced representatives could quickly get approval for an amount above their limit from a more experienced team member, rather than from the vice president.

In the team-based workplace, some people say bringing authority to the front line creates a self-organizing environment where no one is in charge. Not so. By granting the appropriate levels of autonomy and authority, everyone is in charge.

Compensation

One of the most common examples of incongruence in the Critical Influence System observed within client organizations relates to compensation. These organizations have struggled with enabling innovation, but have come to realize that the achievement of innovative results can best be accomplished through teamwork and collaboration. Time after time, architectural and design firms have designed work environments for their clients that are properly engineered to support collaboration and teamwork. Creating a more open work environment and colocating cross-functional team members was believed to be the vehicle to reaching the desired results. Unfortunately, the environment did not produce the desired human behavior.

More often than not, the factor hindering collaborative behaviors is an outdated compensation system, one designed for individual performance, rather than an innovative pay program that motivates teams to achieve high performance. Companies often fail to recognize the power of a compensation plan that is aligned with the way the people within organizations need to work. Slowly, however, the role of the human resources executive is becoming more holistic, and those professionals are being challenged to identify and address barriers that may be standing in the way of optimal workforce performance. While in most businesses today leaders emphasize teamwork, data on how individuals are compensated reflects a disconnect between what employees are asked to do and how they are paid. In a 2006 survey of 10,000 workers in the United States, the Hudson Highland Group conducted research on what the U.S. workforce values in key areas such as pay, health care and retirement benefits, performance reviews, and factors contributing to work-life balance.[8] The survey results revealed the following:

- Forty-four percent U.S. workers surveyed say their bonus is based on individual performance only.
- Twenty-four percent indicate their bonus is dependent on the entire company's performance.
- Only 11 percent of those surveyed say their bonus is based on team performance.
- Nineteen percent of these U.S. workers indicate their bonus is dependent on a combination of individual, company and/or team performance.

University of Michigan's John E. Tropman, author of *The Compensation Solution: How to Develop an Employee-Driven Rewards System*, articulates the importance of including what he calls an "augmentation accelerant" as part of the total compensation equation to maximize the outputs of today's workforce. This accelerant, such as a team incentive pay, must be legitimately earned by employees, and carries no guarantee of automatic payment by the organization.[9]

The federal government has made strides in tying financial rewards to workplace performance. Kevin Kampschroer, director of Research and Expert Services for GSA's Public Buildings Service, shared a powerful concept known as *linking budgets to performance*, used by the U.S. General Services Administration.[10]

You'll learn more about the exciting work being done within the U.S. General Services Administration in a case study on the GSA WorkPlace 20\20 initiative in Chapter 5. The impact of compensation on the other Critical Influences will be addressed in greater depth in Chapter 6.

Rewards and Consequences

When organizations claim a commitment to companywide teamwork, yet continue to reward employees as individuals using outdated practices, it's easy to make a correlation to Steven Kerr's classic theory, "On the Folly of Rewarding A While Hoping for B." First published in 1975, and reprinted in 1995, it is required reading in many MBA programs today. Organizational clarity and alignment surrounding the concepts of collaboration and teamwork, supported by an effective physical workplace solution and a properly designed reward system that recognizes and compensates group achievement, can indeed result in enhanced innovative behavior.

Twenty years after Kerr's theory was first published, the Academy of Management Executive polled its executive advisory panel to determine the progress made in corporate America in addressing the theory. What was true more than three decades ago remains so today: "Managers still cling to quantifiable

TABLE 2-2 What Organizations Hope for and Reward

Organizations Hope For	Organizations Reward
Teamwork and collaboration	The best individual team members
Innovative thinking and risk taking	Proven methods and avoiding mistakes
Development of people skills	Technical achievements and accomplishments
Employee involvement and empowerment	Tight control over operations and resources
High achievement	Another year's effort

standards when they reward others and as their primary explanation for the folly's perniciousness."[11] What an organization hopes for and what it rewards are often at opposite ends of the spectrum (see Table 2-2). Employee reaction to the mismatch of what the individual is asked to do and what he or she observes being rewarded can contribute to a low level of trust of the organization's management, and reluctance to collaborate with peers within their own workgroups, colleagues in other departments, or others from the firm's business units.[12]

Ninety percent of the respondents to the poll conducted by the Academy of Management Executive reported their organizations were indeed still struggling in a number of critical areas. Three major themes surfaced:

- *Difficulty breaking old paradigms of approaching reward and recognition.* Specifically, defining the desired workforce behaviors and developing goals to motivate the appropriate employee performance. These new targets should include non-quantifiable behavior; and rather than emphasizing the employee's job or function in the organization, the rewards should be more holistic and dependent on the overall performance of the system.

Respondents identified barriers to changing old mentalities, including employee belief in entitlement to the rewards, and management resistance to redesigning existing performance management practices.

- *Short-term mentality of both the organization's management and its shareholders.* The emphasis on performance in the short term, without concomitant attention to long-term goals, can be detrimental to the overall health of the enterprise. When those at the highest levels of the organization appear focused entirely on short-term results, the chances of the workforce at large focusing on anything but the here and now are relatively slim.

- *Inability of organizations to view performance results holistically, along with the specific elements to achieve the desired outcomes of the enterprise.* The root cause of this situation is believed to be existing organizational structures. Typical business structures encourage functional, departmental, or business unit "silos" that motivate the maximum results for that particular group. In many cases, that individual performance optimization occurs at the expense of the overall enterprise.

With barriers such as these generating an undercurrent of mistrust of management, an unwillingness to support the efforts of peers, and a general inability to recognize the importance of the long-term goals of the enterprise, it should come as no surprise that a new workplace strategy that encourages teamwork and collaboration has little chance of success. The physical workplace cannot be expected by itself to eliminate deep-rooted hindrances, which need to be addressed holistically within the organization. Just as the emphasis in many companies is on short-term results for performance metrics in sales, market share, and profitability, that same expectation of immediate behavioral change is imposed on the physical workplace solution. Behavioral change takes time. No professional in the workplace field should promise instantaneous results, not when Critical Influences that negatively impact behavior are deeply embedded in the core of the organization's operations.

Performance Management

My husband, Lou, is an avid sports fan and gets totally immersed in watching football and baseball. Our son, Matthew, is equally passionate, and they love nothing more than to discuss the details of the games. I've tried to develop an interest in watching sports, but have given up feigning more than surface-level curiosity. But I have come to understand why so many people become more deeply involved in sports than they do with their work. In sports:

- There is continuous emphasis on practice and improvement.
- Players' goals are clearly defined and reinforced.

- Scores and team performance are measured.
- The coach offers continuous feedback to both individual players and to the team.
- The team knows where it stands at any point in time.
- The rules don't change.

Senior management's expectations for employee performance and overall results cannot be guaranteed simply by articulating 12-month corporate or departmental goals at the beginning of each fiscal or calendar year, then conducting an end-of-the-year review with these individuals to share an evaluation of their performance. Annual reviews are indeed necessary, but clients struggling with less-than-stellar results of employee efforts throughout the year have had much greater success when they've developed and implemented a customized performance management process. A successful process to manage employee performance is one that adds a structural framework to ensure consistency in how managers work with their direct reports, yet balances the ever-increasing need for flexibility as the enterprise finds it necessary to make adaptations to annual plans due to changes in both the internal environment and external, competitive business landscape.

Despite formulating and implementing the appropriate performance management system, measuring employee behaviors—and results—can be difficult, due to barriers created by other elements in the Critical Influence System. For example, in the field sales organization of a midsized service provider, the vice president of sales articulated to all regional sales representatives that each of them had to complete a quarterly sales plan that would identify their top sales pursuits for the upcoming 90 days and the dollar volume potential at stake, and specify any support they might need from others in the company for major presentations, contract negotiations, or other steps in the sales process. A customized, electronic template was user-friendly; the task could easily be completed in 30 to 45 minutes. However, the top sales rep rebelled, stating that he hated paperwork and contending that completing the quarterly sales plan reduced selling time, and would negatively impact his sales results. Rather than enforce this process, which could have improved even this top performer's results, the VP of sales made an exception for him. His justification was that the company needed to keep the rep "upbeat," to prevent him leaving the company to go to the competition.

In this example, leadership behavior, rewards and consequences, and culture erected barriers to success in the field sales group's performance management system. In addition, compensation also emerged as a Critical Influence on the top rep's behavior. Because sales representatives were paid for individual results only, with no compensation for team performance, there was no motivation to focus on anything but their own goals. Nor were there any consequences for noncompliance, further contributing to a culture in the sales group that people were not treated equally, and the perception that the quarterly sales plan initiative would "go away" if enough people resisted it.

As it relates to the physical workplace, some opponents of telework strategies claim that letting individuals work out of their homes prevents managers from monitoring their staff's performance. The fact that a manager cannot see the minute-by-minute activities of an employee does not mean that he or she is unable to measure performance. It is the results that should be measured, not the minutiae of every task. And if the employees cannot be trusted to complete their work, then managers may have the wrong employees onboard, or are using the wrong performance management system—one that measures activities, rather than results.

Communications

I received an interesting e-mail message not too long ago from Vladimir Pravotorov, editor-in-chief of *Human Resource Management (HRM)* magazine, in Moscow, Russia.[13] *HRM* is the largest Russian media resource for the country's personnel management market, with a focus on important trends in managing people at large companies throughout the world. Pravotorov had heard about my work through the Society for Human Resource Management[14] (www .shrm.org) and requested an interview with me for the December 2006/ January 2007 issue of the publication, whose central topic would be communications. I would be asked to comment on "storytelling, corporate myths, and legends" and how organizations in the United States apply this type of communications in the context of change management. (Many members of the workforce today would say there's a great deal of "corporate myths and storytelling" going on when the "legends" to whom they report try to convince their employees how wonderful an upcoming change will be.) Eventually, we agreed on the topic of internal branding as a communication mechanism in the context of change management within organizations in the United States. Key thoughts from that interview are given in the accompanying sidebar.

Of course, communication within the enterprise takes numerous shapes, many of which are less colorful than what the Russians refer to as storytelling, corporate myths, or legends. Organizations that are

most successful in driving workplace change tap into multiple media to get their messages across. It is not enough, for example, to distribute a single announcement from the vice president of corporate real estate describing the decision to move all managers out of private offices into the open plan. Communication is a two-way process. If information is flowing in one direction only, the audience perceives the message to

CORPORATE STORYTELLING

"Communications is one element of the Critical Influence System, and corporate storytelling falls within this important category that must be taken into account throughout the change management process. Storytelling, often called internal branding in the United States, serves the purpose of positioning the desired organizational culture in the minds of employees. It also acts as a support mechanism for companies' strategic plans for the attraction and retention of talented employees.

"Some corporate stories may be internal messages, intended to guide employees in making decisions in their day-to-day work lives. An example of this is a manufacturing client with whom Stegmeier Consulting Group worked. The organization had been very operations-driven, and over time, customer service representatives made decisions to please their internal supervisors and managers rather than make decisions in the best interest of the external customers. Stegmeier Consulting Group developed a comprehensive change management plan focused

on customer centricity. Our work involved educating the company's executive leadership team on the importance of clearly communicating to all new hires and existing employees that each person was to perform his or her job with customer service excellence at the center of all they did. Specific examples of customer service representatives who had exceeded client expectations were gathered and woven into Centricity Training, which was mandatory for all representatives.

"Stories may be necessary to help employees understand the need for change when a company is restructuring, acquiring another company, or merging organizations. Sharing new information in an honest manner can increase employees' trust in the organization's leaders. In cases such as this, the stories provide explanations of why changes must take place. The message may not be what employees want to hear, but they appreciate the honest delivery of the information. To help train clients, educational workshops such as Straight Talk About Reorganization

(STAR)[15] signal to the members of the workforce that they are an important part of a changing organization, and that their enthusiastic participation in events surrounding the changes is much needed.

"Lastly, corporate stories may be geared towards external audiences. More and more companies in the United States are challenged with the need for highly skilled, younger workers as the entire wave of baby boomers (the generation of 75.8 million Americans born between the years 1946 and 1964, inclusive) face retirement. Many organizations have developed strategies to become an employer-of-choice, or are aggressively competing in local, regional, and national competitions such as the Fortune 500 Best Places to Work®. Companies share examples of what it's like to work at their establishment. Businesses often involve their marketing or public relations departments to create an information portfolio that includes stories aimed at getting potential employees excited about coming to work for that organization."

be a lecture or an edict, and thus, "change is being done to them." Better to encourage employee feedback as a means of engaging the workforce in the change process.

Interestingly, Pravotorov emphasizes the context in which communication takes place. Strong leaders are typically excellent communicators and are deliberate in aligning the appropriate message with the context in which it is delivered. These men and women understand the power of face-to-face dialogue with employees at all levels of the enterprise and are more apt to listen rather than talk during interface with staff members. The messages from senior executives may provide the who, what, when, and how of the imminent changes employees will face, but the physical workplace provides the where. It is the context in which the change

occurs. How is the workplace being positioned in company communications as a support mechanism to enable the transformation?

The physical workplace environment that incorporates a variety of spaces to accommodate and invite interaction will support the goal of improved communication. Figures 2-11 and 2-12 show two examples from Whitney, Inc., and reflect well-planned solutions that encourage communication, whether in a meeting for a large group that is arranged in advance or in a spontaneous exchange of information by two colleagues over coffee.

When a client in the pharmaceutical industry merged with one of its former competitors, the organization began developing a strategy for the transformation of the workplace to facilitate its business drivers—building the new

Figure 2-11: Whitney, Inc. updated this large conference room for Mesirow Financial in Chicago, personalized to the client's standards. New paint and carpeting, as well as custom woodwork and a built-in coffeemaker, make this generous space for meetings welcoming.

© 2007 Whitney, Inc.

Figure 2-12: Reflecting the vibrancy of its client, Talent Partners, New York, Whitney, Inc. based this design around unorthodox finishes, modern furniture, and crisp, clean lines. This lunchroom conveys the character of the company, inviting individuals to socialize during a meal or gather for a spontaneous meeting over coffee.

© 2007 Whitney, Inc.

consumer health care product portfolio and increasing the speed of product commercialization. The new office would need to support new behaviors focused on collaboration and innovative results. This firm was passionate about the impact communications would have on the workplace project, as evidenced by the director of communications who had been appointed to the core team overseeing the physical space project. The communications plan for informing employees of the numerous changes affecting them was carefully developed and executed throughout the entire workplace project. One collateral piece was especially notable. It was a colorful brochure entitled "Day One," which articulated that the employees of the merged companies were linked by more than a common name and vision; they were

also linked by their computers, video-conferencing, phones, and e-mails. This corporate communication was, itself, about communication.

In this brochure, the communications, marketing, and information technology teams had joined forces to anticipate as many questions as possible on the first day in the effort to communicate effectively to the newly merged enterprise. The cross-functional group addressed, in advance, any potential confusion that might surface. New workplace protocols established a heightened awareness of sound levels in communicating in a much more open office environment. The brochure also contained how-to sections, ranging from common questions related to two separate e-mail systems that would "talk" to each other to guidelines for using the templates for letters, faxes, and PowerPoint presentations, each of which were ready to incorporate into employees' daily tasks on day one.

Knowledge Management

Many organizations develop sophisticated knowledge management systems, categorizing data on competitive pricing analyses, market studies, and technical information. The reasoning behind gathering and storing data is to allow easy access, retrieval, and leverage of company intelligence for the benefit of the organization. The data is meant to be readily available 24 hours a day to enable employees to make wise business decisions. But what happens when the executive team does not trust the interpretation and application of the data by lower-level employees? This creates a culture of mistrust, thereby erecting a barrier to the maximization of the knowledge management system.

As it relates to physical space, a workplace strategy to allow employees to telework from home may be technologically possible thanks to a robust knowledge management system. But, though the physical space supports the optimization of the data that has been carefully gathered and categorized, not trusting employees to put in a full day's work will undermine both the workplace strategy and the knowledge management initiative.

Even in an organization where trust is not an issue, the increased mobility of the workforce may still impede data access. Data that is available to an employee while he or she is in the office may fail to be optimized if critical information cannot be accessed when the employee

is face to face with a key customer who is concerned about the company's products and/or services. In the words of Sandy Price, Sprint Nextel's senior vice president of human resources, "You should have what you need, when you need it, embedded into your tool at the point of business impact."[16]

An interesting design challenge presented to HOK Canada involved a complex requirement for knowledge management. Don Crichton, vice president of workplace solutions, shared his firm's experience in developing an office solution for a group of separate entities, each dedicated to prevention of workplace injury and illness. The project began as a consolidation study focused on the real estate holdings of four distinct health and safety organizations: the Electrical & Utilities Safety Association (E&USA), the Industrial Accident Prevention Association (IAPA), the Ontario Service Safety Alliance (OSSA), and the Transportation Health and Safety Association of Ontario (THSAO). Together, these four enterprises served 80 percent of workers in Ontario, Canada; yet at the time of the real estate study, they did not have the benefit of being colocated, to support an exchange of knowledge between the individual groups, nor their external interactions with the research community and diverse businesses.

Each of the four founding partners wanted to maintain its unique identity and have the new location support its physical space requirements. Shared spaces and business services would not only serve the goal of improved knowledge sharing, but also result in cost efficiencies for the collective partner group. HOK Canada's solution was to design a suite of offices for each of the four founding partners. Areas that would be shared by all included conference rooms, training and meeting rooms, a resource center, a retail store, a wellness facility, and a full-service cafeteria. Designed to exist in harmony under one roof, these individual and shared spaces, totaling 120,000 square feet, became known as the Centre for Health & Safety Innovation (CHSI).

The importance of knowledge exchange was reflected in HOK's dramatic design of the Promenade, a spacious circulation path bathed in natural light (see Figure 2-13).

Benches were placed in the wide corridor to invite casual, open conversations, yet were strategically positioned to allow private dialogue.

One of the core values of the organization is to "lead by example in creating a healthy and safe environment." To that end, HOK incorporated sound principles of ergonomics in the individual workspaces for the 400 employees working in the Centre's offices. CHSI's commitment to knowledge sharing on health and safety principles, coupled with its value of leading by example, resulted in a workplace solution that "walked the talk." Proper lighting was installed to reduce eyestrain, complemented by

Figure 2-13: HOK designed the offices for the Centre for Health & Safety Innovation in Ontario, Canada. The Promenade provides circulation through the 120,000-square-foot space, and offers a pleasant, natural-light-filled corridor where colleagues can converse.

© 2006 Tom Arban Photography.

access to natural light and an appropriate balance of task and ambient lighting. The full-service cafeteria, too, was designed for exposure to natural light. Decorated with vibrant-colored tables and chairs reminiscent of a diner, it looks out to the street level (see Figure 2-14). Other break areas adjacent to clusters of workstations enable employees to gather for informal knowledge exchanges, or just for a quick respite from their workstations (see Figure 2-15).

And to highlight the pride the Centre for Health & Safety Innovation takes in its dynamic training and educational programs, HOK added a wide, glass sidelight next to the training room door, and designed a learning environment where program participants can study without the feeling of isolation inherent in windowless training facilities (see Figure 2-16). Similarly, HOK's design

of a variety of small meeting areas, to support spontaneous interactions among employees of the four groups, effectively addressed the nuances of diverse user preferences. For example, two small rooms placed side by side were designed differently. One features side chairs and a more conventional round meeting table. The other contains oversized, mobile chairs with tablet-arms (see Figure 2-17).

Technology

Technology is a primary enabler of enhanced productivity in the workplace. In general, technological concepts appear in the workplace, followed by less expensive versions for home use. Heavy-duty office copiers and fax machines, for example, are now available in more affordable and smaller versions suitable for use in the home or home office. An example of the reverse of this phenomenon

Figure 2-14: HOK Canada met CHSI's requirement for access to natural light for its staff throughout the facility. The full-service cafeteria is bathed in sunlight, for all to enjoy.

© 2006 Tom Arban Photography.

Figure 2-15: The work environment for the Centre for Health & Safety Innovation's 400 employees emphasizes ergonomics, appropriate lighting, and conveniently located spaces to take brief breaks throughout the workday.

© 2006 Tom Arban Photography.

Figure 2-16: In designing space for CHSI's numerous training and educational programs, HOK incorporated glass sidelights or glass fronts, to create additional openness in the spaces.

© 2006 Tom Arban Photography.

Figure 2-17: Small meeting rooms in the Centre for Health & Safety Innovation have unique characteristics to satisfy user preferences.

© 2006 Tom Arban Photography.

Figure 2-18: Businesses that want to provide a "touchdown" spot where employees can check e-mail, instead of dedicated workstations or private offices, can borrow from the concept of a computer laboratory employed in universities, such as at Davenport University, shown here.

Rockford Construction Company; © 2005 Kevin Beswick, People Places & Things Photographics.

was the introduction of the cordless phone, which enabled movability throughout the home. Yet in corporate America, too many workers are still tethered to their workstations by their corded telephones, making it difficult for them to give a customer an immediate answer to a question should the reference material they need not be at their fingertips. With many new workplace strategies focusing on cost reduction by reducing the overall footprint of individual workspaces, the decision is made to replace duplicate reference materials with a single set of documents for use by an entire department. When this happens, outdated phone equipment prevents optimal use of the new workplace design.

Perhaps nowhere is the gap between generations so apparent as in the use of technology. Understanding one generation's perception of technology must go well beyond interpreting an individual's level of comfort in using the existing electronic work tools the enterprise provides, or a willingness to learn the latest software release prescribed by the company. Bob Johansen of the Institute for the Future has explored the social and organizational impact of new technologies. As a social scientist, he has studied the human aspect of technological advancement. He describes these different perceptions of technology in *Get There Early: Sensing the Future to Compete in the Present* (see side bar).

Reflecting on Johansen's insights on how technology might be perceived differently by members of an organization's workforce, and then applying them to the design of the physical office space, the architect or interior designer no doubt will notice misalignment between what technology can do and what the client is willing to do with it. Consider reducing numerous workplace design options to the lowest common denominator to accommodate four different generations. This is a difficult challenge, to be sure. Even the presence of mobile technology and wireless access to data in an organizational culture that truly trusts employees to work wherever they choose does not guarantee that members of the aggregate workforce will be productive. Certainly, the "digital youth" identified by Johansen are adept at operating among multimedia influences and interruptions. Conversely, baby boomers often feel distracted by similar influences, and so prefer to have some space between themselves and others, to better focus on their work. That is not to say they cannot multitask—they may indeed be performing a number of different tasks. It is to say they may prefer a quieter space in which to conduct their activities.

Bill Weldon, CEO of Johnson & Johnson, and LaVerne Council, the company's chief information officer, recently gave a joint presentation on "Change Artists," hosted by IDG Communications, Inc., a leading information technology media and event company that publishes a variety of technology-specific magazine and newspapers, and hosts Web sites.[18] In this presentation, where competitive business advantage was emphasized, Weldon described a Johnson & Johnson initiative called "Links," where technology is used to reduce the time needed for problem resolution. Using the Links program, for example, a scientist can go online within the enterprise and state a problem and ask for help. Other scientists track the questions and respond with potential solutions. Using this technology can generate answers to key issues arising in the development of new drugs in record-breaking time.

The point here is not that Johnson & Johnson has invented a new technological forum in which employees can exchange ideas. Many organizations have done as much. The point is that the system works at Johnson & Johnson because *it is being used*. Frequently, organizations develop a process for information exchange between its employees, and generate enthusiasm with the initial launch. But in most cases, the system is not reinforced by the company's management, and so it goes unused or, at best, is underutilized.

Critical Influences may raise barriers to the optimization of future technologies that will be invented to share knowledge. Even if the appropriate office or laboratory space is designed for collaboration, and the technology is developed, the organizational culture could become a hindrance to employees' exchange of data. If the culture of an enterprise is focused on the "I" rather than on the "we"; if staff members feel their ideas are not fairly recognized by the leaders of teams, departments, or business units; or if managers take credit for the concepts developed by their direct reports; then knowledge exchange within the organization will be stifled. A company that needs to produce innovations on an ongoing basis to survive in the industry in which it operates could find itself failing in its field if it cannot motivate collaboration and the sharing of knowledge among members of its workforce.

Business Processes

Changes to the physical workplace are often planned to move an organization's business processes from a linear method, whereby a customer's request is slowly transferred from department to department, to one of cross-functional teamwork wherein members process the necessary documents simultaneously, thus reducing response time. If the technology required to allow employees immediate access to shared electronic files is not in place, or if the culture is not centered on teamwork and collaboration, though the cross-functional staff members may be physically colocated within a shared space in the office, the business process may continue to be carried out as it was prior to implementation of the new workplace strategy. Holding onto a customer's files by an employee until his or her individual tasks are completed, before passing on information to a teammate, signals the organization that the team may need training in working collaboratively.

Recall Bill Weldon and LaVerne Council's experience at Johnson & Johnson, which illustrated how the corporation leveraged electronic tools to quickly tap into the specialized knowledge of its scientific staff members. Another aspect of their strategy had to do with accelerating the speed of business process completion to create a competitive advantage in the field of drug discovery. Weldon emphasized the importance of making a paradigm shift in light of the company's acquisition of Pfizer Consumer Healthcare. That shift had to expand beyond the internal company boundaries to the external environment, and incorporate what the enterprise brings to the consumer. Council explained that technology is not the competitive advantage for Johnson & Johnson; rather, it is the company's intellectual capital that is its differentiating advantage. The technology can enable differentiators the closer one gets to the customer, which is where an organization needs the competitive advantage.

In the field of drug discovery, accelerated speed in performing business processes is critical to becoming the "first to market" with a medical breakthrough. Streamlined business processes thus can result in a competitive advantage. Business processes necessary to improving existing drugs and inventing new ones have historically been time-consuming, when conducted manually and in linear steps. Using advanced technology, processes can be expedited greatly. Clinical trials can be completed faster, and digital signatures to the Food and Drug Administration can supplant the submission of truckloads of paperwork mandatory for FDA approval.

Just keep in mind, as the 10-year research study on the Critical Influence System proved, if the physical workplace is designed so that people must work in departmental silos, isolated from others involved in a mission-critical process, no matter how good the technology, it may not be fully optimized. A workplace strategy that colocates cross-functional team members involved in time-sensitive business processes would benefit those accountable for the on-time completion of individual steps in the respective processes. A given member of the workgroup would then be able to recognize when a colleague was struggling with an issue, and be able to offer immediate assistance, thereby preventing delays in the workflow. Such time savings

could make the difference between the enterprise being first to market with a new drug discovery and being left behind by the competition.

Physical Workplace

This topic is the last of the Critical Influences discussed in this chapter, for good reason. Perhaps you may even have skipped over the others to quickly "get to the important one." But if you're passionate about the power of place, adamant about the importance of the workplace in driving the changes your client needs to make to meet its goals, and committed to the successful execution of the workplace strategy you've determined will transform the way the client's workforce will operate, you would be wise to return to the beginning of the chapter and read about each Critical Influence in the order presented.

Consider what Chris Turner, author of *All Hat and No Cattle: Tales of a Corporate Outlaw*,[19] had to say in an article titled "Leading in Interesting Times," regarding the importance of the context in which we work (see side bar).[20]

To continue Turner's metaphor, too often, clients expect their architects and interior designers to improve the water to provide a healthier environment in which the fish can swim, but fail to identify and address other elements within the aquarium that are preventing our fine-gilled friends from productive travels within the tank. The seaweed and other vegetation (i.e., business processes and levels of authority) have become overgrown, and often strangle the fish as they go in circles. The fish food (i.e., compensation) sprinkled on the surface of the water then generates competition among the fish, even though they operate most effectively in schools (teams). And that deep-sea diver statue (technology) that was supposed to generate life-saving oxygen never seems to work.

As noted previously, incongruence between the physical workplace and other Critical Influences may erupt when organizations institute telework initiatives. The decision to allow employees to choose their home as their physical workplace is not an easy one. Various clients handle this in a number of ways. Some develop telework programs with sophisticated guidelines and a complete infrastructure to support the initiative; others follow a one-page sheet that documents how to handle a request to telecommute. The barrier that often emerges, regardless of the size of the enterprise or the level of sophistication of the telework program, is a cultural one. The perception of people within the organization that telework isolates employees from opportunities for career advancement can result in underutilization of a program that otherwise has the potential to increase worker productivity. Similarly, the view that employees choosing to telecommute are not as committed to the enterprise can stifle chances for the teleworker to be invited to lead an exciting, new project that would provide learning, personal growth, and engagement within the organization.

In January 2007, global talent management company Korn/Ferry International announced the results of its survey of business executives from 71 countries. The organization's Trends@Work research revealed:

- Of more than 1,300 business leaders, 61 percent believe teleworkers have a lesser chance of career advancement than those who work in conventional work environments.
- More than one-third believe teleworkers are more productive than their peers who do not telework.[21]

This data has been corroborated by the research results of the Center for Excellence in Service at the Robert H. Smith School of Business, University of Maryland, which were published in the Society for Human Resource Management's *HR News*.[22] In its annual National Technology Readiness Survey (NTRS), the center gathered feedback from 1,015 adults in the United States. In 2006, survey results indicated that although 25 percent of the respondents were given the option to telework, only 11 percent chose to do so full- or part-time.

Telework is a great concept, yet complex issues surround the decision to implement such an initiative. In Chapter 4, we'll explore the case for—and against—telework, and look more closely at the positive impact it can have on worker productivity. You'll also read about key stakeholder issues regarding telework, including the perspective of employees within the enterprise who are not eligible to participate in such a program.

If you could inform your client organizations that they could reduce their real estate costs from 35 to nearly 50 percent, wouldn't that capture their attention? If a company's goal is to cut costs, would its business leaders be willing to do whatever was necessary to achieve such significant savings? In fact, cost savings this significant are being realized by a number of enterprises today. The driving force behind these attention-getting savings is the transition from measuring the effectiveness of the organization's real estate investment in terms of occupancy to metrics centered on utilization. The traditional emphasis on building occupancy focuses on the number of individuals the facility can hold based on the assignment of one workspace per person. But take a walk through the typical office environment today and notice how many workspaces, whether private office or workstation, are unoccupied, regardless of day of week and time of day. Feedback from facilities and corporate real estate professionals that, currently, individual workspaces are often vacant 65 percent of the time due to employees traveling; working in other parts of the building or office campus; or gathering in conference, meeting, or team spaces. By shifting to the real estate measurement of space utilization, the enterprise analyzes the number of individuals who actually use the facility at a given time. And by switching to an office environment composed of unassigned workspaces, a significant reduction in total real estate requirements can be achieved, leading to major cost savings. Research commissioned in 2006 by CoreNet Global indicates that, by the year 2010, 20 percent of large companies anticipate having 25 to 50 percent of their employees working in unassigned workspaces. With the growing adoption of this approach to support cost reduction and improve deployment of real estate holdings, according to this research, by 2020, the majority of large enterprises can be expected to shift to the use of unassigned workspaces to some degree.[23]

Leadership behavior can impede the adoption of a program that incorporates unassigned workspaces. Executives who have successfully halted the transition from private offices to the open plan in the past will most likely resist moving from private offices to partially or totally unassigned workspaces. Another Critical Influence impacting the shift to unassigned workspaces is technology. But taking simple plug-and-play technology to a higher level may help to eliminate many concerns about working in such an environment. The ability for an employee's telephone extension to follow wherever he or she chooses to work in the facility, or providing advanced technology to capture and share meeting notes, rather than relying on paper, can support the successful execution of a workplace strategy employing unassigned workspaces. Finally, corporate culture can impede the transition to unassigned workspaces for a portion of the workforce. When supervisors, managers, and other executives are moved from dedicated places to work in the unassigned work environment, those maintaining their private spaces may react negatively, perceiving that they're "not important enough to switch to the new way of working." Their interpretation of the decision to keep them in their cubicles is that the organization lacks trust in them. That dedicated workspace has just taken on the connotation of a cage or prison cell to "contain" them rather than as a tool to support their productivity.

With the increasing emphasis that business leaders are placing on improving innovative organizational outputs, workplace professionals charged with developing environments meant to enable innovation would be wise to heed warnings of barriers that may undermine their office design solutions. Fortunately, understanding the interrelatedness of the Critical Influence System factors can help to explain why previous workplace designs have failed to achieve their project objectives. My advice to any organization frustrated with less than stellar results produced by a newly designed workplace environment is to avoid assuming a large dollar investment is required to redesign that solution. Better to invest the time in exploring the various elements of the Critical Influence System to identify incongruence among the interdependent factors. The office design may in fact be quite appropriate. Environmental adaptations needed, if any, may be minor, and carry little or no cost. The key learning is that the physical workplace needs to be considered simultaneously with the other elements. A change in one element often causes a disruption elsewhere in the system. All factors within the Critical Influence System need to be congruent, and working in harmony.

NOTES

[1] Stegmeier, Diane, "Improving Collaboration and Teamwork to Create Better Results," presentation to the American Institute of Architects, Tri AIA Convention, Pittsburgh, PA, March 9, 2002.

[2] Grossman, Robert, "Space: Another HR Frontier," *HR Magazine*, Society for Human Resource Management, Vol. 47, No. 9, September 2002. http://www.shrm.org/hrmagazine/articles/0902/0902covstory_space.asp (accessed November 13, 2006).

[3] Daft, Richard L., *Organization Theory and Design*, 6th ed., Cincinnati, OH: South-Western College Publishing, 1998.

[4] Johansen, Robert, and Rob Swigart, *Upsizing the Individual in the Downsized Organization: Managing in the Wake of Reengineering, Globalization, and Overwhelming Technological Change*, Reading, MA: Addison-Wesley, 1994.

[5] Johansen, Robert, *Get There Early: Sensing the Future to Compete in the Present*, San Francisco: Berrett-Koehler, 2007.

[6] Johansen, Robert, communications with the author, January 11, 2007.

[7] Gensler, *Well-Designed Office Key to Improving Employee Performance: New Survey*, July 20, 2006. http://www.gensler.com/news/2006/07-20_workSurvey.html (accessed April 21, 2007).

[8] Hudson Highland Group, www.hhgroup.com.

[9] Tropman, John E., *The Compensation Solution: How to Develop an Employee-Driven Rewards System*, San Francisco: Jossey-Bass, 2001.

[10] Kampschroer, Kevin, Research & Expert Services, Office of Applied Science—Public Buildings Service, U.S. General Services Administration, interview by the author, September 8, 2006.

[11] "On the Folly of Rewarding A While Hoping for B," *Academy of Management Journal*, New York: 1975, pp. 769–783.

[12] "More on the Folly," Academy of Management Executive: The Thinking Manager's Source, New York: February 1, 1995, pp. 15–16.

[13] *Human Resources Management Magazine*, Interview with the author, Moscow: December 2006–January 2007, www.hrm.ru.

[14] Society for Human Resource Management, www.shrm.org.

[15] Straight Talk about Reorganization Workshop (STAR), Diane Stegmeier, 2002, www.stegmeierconsulting.com.

[16] Wunder, Sarah Stone, "Sprint Nextel: Bringing Mobility to Talent Management," *Workforce Performance Solutions Magazine*, September 2006, pp. 34–51.

[17] Johansen, Robert, *Get There Early: Sensing the Future to Compete in the Present*, San Francisco: Berrett-Koehler, 2007.

[18] Weldon, Bill, and LaVerne Council, "Change Artists," Webinar, IDG Communications, Inc., January 18, 2007.

[19] Turner, Chris, *All Hat and No Cattle: Tales of a Corporate Outlaw*, New York: Perseus, 2000.

[20] Turner, Chris, "Leading in Interesting Times," *BUSINESS: The Ultimate Resource*, New York: Perseus, September 2006, pp. 273–274.

[21] Korn/Ferry International, www.kornferry.com.

[22] Gurchiek, Kathy, "Workers Choose Office Over Telecommute Most Days," *HR News*, Society for Human Resource Management, July 27, 2006. http://shrm.org/hrnews_published/ARCHIVES/CMS_017909.asp (accessed January 30, 2007).

[23] Durfee, Don, "Take My Desk—Please: By Rethinking Office Design, Companies Are Cutting Real-Estate Costs by Nearly Half," *CFO Magazine*, October 1, 2006, pp. 99–102.

CHAPTER 3
CREATIVITY, INNOVATION, AND THE INNOVATION-FRIENDLY WORKPLACE

What do the following inventions have in common: dynamite, Caesar salad, Post-It Notes, Teflon, Velcro, birth control pills, X-rays, penicillin, nylon, photography, and Super Glue? Each of these famous discoveries was made by accident. Unexpected breakthroughs are a result of serendipity, according to the thought leadership of Royston M. Roberts. In his book *Serendipity: Accidental Discoveries in Science*, he draws from his exploration of hundreds of innovations that have improved our everyday lives. Some of the discoveries, such as artificial sweetener, have become so commonplace they may be taken for granted. Others are life-saving, such as the accidental discovery of the impact of nitrogen mustards on white blood cells, the revelation that led to chemotherapy treatment for cancer.[1]

There is a growing awareness that very different physical work environments are required to support innovation. How can we connect this concept of the accidental discovery of inventions to the emphasis many businesses today place on improving collaboration to produce more innovative organizational results? How can we leverage academic theory and empirical evidence on human behaviors that lead to innovative results and translate that knowledge into workplace design? Let's begin connecting the dots.

Chapter 1 introduced you to the importance of integrating the ideas of professionals from various disciplines to produce the richest and most innovative workplace design solution. As research results have revealed, providing the ideal office design does not guarantee that the physical space will be used as intended. Furthermore, even when end users make every attempt to use the space as the physical cues suggest, other Critical Influences may hinder the type of behaviors the organization requires to achieve its goals of innovative results. As I explained in the Introduction, I did not discover the Critical

> *"Creativity is the input, while innovation the output."*
> —S. VICARI

Influences impacting behavior in the workplace in an accidental, serendipitous fashion, rather as part of an evolving process over ten years.

DEFINING CREATIVITY AND INNOVATION

Most business leaders would no doubt acknowledge that creativity and innovation are critical to the growth, competitive advantage, profitability, and market success of their respective organizations. Still, one is hard-pressed to find a consistent and universal definition of either word in business language today. Moreover, the words *creativity* and *innovation* are commonly used interchangeably, leaving little to distinguish them. So, for the purposes of this book, the following definitions will be assumed:

- *Creativity* is the ability to approach the situation at hand with a fresh perspective, and link together previously unrelated or uncombined concepts, to generate new and unexpected ideas that solve a problem or capture an opportunity.
- *Innovation* is the synthesis of knowledge and ideas; the transformation of that knowledge and those ideas into new products, services, or processes; and their subsequent commercialization and diffusion through society and the economy.

BUSINESS CASE FOR DISTINCTION

As just noted, the words *innovation* and *creativity* are often confused and misused. Many in the business

world don't take the time to make the distinction, despite their organizational leaders pushing for better innovative results throughout the company. Architects and designers charged with developing a physical space to enable collaboration and creativity would be wise to tie their office design solution to a business case for supporting organizational innovation. If the client does not specifically articulate the requirement that the workplace support the business goal of increasing innovative results, questions should be posed to discover why a collaborative workplace is wanted in the first place. Legitimately, an organization may be struggling seriously with attracting and retaining the talent needed for future success, so the decision to create a collaborative workplace might be driven solely by an attraction and retention strategy. In a situation such as that, a business goal of producing richer innovative outputs may not be voiced specifically by the workplace project's decision maker. Yet, chances are, at the highest level of that client organization, top executives are losing sleep over their competitive status in the market via the introduction of innovations.

Creativity does indeed differ from innovation. Creativity may be considered the foundation for innovation, yet it does not always lead to innovative outputs. Conversely, innovation cannot occur without creativity. To reiterate the definitions just given, creativity generates novel and unexpected concepts; innovation is the transformation of those concepts into commercial reality. We can best examine the fundamental distinction between creativity and innovation through the thought leadership of those involved with the Creative Processes for Enterprise Innovation's CREATE project, funded by the European Commission and coordinated by the University of Udine in Italy. Centered on the importance of organizations creating competitive advantage through creativity and innovation, the CREATE project focuses on enterprise capacity for creativity, which is the first step of the innovation process. The necessity for organizations to manage creative capability, transform new concepts into value in competitive markets and, subsequently, into profits for the firm introducing the innovation, has been a driving force for business leaders to better understand the dynamics of creativity and innovation, and to develop and execute strategies to leverage the workforce, intellectual capital, and the physical workplace to increase innovative output for the organization.

Professor Alberto Felice De Toni of the University of Udine, along with an international consortium of academic, research, industrial, and consulting partners of diverse backgrounds and expertise, examined 16 methodologies and more than 200 techniques centered on promoting creative work environments and producing innovation through the generation of new ideas. "Creativity is the context where innovation might develop" was a phrase heard at the March 2005 CREATE Conference held at Palazzo Torriani in Udine, Italy.[2] Of particular interest to the architectural and design communities should be the group's strong emphasis on the "where" in this comment, and how the research results can be interpreted

and applied to the design of the physical workplace. The initial phase of the methodology recommended by the CREATE team, predisposition, suggests the business enterprise constitutes creative groups, identifies catalysts and facilitators, and "creates a work environment to allow the employees to free their creativity."

To further clarify the difference between creativity and innovation, and to articulate the importance of the context in which both occur, it's recommended that architects and designers create a business case that ties the workplace design solution to the client's goals to increase organizational innovation. The messages of several experts on creativity and innovation were shared at the CREATE Conference, exemplifying the positioning of the three:

"Organizations increasingly perceive the development of conditions that encourage creativity within their working environment as a long-term process rather than a quick fix to their current problems."[3]

"Creativity is the input while innovation the output."[4]

An innovative change is a "sequence of events where creativity is the cause, while innovation is the effect."[5]

"If implementation is putting an idea into practice, creativity is coming up with the idea in the first place. Creativity is an essential part of innovation, the point of departure."[6]

"Innovation is the outcome, the result, while organizational creativity is the condition."[7]

"Creativity is the generation of ideas, while innovation consists of transforming these ideas into action through a selection, an improvement, and an implementation."[8]

THEORY OF MULTIPLE INTELLIGENCES

Harvard psychologist Howard Gardner, author of *Frames of Mind: The Theory of Multiple Intelligences*, has revolutionized theoretical views about intelligence and creativity.[9] He challenged the more traditional view of intelligence as a one-dimensional measurement of mental capacity with his theory of multiple intelligences, identifying nine distinct forms of intelligence possessed by all human beings to varying degrees. Each individual, he contends, has a unique intellectual profile comprising the following (reprinted by permission of BASIC BOOKS, a member of Perseus Books Group):

- *Verbal-Linguistic Intelligence*: The strength of an individual's verbal skills and his or her sensitivity to the sounds and rhythms of words and their meanings.
- *Mathematical-Logical Intelligence*: The capacity for abstract and conceptual thinking, and for recognizing orderly patterns of numbers.
- *Musical Intelligence*: Developed skills in identifying and creating sound properties.
- *Visual-Spatial Intelligence*. The ability to understand the relationship of space and to visualize abstractly in images.
- *Bodily-Kinesthetic Intelligence*: Developed sense of body motion and controlling the movement of physical objects.
- *Interpersonal Intelligence*: Developed sensitivity to temperament and what drives the desires of others.
- *Intrapersonal Intelligence*: The ability to be self-reflective with one's own values, perceptions, opinions and thought processes.
- *Naturalist Intelligence*: The capacity to identify and classify living organisms in nature.
- *Existential Intelligence*: Sensitivity to complex issues surrounding our existence, and developed skills in pondering deep questions.

Gardner's theory has been primarily applied to the process of independent learning, examining how diverse individuals learn best, based on the composition of their intelligence profile. His research can also provide great insight to business leaders seeking to improve collaboration in the workplace for the purpose of increasing organizational innovation. Certainly, a deeper understanding of how mutidisciplinary team members perceive a given situation differently, or how they convey ideas, would help us operate more effectively in today's fast-paced work environment. Or, if you are responsible for selecting multidiscipline team members to support a client's project, this understanding can help you to form a stronger workgroup, by ensuring the appropriate intelligence categories are reflected in the skills of the specialists chosen.

Further investigation of Gardner's work led to the establishment of the Harvard research group, Project Zero, where his thought leadership has contributed to the exploration of understanding, enhancing, and promoting critical and creative thinking. As part of my own work in understanding influences on employee behavior, I began asking myself how I could interpret Howard Gardner's theory of multiple intelligences in order to apply it to the design of physical space intended to improve collaboration in the workplace, and in turn, raise the level of organizational innovation.

The first step was to analyze my own skills to determine how I use them to solve my clients' complex challenges. Keeping in mind Gardner's claim that the multiple intelligences of each individual can be strengthened by nurturing or, conversely, weakened by lack of attention to them, I set out to identify my own forms of intelligence by taking the Multiple Intelligences Self-Inventory, available online at www.thirteen.org/edonline/concept-2class/mi/index.html.[10] Specifically, because a large part of my work as a consultant involves working as a member of diverse interdisciplinary teams, I wanted to understand which particular intelligences I contribute most to my colleagues. Are there areas I need to enhance? Which

specific intelligences are my weakest, and require improvement? Do other team members typically complement my weaknesses, or would I be a better team member if I embarked upon training to better understand their strengths? You can see my Multiple Intelligences Profile in Figure 3-1.

How can we apply Gardner's Theory of Multiple Intelligences to the design of workplaces focused on improving collaborative behavior? For starters, all architects and interior designers should take the Multiple Intelligences Self-Inventory. By doing so, you can begin to translate specific characteristics of the multiple intelligences into physical manifestations in the workplace. For example:

- *"Likes to read"*: To improve Verbal-Linguistic Intelligence, take a different approach to, for example, a client's request to include a reference library in their new facility.

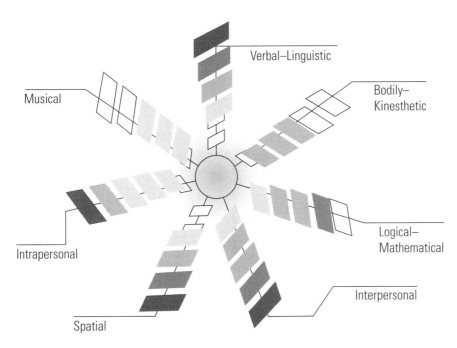

Figure 3-1: The Multiple Intelligences Self-Inventory is based on Howard Gardner's Theory of Multiple Intelligences. The resultant profile identifies the degree of each intelligence for the person taking the inventory.

Adapted from Concept to Classroom, produced by Thirteen/WNET New York, http:www.thirteen .org/edonline/concept2class.

Whereas the public library enforces silence, encouraging individual learning by discouraging distractions, you might, instead, develop a group innovation library—perhaps within the break room. This is what one architectural firm did to reinforce collaborative learning. You might also stock the shelves with thought-provoking articles on innovation from very diverse sources.

- *"Analyzes numbers quickly"*: To enhance Mathematical-Logical

Figure 3-2: The IDEO Tech Box takes the Montessori approach to visual and tactile learning. The firm considers the collection of objects its "corporate sparkplug" to ignite innovation.

Courtesy of IDEO/Joe Watson.

Intelligence, resist the temptation to assume statistical interpretation occurs only in the finance department. At one of my clients, the customer service team was passionate about improving their performance. To that end, the workplace design included a small, yet prominent space in the main corridor just outside their call center that was equipped with a tackable surface, colored paper, markers, and pushpins. Colleagues from other departments passing by throughout the day were encouraged to read the current posting on a performance statistic and share ideas on methods for improvement. In addition to this giving the customer service professionals some great ideas for optimizing performance, others in the company, who did not ordinarily have direct contact with customers, came to better understand client issues and expectations.

- *"Appreciates the visual world"*: Gardner's research results on Visual-Spatial Intelligence can be interpreted by architects and interior designers to produce some of the most interesting applications in the physical work environment. The investigation of how organizations can strengthen and leverage these competencies can be illustrated by my personal experience with a European client on their visit to IDEO in Palo Alto, California. Renowned for their work in helping companies innovate through design, IDEO's emphasis has expanded from product design and development to the application of divergent thinking to social issues, including sustainability, health and wellness, and enterprise in lower-income groups. The IDEO work environment and multitude of groundbreaking innovations, which were displayed on-site, made it clear this is an organization that walks the talk. The organization's workplace is filled with interesting artifacts that stimulate the senses. Most notable, however, was the firm's adoption of the Montessori approach to learning through visual and tactile objects. The Tech Box, for example, an ever-changing collection of gadgets and materials (shown in Figure 3-2), is, in the enterprise's description, the "corporate sparkplug" for igniting innovative thought.[11]

DESIGNING FOR DIVERSITY

Ideally, by reading about Howard Gardner's research, you will make the connection between the power inherent in combining individuals with diverse multiple intelligence profiles and producing more innovative results. As the saying goes, the whole is greater than the sum of its parts. By improving collaboration in the workplace, not only can the organization increase the *quantity* of innovative outputs, but it can also realize significant improvement in the *quality* of innovations as well.

Consider my experience at Steelcase Inc., where I was fortunate to hear a keynote speech delivered by R. Roosevelt Thomas, Jr. Recognized for his groundbreaking work on managing diversity, Thomas has consulted numerous clients on maximizing organizational and individual potential. He had been engaged by Steelcase to address a group of diverse individuals employed at the company who were passionate about helping the enterprise leverage the talent of its workforce. Each was committed to becoming an "employee on loan" to our own company, a team that would take on the major task of training all management levels of the enterprise on valuing and leveraging the increasingly diverse workforce. Through training, coaching, strategic planning, and performance management, the company was determined to instill accountability from the C-level executives to the first-time supervisor to maximize the talent in our workforce.

Thomas told a story that featured a clear jar holding a large number of jelly beans, primarily yellow. Mixed in was a handful of red jelly beans, plus a few purple jelly beans, and two green jelly beans. Thomas asked the group, "Which jelly beans are the diverse jelly beans?" He paused to let each member of the audience reflect. He suggested that participants put themselves in the place of a yellow jelly bean, then in the place of each of the other colors. "Which color jelly beans are the diverse ones?" Chattering was heard throughout the auditorium. Eventually, Thomas told us the answer: that all the jelly beans—the entire collection—were diverse, not just the ones represented by smaller numbers.

The same is true in the workplace. It is crucial to examine the diversity of the workforce on a much deeper level if we are to use uniqueness as a springboard for innovation and business growth. The entire workforce comprises a diverse blend of individuals, each of whom possesses a unique background, perspective, knowledge, opinion, work style, and approach to problem solving. Typically, these characteristics are not being used to strategic advantage as much as they could be.

As we reflect upon how an enterprise can leverage diversity to optimize both organizational and individual performance, we should keep in mind that stereotyping can place limitations on innovative results. We cannot assume that innovation should be a task dedicated only to the research and development team or the marketing department. The business enterprise needs to challenge every cog in the workforce wheel to discover better ways of doing things.

How can we interpret the concept of diversity when examining the use of the physical workplace? When employees are offered alternative work spaces, is it obvious which of the spaces are "alternative"? In most cases, employees moving into a new office facility are not provided enough training on how to use alternative work spaces. Rather than educating the workforce on how to use the entire work environment, often employees are sent an apologetic message: "Even though you no longer have a large, private office, we are providing you with a small space in the open area. And, by the way, if you really need to find some privacy, check if one of the small conference rooms is available." It should come as no surprise, then, when the new office design is met with great resistance.

One good way to help employees better understand how to fully utilize the work environment is to ask them to consider how they make use of their own homes. For example:

- One may ordinarily pay his bills in the kitchen, but when his teen-aged daughter and her friends are making a mess there baking cookies for the school fund-raiser, he grabs his laptop and a soft drink and moves to the deck, where he can use wireless access to the Internet to pay the bills online while enjoying the warm, sunny day. The kitchen and the deck are shared resources in his home.
- Another may sit in the great room to wait for a phone call from one of her employees while her husband is reading in the same room. When she receives the call, she takes the cordless phone into the den where the conversation will not distract her mate. She did not reserve the den for the entire day for her own dedicated use, given that she could not predict exactly when the phone call would come.

The successful architectural and design firm will challenge its clients to engage in dialogue to address some tough questions about the use of shared spaces. Are the diverse work settings utilized as exceptions to the rule rather than spaces that are consciously sought to conduct work? If a midlevel manager does have a private office, is it damaging to his or her status to be seen meeting in the open, shared spaces of the facility? Will his or her private office be taken away because he or she doesn't need a space to conduct confidential conversations 100 percent of the time? Do we only enter a free-address workspace as a last resort when all "regular" work areas are occupied? Is the reason we're meeting in the cafeteria with colleagues because all the conference rooms are already taken? A culture that forces employees to perceive physical space as a currency to reward status, or whose members feel they must make excuses for where they've chosen to work, is not in line with a culture essential for driving innovation and change in today's competitive business environment.

How can we apply this principle to the design of the physical workplace? How can architectural and design professionals convince the decision makers in their client organizations to break out of the reference scheme that says the enterprise must provide a dedicated, individual workspace (regardless of private office or semiprivate workstation) to each employee? Do we think that an individual's primary work style—for example, concentrated focus on financial data—means that he or she must conduct interactive work from that same quiet place? Planning workplace design based on titles and status must be supplanted by strategic design that supports the activities being performed within the organization.

Educating clients early in the design process is essential. Articulating from the outset the impact of Critical Influences on behavior in the workplace can mean the difference between the designer creating an office that will transform the way people work, using a blank canvas, and squeezing incremental improvements onto a partially completed paint-by-number kit, which will, in the end, be insufficient to guide the necessary employee behaviors.

DICHOTOMIES OF THE INNOVATION-FRIENDLY WORKPLACE

Upon earning my MBA with a concentration in Leading Organizational Change, I became committed to expanding my knowledge in the areas of change and organizational innovation. I am, in short, a student of change. After graduation, I began exploring the more structured aspect of my continuing education, ultimately deciding to participate in a Harvard University program on innovation and organizational change. My goal: to gain knowledge that could be applied to the design of physical workplaces centered on improving collaborative behavior for the purpose of increasing innovative organizational results. Seven years later, when solving my clients' complex problems, I continue to tap into the approach to innovation and organizational change I learned at the Harvard program. Therefore, one of my goals for this book is to apply that approach, along with complementary ideas of my own, to the practice of physical space design for environments that support innovation and other performance processes.

There is no shortage of self-proclaimed experts, gurus, and consultants intent on selling training, leading workshops, and offering other services to improve creativity. Consequently, many of my clients are relieved to find a methodology of substance, the Critical Influence approach. These organizations seek research-based processes, supported by effective systems and a physical infrastructure for innovating successfully—along with similar provisions for carrying out other performance processes, as needed.

Unfortunately, a specific recipe or magic formula for innovation does not exist. Instead, we can make use of a specific innovation-generating process based on behavioral studies and tested in workplace applications. This process can be adopted to analyze complex performance situations, determine specific needs for creativity, find specific ways to address those needs, and greatly improve our chances of developing innovative products and services.

The next section highlights elements of the comprehensive framework on leadership and human performance from the Harvard course just mentioned. Drawn from *Promoting Innovation & Organizational Change*, it represents a portion of a curriculum developed by Sherman D. Roberts. (Note: Since taking the course, an updated framework, "Optimal Performance and Leadership: The Five Process Model," has been released based on further research conducted by Roberts, © 2007, *Ivy Faculty Reports*, Number 07-3.) Then director of executive seminars at Harvard's Kennedy School, Roberts' impressive background includes work on several research projects under eminent Harvard psychologist B.F. Skinner. He is now affiliated with Oxford University's Saïd School of Business, and is the founder and director of the Ivy Faculty Consortium (www.ivyfaculty.org), where I am an associate faculty member and serve as director of Organizational Change Initiatives.[12]

Innovation versus Performance Maximization

It's important to note where innovation falls among the types of performance processes that executive leaders must understand and learn to handle skillfully. The Harvard program, designed by Sherman D. Roberts, introduced a useful way of looking at innovative performance in the context of performance in general. The course highlighted four fundamental leadership processes:

- Decision making
- Persuasion
- Performance maximization
- Innovation

Everything a business leader does is an aspect of one of these four processes, or a combination of two or more of them. Of the four, two form an interesting relationship— performance maximization and innovation—when translating the academic theory into practical advice that architects and interior designers can follow to design effective workplaces that will contribute to organizational innovation. That said, these two very different types of behaviors can be the most perplexing to support through workplace design, especially as more and more organizations begin to challenge their managers to motivate optimal performance from their employees for "business as usual" tasks, while simultaneously setting expectations to find innovative ways to strengthen the enterprise within their areas of responsibility—or to enable "business as *unusual*."

To elaborate on these important concepts, let's look at Roberts' definitions.

Performance maximization is the process of "using consequences deliberately to shape behavior, so that over time, it progressively approaches and 'hovers around' the maximum possible."

Innovation is the process of "using consequences and antecedents deliberately to cause behavior to vary more widely in order to generate new alternatives from which to choose."

Thus, these concepts are antagonistic at the behavioral level, as defined here by Roberts, then applied to the design of the office environment in support of the desired workplace behaviors (see Figure 3-3):

"Maximizing emphasizes choosing the best performance and then motivating that performance so that it varies less."

"Innovating emphasizes motivating performance, so that it varies more, and then choosing the best variations."

A critical point in comparing these two very different strategies is that most organizations should both maximize performance and innovate. Consider the example of a food processing company, where process improvements conducted over time have been focused on streamlining activities on the plant floor, specifically, to identify and eliminate any wasted steps in the conversion of fresh fruit into strained baby food. A year ago, it might have taken 17 steps to transform the fruit into a jar of baby food, to be sold by the grocery store. A new technology being launched by a supplier of food processing equipment claims that the process can now be completed in only 13 steps, an estimated 23.5 percent improvement in time savings. The plant manager of the corporation, through time studies, analysis, and testing, decides what the best performance is (13 steps versus 17), while weighing the cost of the investment in new equipment and the impact of the potential technology purchase on the wholesale price of each case of baby food. She may need to persuade others in the firm that this is the right direction to take (the process improvement will save the company time and money, while increasing the freshness of the baby food, with minimal increase in wholesale price). Employees are motivated to have less variance in their performance through training on the new process, communications detailing why things are changing, and developing written instructions on operating the new equipment.

**Antagonistic workplace behaviors
are supported by a variety of workplace settings.**

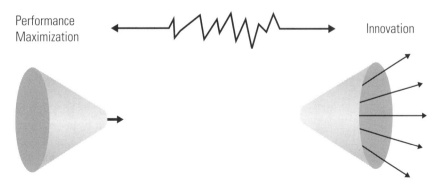

Performance Maximization

Innovation

Figure 3-3: The design of the office environment needs to support both performance maximization and innovation through a variety of workplace settings.

© 2001 Diane Stegmeier.

Three leadership processes were deployed: performance maximization, decision making, and persuasion. The physical space design to support this highly defined process should discourage variance in behavior. The tasks to be performed using the heavy-duty equipment, which is regulated by temperature control devices, have to be precisely calibrated, thus are surrounded by safety mechanisms. To comply with food-handling regulations, the fruit must only be processed in a dedicated area in the plant; the fruit preparation team is not permitted to deviate from the process by pureeing peaches in a blender in the company's shipping and receiving department. The tasks must be conducted sequentially, so the enterprise cannot have a person decide to work nine to five one day, to try to catch up with the food processing shift that began at 7:00 A.M. The situation dictates a precise process and an equally precise physical work setting.

Somewhere else in the company, five members of the field sales staff are chatting in an office corridor about their desire to improve sales. The group decides to leave the building to get some fresh air, and ends up huddled elbow to elbow around a small table at the local coffeeshop. Individually, each has discovered a new tactic the competition has been adopting market by market to win over established customers. They decide to strategize on how to increase the loyalty of their existing customers, and brainstorm other uses for the pureed fruit the company has historically sold only in the increasingly competitive baby food market. Away from the typical interruptions in the office environment, the team

comes up with three new ideas: to promote the entire line of baby foods for use in nursing homes; sell the more expensive, pureed apricots as the base ingredient for glaze for pork tenderloin to restaurants and gourmet food shops, and position to consumers the best-selling strawberry-banana fruit combination as an additive to stir into yogurt or blend into fruit smoothies. Following their meeting these field sales professionals were energized, and looked forward to presenting their ideas to their vice president of sales.

The activities of these five individuals were heavily focused on innovation. And in sharing their ideas with their vice president for new uses of the company's products, they will be deploying the fundamental skills of persuasion. If the enterprise is anything like those I've worked with in the past, the sales professionals' vice president will also engage in persuading others in the organization prior to any decision making.

What lesson can we apply to the appropriate workplace design in this case? The variation in physical spaces from which the field sales team could choose to meet contributed to their relaxed and uninterrupted brainstorming session during which the group uncovered new applications for the company's products. Certainly, they could have met on-site in the employee cafeteria and had the same conversation over coffee, but what's important here is the presence of an organizational culture that trusts its employees to meet—and exceed—their goals as they see fit. The architectural and design partners developing an office design to support this type of collaboration might decide to include a variety of team meeting spaces ranging from a totally open, public space where any peers could join in to an enclosed "huddle" room with a do not disturb protocol, enabling teams to remain sharply focused on solving a critical problem, such as combating the competition.

Divergent versus Convergent Thinking

As just mentioned, performance maximization and innovation can be the most perplexing processes to support in the design of workplaces, because they are at the opposite ends of the behavioral spectrum. In emphasizing performance maximization, behaviors are well defined and predictable, requiring little or no variation, until which time a process improvement is deemed appropriate. With innovation, the emphasis is on wide behavioral variation, by leveraging the diverse backgrounds, talents, and approaches of employees in order to come up with numerous alternatives from which to choose. As we continue our focus on the dichotomies of the innovation-friendly workplace, it's helpful to gain a heightened awareness of the differences between divergent and convergent thinking, and how they relate to performance maximization and innovation.

- Convergent thinking involves gathering data, materials, evidence, or experiences from a variety of sources to solve a problem. Strengths in analyzing and selecting the best choice from a large group of possibilities complement the convergent thought process. In most circumstances, there is only one answer to the problem being solved. With the goal of producing that one "correct solution," convergent thinking is typically used in the fields of technology, mathematics, and science (see Figure 3-4).
- Divergent thinking begins with a catalyst that stimulates thought. Key attributes of the divergent thought process include both the quantity and diversity of the alternatives produced, the ability to express new concepts or convey new connections to unrelated ideas, and the capability to easily switch between concrete and abstract thought. Rather than

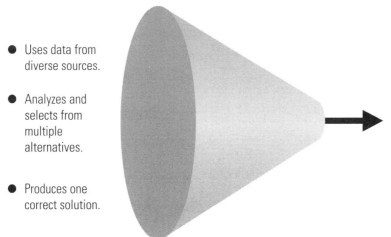

● Uses data from diverse sources.

● Analyzes and selects from multiple alternatives.

● Produces one correct solution.

Figure 3-4: Convergent thinking.
© 2001 Diane Stegmeier.

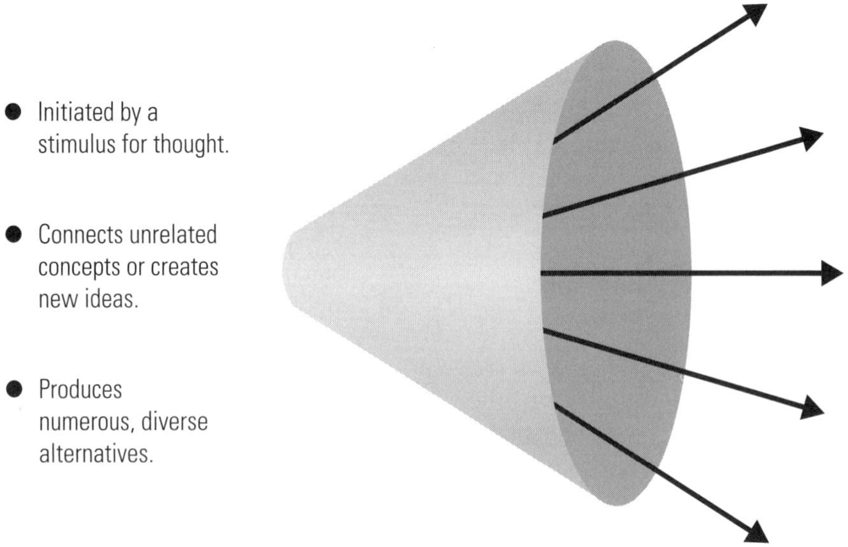

- Initiated by a stimulus for thought.

- Connects unrelated concepts or creates new ideas.

- Produces numerous, diverse alternatives.

Figure 3-5: Divergent thinking.
© 2001 Diane Stegmeier.

seeking the one correct answer, as with convergent thinking, an important goal of divergent thinking is the generation of a multitude of possible solutions (see Figure 3-5).

It is critical to note that convergence and divergence are not mutually exclusive. In today's complex business environment, organizations have strong requirements for both styles of thinking. While many individuals are clearly comfortable with one or the other approach, there are people who can quickly switch between convergent and divergent thought with little effort.

How can both convergent and divergent thought processes be supported in the office design? Do work spaces for individual convergent thought differ from those required for group convergent thought? Are workplace settings to accommodate the divergent thought process for an individual the same as the type needed for teams employing the

divergent thought process? In general, both divergent and convergent thinking can be supported by a variety of workplace settings. In comparing either thinking style as it relates to an individual versus a group, the principle of designing meeting spaces in several sizes to comfortably hold different teams is a logical solution. However, it's important to be aware of two common mistakes: assuming that because convergent thought is more analytical, it is always conducted in a private space, and believing that work settings for divergent thinking should be designed with only groups in mind, rather than for the individual.

Discontinuity versus Continuity

Along with other dichotomies of the innovation-friendly workplace, the concepts of continuity and discontinuity may create organizational friction by the very nature of their coexistence. Businesses are generally founded with a goal to remain viable for the long term. While an enterprise may be born out of an innovation introduced by an entrepreneur, eventually, as it grows and prospers, the business gravitates toward routine processes and operational excellence. Incremental improvements are sought, to protect profitability and strengthen the enterprise as a living entity.

At the same time, as the organization develops and commercializes new innovations, it creates disruption, and often the replacement of existing products, services, or processes. The phrase "creative destruction," coined in the 1930s by Austrian economist Joseph Schumpeter, reflects his theory of business cycles and the role of innovation in destroying that which already exists. Waves of innovation shape the market, creating opportunities for those who embrace discontinuity.

In applying the concepts of continuity and discontinuity to workplace design, flexibility of the components (e.g., mobile furniture, technology, work tools, etc.) used in the physical space is paramount. For example, even though mobile furniture is highly durable and designed to be moved many times throughout the course of a day, consider for a moment the movement of these furniture components orchestrated with business cycles. If you visualize a research and development team eagerly beginning the first day of a new product exploration initiative, they select furniture components from a "kit of parts" to configure their ideal office environment suited for the types of tasks they will be performing and their desired innovative results. The team may be together for only 8 to 10 months before disbanding, and during that time, they will make incremental changes to their group workplace as necessary. At the end of that particular assignment, a cycle, or wave, ends and another begins. The collection of furniture components—and the people— scatter in different directions, each moving on to the next initiative.

Figure 3-6 illustrates a single "wave of innovation" as it coincides with the classic marketing approach of viewing

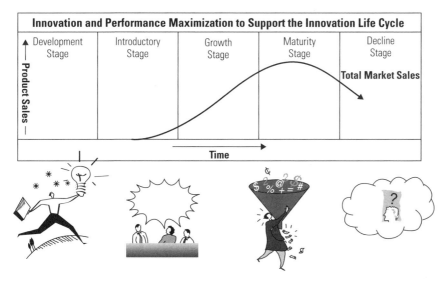

Innovation and Performance Maximization to Support the Innovation Life Cycle

Development Stage | Introductory Stage | Growth Stage | Maturity Stage | Decline Stage

Product Sales

Total Market Sales

Time

Figure 3-6: The innovation life cycle represents a single "wave of innovation" coinciding with the life cycle of that product. The graphic illustrates how divergent and convergent thinking—and the appropriate workplace settings to support those processes—play a role in the decisions surrounding the commercialization of a new product.

© 2006 Diane Stegmeier.

product sales over time throughout that product's life cycle. Starting with a stimulus, divergent thinking emphasizes increasing and expanding the number of innovative alternatives generated. Shifting to a convergent thought process, a breakthrough concept is discovered from the many possibilities that were explored. The organization as it exists today is now facing a situation of discontinuity. The excitement of planning a new product or service launch to the market, and the anticipation of a new revenue stream, come face to face with the current state of the enterprise. Do other products the company manufactures now become obsolete? If so, will obsolescence necessitate downsizing staff in business units that would be affected by this decision? Does the enterprise need to radically change its internal structure to reflect a new business direction?

As the commercialized innovation approaches maturity, emphasis is placed on improving processes to protect declining profitability. Convergent thinking is employed to reduce and refine all options down to the single best solution, enabling performance maximization. Meanwhile, as the innovation experiences a decline in its usefulness, or when competitors' "me too" introductions have positioned the product or service as a common commodity in the minds of consumers, proactive efforts may include assigning a research and development team to brainstorm the next new product. During these stages, the organization is focused on continuity. Typical activities to support the long-term success of the enterprise may include benchmarking tactics deployed by others in similar or dissimilar industries,

identifying and adopting best practices aimed at protecting profitability, or establishing an operational excellence initiative to be adopted throughout the organization.

Please note that this concept of innovation waves has been highly simplified here, to focus on the fundamental leadership skills of innovation and performance maximization. Intentionally, a great number of activities that support taking a new concept to market have not been shown graphically or included in the narrative description, so as to emphasize the dichotomies of innovation versus performance maximization, divergent versus convergent thinking, and discontinuity versus continuity. There is no prescriptive timing of the stages, and within the innovation wave, it is essential to understand that the various activities reflecting these elements will overlap. The most important point is that the innovation waves themselves overlap, with a potential new innovative concept surfacing before the prior one reaches the end of its life cycle. This overlapping of waves is especially evident in a large corporation where different divisions or business groups are working on developing new innovations on an ongoing basis. As the organization morphs and adapts to changes based on the dichotomies, ideally, the design professional will have developed a physical workplace solution that can respond to the shifting requirements of end-users at any moment in time. The need for maximum flexibility, mobility, and adaptability will not decrease anytime in the near future. It will, in fact, increase as a function of greater organizational change on the horizon for clients in diverse industries engaged in workplace transformation initiatives. The fact that there is no one prescription for precise office design to support the fluidity that occurs in an organization is exciting. An architectural or design firm that understands and applies the knowledge of these nuances of the dichotomy can most effectively clear the design canvas of obstacles in the way of truly leveraging their talents, skills, and creativity to design the innovation-friendly workplace.

AN INFRASTRUCTURE FOR INNOVATION

Organizations focused on improving innovative results can benefit from adopting the systematic approach developed by Sherman D. Roberts to create an infrastructure for innovation centering efforts on these six components:

1. Targeting domains.
2. Shaping a culture of innovation.
3. Engaging employees.
4. Making decisions in innovative contexts.
5. Developing implementation strategies.
6. Designing the innovation-friendly workplace.

Targeting Domains

The organization's leaders must determine areas where innovative alternatives are most needed, and whether support from external resources would be beneficial due to specific skills lacking internally. Primary targets for innovative efforts may be driven by the changing competitive landscape or a general

decline in sales over time due to the maturity of the product. These domains should be pursued strategically and proactively, and the appropriate financial investment allocated. In addition, the executive team should be asking tough questions about their expectations at all levels of innovative results:

- Where do we currently stand in our industry in terms of introducing product or service innovations relative to our competitors?
- What have we learned from failed attempts at innovation in the past?
- Are funds available for employees to explore innovative alternatives that may only lead to incremental improvements rather than a breakthrough discovery?

Shaping a Culture of Innovation

As the organization strengthens its infrastructure for innovation, emphasis must be placed on guiding the appropriate behaviors necessary to produce the desired results. A strategy should be developed that incorporates tactics to shape a cultural of innovation. Business leaders, themselves, must be willing to adapt their own behaviors at times, as well as insist on accountability at each level of the organizational hierarchy to drive behavioral change. The following key components of an innovation-centered culture can serve as thought-starters for organizations developing the cultural aspects of their strategy.

- *Raise the level of trust.* A lack of trust, between managers and direct reports, between peers, or between corporate headquarters and field locations, is often one of

"The only time that you can't afford to fail is the last time that you try."
—CHARLES KETTERING, INVENTOR

the highest barriers to organizational innovation. Employees may fear being ridiculed for a radical idea, or not feel confident they will receive credit for one of their concepts. Friendly cooperation on the surface may produce a false sense of collaboration, but without a high level of trust, individuals may withhold important ideas that could accelerate the attainment of the goals of the enterprise.

- *Reinforce all ideas.* Employees need ongoing, positive reinforcement to encourage them to take the initiative to find better ways of doing things, whether within their area of responsibility or related to the business outside of their span of control. The leadership of the enterprise must value and express appreciation of all ideas, not just the handful of concepts that are approved, implemented, and proven successful. Risk taking must be encouraged, which also means that failing is acceptable as long as lessons are learned from failures and applied to future innovative pursuits.

- *Reduce the punishment.* The responses employees receive when sharing new ideas often discourage them from expressing ideas in the future. What does that individual hear? "That's nice, but you're not here to come up with improvements. Just go and do your job!" "Are you crazy? We've never done anything like that before!" Sometimes even the most positive response can be perceived as a negative. "Great idea! Now go back and prepare a 75-page implementation plan for me in triplicate. And, by the way, where's that report you're working on for my

important initiative?" If a new idea sounds promising, a much more positive response would be for the manager to ask how he or she can best support the employee while further investigation of the concept takes place.

- *Leverage diversity.* Decision makers should avoid stereotyping when selecting individuals to be involved in a new initiative. They should encourage project leaders to tap into cross-functional knowledge and experience to create both depth and breadth in solving the challenge at hand. Breakthrough innovations often are a result of different levels of experience, so managers should hesitate before automatically forming a team of individuals all from the same level within the enterprise. Including diverse talents on the team will increase the chances of coming up with more innovative outputs. The company should hire with diversity in mind, to gain fresh perspectives, rather than bringing onboard only those individuals who mirror the education and experiences of the existing workforce.

- *Capture and preserve creativity.* How does the enterprise capture the initial sparks of a new idea? How can the company avoid losing ideas amidst numerous organizational changes, doing more work with fewer people as a result of downsizing, people accepting new roles, or individuals taking on additional responsibilities? The organization's strategy should ensure its technology is being fully utilized to document ideas that may not be appropriate today but may be worth revisiting in the future.

- *Reframe the challenge.* Avoid the trap of immediately attempting to find a solution without first fully exploring the problem. Quickly diving into discussions with the purpose of finding the one right answer often results in less innovative alternatives. A richer set of options can be obtained by first coming up with as many ways as possible to express the challenge. In addition, identifying any and all constraints early in the process will result in the discovery of potential solutions that are more appropriate.
- *Give cues for conduct.* To drive innovation, the organization must surround the workforce with multiple antecedents—signals to drive the desired behavior of the workforce. Antecedents are sensory inputs or cues deployed by the organization's executives to lead employees. The cues can take numerous forms, and include, for example, clearly written and documented job descriptions, policies and rules, annual departmental plans, and commitments made by management. Signals may also include a clear statement of the overriding vision of the firm, which sets direction for employee activities, a "call to action" speech to enlist employee involvement in developing significant improvements in a specific area, or a challenge presented by the leaders to find a solution to a company-wide problem that creates collegial internal competition.

Engaging Employees

The Employee Involvement Association (formerly known as the National Association of Suggestion Systems) focuses on keeping workers engaged in their organizations through open communication, teamwork, positive relationships with coworkers, respect, and trust. The EIA also compiles data on productivity and statistics on the generation of new ideas by the workforce. With the emphasis that American businesses are placing on innovation as a competitive advantage, there has been significant improvement over the past three decades in better understanding what drives the generation of new ideas, and in quantifying the manifestation of innovative behaviors. In 1980, the average number of suggestions per employee in the average U.S. workplace was .20, meaning it took five people to develop one idea. That means the Fuji Company, with 1,500 employees in that same year, should have had a total of 300 suggestions by U.S. standards. Instead, the Japanese company produced 193,330 new ideas, and that was not considered its best year.[13]

The United States has been considered by many global thinkers to be behind the eight ball in driving business innovation. There has been a great deal of focus on improving innovation as a strong contributing factor to competitive advantage, not just U.S. enterprises competing against each other, but also focused on developing the innovative strength of the American business landscape at large. And while statistics have improved dramatically (more recent statistics indicate the organizations with sophisticated infrastructures to gather and implement new concepts are "exceeding 40 ideas per person annually, with greater than 80 percent implementation rates, and high levels of participation,"[14] those of us who are asked by clients to remove every possible barrier to optimal organizational performance know that the workplace still has significant room for improvement in supporting these goals.

Many companies are turning to architects and designers to develop workplaces that will inspire the workforce and increase innovative output. In Chapter 4, we'll look at "best places to work" initiatives and untapped opportunities for architectural and design firms, which could result in a competitive advantage for both the A&D firm and its client.

Making Decisions in Innovative Contexts

As stressed previously, many executive leaders are concerned that their organizations are not producing results as innovative as they feel critical for the long-term success of the enterprise. While a great number of these leaders are concerned with the quantity of new concepts resulting in commercialization, others feel the problem is not a dearth in the number of ideas generated but rather one of deciding in which, among alternative suggestions, the organization should invest time, talent, and capital. In either case, decision making in innovative contexts must be addressed strategically.

How to select from new ideas for products, services, and procedures from the multitude of concepts produced by the enterprise was the question posed at the CREATE Conference in March 2005 as part of the evolutionary process of creativity. "Creativity is not just producing something new, but it is also the result of the mechanism that selects or refuses variations that have been produced."[15] In my consulting work, I've heard leaders express frustration over the inconsistency of methods managers use to make decisions, corroborating the importance placed by thought leaders of both Harvard and the CREATE initiative on the principle of structured decision making. Further, the executives within my client organizations recognize that the choices made are frequently not aligned with the strategies and tactics already in place to guide managers in the appropriate direction. When enterprises develop the proper infrastructure to enable an increase in the number of new ideas generated, managers will be approached more frequently by employees, proposing that the company invest its resources in exploring the viability of their suggestions. If those managers are ill prepared to make sound decisions surrounding common, everyday issues, they most likely will struggle with decision making involving many unknowns and greater risks. Drawing from stepwise, computational methodology, such as that of Charles Kepner and Benjamin Tregoe, experts in the field of decision analysis, can help managers become better decision makers.[16] As pointed out earlier in this chapter, organizations enabling divergent thinking will gain a greater number of innovative alternatives from which to choose. The expectation should be set that the business case be properly presented for the possible innovation to be given consideration for approval.

This, of course, brings in the important fourth leadership process—persuasion. Decisions cannot be made by managers unless the employee has thought through the issues; identified what could go wrong, as well as what he or she expects to go smoothly; and prepared for the potential questions executives may ask. Training managers throughout the enterprise on a single decision analysis method, and holding them accountable for using a logical, step-by-step process, can result in improved consistency in decision making. An added benefit of using a formal process is that it provides a permanent record of ideas proposed by the firm's employees, and creates a method of documenting concepts that may not be appropriate for further exploration at the time, but may be ideal for commercializing in the future.

Developing Implementation Strategies

In too many cases, innovation strategies fail due to poor execution. Implementing a strategic plan for a specific new product or service idea requires discipline from many levels in the organization. Enterprises that are anticipating an increase in new ideas from members of the workforce can create structure for the implementation of new concepts while still maintaining a strong sense of *intrapreneurialism* (in essence, the entrepreneurial spirit applied internally within a corporation, transforming an idea into a finished, profitable product or service to be sold externally):

- *Set expectations.* Employees who have earned the privilege of implementing their innovative concepts still need to respect the company's guidelines and formal procedures. Errors should be kept to a minimum and emphasis placed on reducing risk.

- *Understand intrapreneurialism.* The employee whose concept is being explored for possible commercialization is using the company's resources, be that funding, physical space, time, or assistance from other staff members who could be devoting efforts to other initiatives. In most circumstances, that employee is passionate about the innovation and eager to work on the implementation. However, if he or she were an independent entrepreneur, investing his or her own money to bring a new idea to market, there may be a stronger sense of urgency to move through the execution of the strategy. At minimum, there would be a heightened sensitivity to keeping expenses under control. An entrepreneur's risk is high, sometimes requiring he or she take out a second mortgage on their house or existing without a paycheck while developing and commercializing a new concept. An intrapreneur still gets a weekly paycheck, benefits, the physical space to work, technology, and so on. If the innovation fails, he or she will most likely keep his or her job if the failure is handled professionally. The intrapreneur should spend the company's money in developing the idea as if it were his or her own.

- *Document decisions.* The organization would be wise to expect the intrapreneur and his or her manager to come to an agreement on the timeframe of the exploration and establish a budget for expenses, to avoid the project exceeding reasonable investments of time and money. These and other pertinent details should be put in writing. Certainly, new ideas for incremental improvement can be categorized as innovations, and are typically welcomed by the organization. When the innovative idea is a frame-breaking concept, however, one that can be translated into a product or service the enterprise will sell in the marketplace, that innovation is owned by the company, not by the employee functioning in the role of an intrapreneur. Today, many on-boarding procedures in companies include a document that new employees must sign stating that the enterprise is the sole owner of any innovation in which he or she may take a part during his or her employment.

■ *Balance support with accountability.* The organization should support its intrapreneurs with the resources appropriate to quickly bring new concepts to market. In many enterprises, decision making is much too cumbersome for the speed needed to commercialize an innovation in a highly competitive industry. Companies that have been successful in introducing new products and services on a regular basis have developed an expedited decision-making process for new issues that may arise during the innovation's implementation phase. When offering resources, leaders should not overlook things such as tapping into the company's brand recognition, leveraging the firm's database to understand patterns of buyer behavior, or involving current customers in the validation of the concept prior

to commercialization. To reiterate a key difference between intrapreneurial employees and independent entrepreneurs: these members of the workforce are using the resources of the enterprise, and must be held accountable. It should be made clear that they are responsible for meeting deadlines and providing updates on their progress.

■ *Embrace constructive failure.* The reality is that the more attempts the organization makes to create innovative alternatives, the more failures it will have. It's a numbers game. The implementation strategy for exploring a new concept should include a contingency plan. Intrapreneurs can move forward, keeping things as small as possible to ensure maximum speed and flexibility. Once initial success has been realized, the efforts can be scaled up as appropriate.

■ *Provide shelter.* The Rolling Stones had the right idea to "gimme shelter," but many enterprises struggle with relieving intrapreneurs from their day-to-day roles during strategy implementation, to ensure their attention is spent only on the innovation.[17] If intrapreneurs cannot be relieved from their current responsibilities, perhaps they can be given support via college interns or temporary help, to allow them to spend more time on executing the strategy. A physical space can provide much needed shelter as well—for example, a team room that inspires interaction and the generation of new ideas as captured by photographer Kevin Beswick in Figure 3-7.

Figure 3-7: Organizations can provide much-needed "shelter" to teams charged with specific goals by designating a space that can be used for collaboration and the generation of new ideas.

Rockford Construction Company, © 2005 Kevin Beswick, People Places & Things Photographics.

Designing the Innovation-Friendly Workplace

Let's reflect back on two statements made earlier in this chapter to interpret what they mean to workplace professionals designing new office environments focused on improving innovative organizational results.

- "Creativity can be considered the foundation for innovation, yet creativity does not always lead to innovative outputs."
- "Creativity is the context where innovation might develop."

The good news to architects and designers is that the potential impact the physical workplace can have on enabling creativity is significant, which is a critical precursor to innovation. The bad news? There is no guarantee that the workplace will automatically drive creative behavior. What advice can the architectural and design community take away from these messages to protect their workplace strategies from failure?

When developing workplaces to foster creative and innovative behavior, the designer should go beyond "the look" of creativity on the surface. We've all seen them, and can quickly recognize a mismatch with the culture, management style, level of autonomy, and processes for getting things done in the organization. The workplace may be drenched in a brightly colored palette and incorporate numerous teaming areas sprinkled throughout the space. The surface materials chosen may be visually stimulating, with thought-provoking statements stenciled on the walls. But physical space solutions such as these can quickly fail when sound principles of behavioral psychology centered on driving change are not integrated into the workplace strategy. Designing the physical workplace that "looks" innovative does not guarantee alignment of the Critical Influence context in which the organization's employees work. Did the office design solution evolve from a deep exploration of the employee behaviors necessary to achieve its long-term goals? Was there a thorough evaluation of its leaders' current behaviors, and was any incongruence to driving the desired work culture addressed? Did the executive leadership team make—and sustain—a conscious commitment to identifying and removing operational barriers to the successful implementation of the new workplace strategy?

In Chapter 5, you will learn about the work environments of diverse organizations that have successfully contributed to the achievement of the establishments' short-and long-term objectives, as well as supported these public and private businesses throughout changes, both planned and unpredicted. But first, let's look at the innovation-friendly workplace in greater detail.

THE INNOVATION-FRIENDLY WORKPLACE

To introduce you to the principles of Variation Enabling Innovation & Performance Maximization, let's first look at the concept visually in the form of a graph. We'll then use a specific example to point out the nuances of its practical application to the workplace. Figure 3-8 represents the impact that workforce behavioral variance, combined with variety in workplace settings from which employees can choose, has on organizational output.

- Employing convergent thinking, a low degree of behavioral variance,

and selecting from a smaller number of workplace setting alternatives, results in individual performance maximization (represented by the bottom left quadrant).

- By increasing the behavioral variance by using divergent thinking while maintaining the same degree of work settings from which to choose, the combination results in individual innovation (bottom right quadrant).

- As we increase the degree of variety of the workplace settings, while maintaining a low degree of behavioral variation by employing convergent thinking skills, the result is organizational performance maximization (top left quadrant).

- It is with the combination of a high degree of behavioral variation using divergent thinking and a high degree of variety in workplace settings that organizational innovation is best enabled (top right quadrant).

Individual Performance Maximization

Let's walk through Figure 3-8 again, making the description more meaningful through an example of an individual we'll call Jon Matthews. Jon is a member of the Millennial Generation, a 24-year-old employed by an international law firm, in its finance department. Jon interned at the firm on winter and summer breaks during his last year and a half in college, prior to earning his bachelor's degree in finance. He is very bright and gives 100 percent in all that he does; however, he requires intellectually challenging work to stay engaged. He loves the strong team culture of the firm and wants to contribute positively by sharing new, innovative ideas that will significantly improve the ways his department works.

The bottom left quadrant of the graph, Individual Performance Maximization, reflects the combination of lower degrees of variation in both workplace settings and employee behavior. When Jon is performing activities in this quadrant, his tasks are routine and rather predictable. In seeking ways to be the most productive (which equates to performance maximization), he may employ convergent thinking skills to identify and reduce or eliminate certain steps he performs in his work assignments, to streamline the various workflows for which he is accountable.

Individual Innovation

The bottom right quadrant, Individual Innovation, reflects an increase in the variation of Jon's behaviors as compared with his behaviors described in the quadrant for Individual Performance Maximization. The general level of diversity of workplace settings available to him, however, remains similar. When Jon encounters a perplexing challenge or problem related to his area of responsibility, he switches his approach in an attempt to find an alternative to the extremely time-consuming method others in his work group have used. Leveraging the same physical work environment, he engages in more divergent thinking than the convergent thought process he used in the Individual Performance Maximization quadrant. As a result of expanding his attention to encompass a greater number of alternative solutions to the situation,

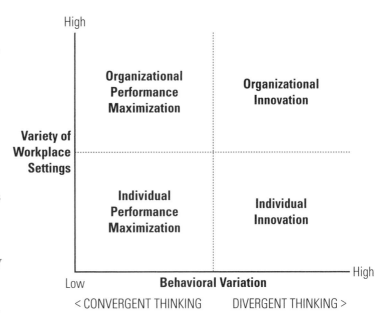

Figure 3-8: The Variation Enabling Innovation & Performance Maximization graphic illustrates the impact that variation in employee behaviors, combined with the degree of variation in workplace settings, have on organizational output.
© 2006 Diane Stegmeier.

Jon adapts to the physical workplace provided and discovers two possible innovative methods of solving the problem, each of which would save significant time.

Organizational Performance Maximization

In the top left quadrant, Organizational Performance Maximization, the degree of variance in workplace settings is high, offering individuals a number of alternative spaces in which to work. The focus, however, remains on improving productivity of existing workflows rather than "reinventing the wheel." The chief financial officer has sent an e-mail to all members of the finance department announcing the location of this month's staff meeting. When Jon arrives for the staff meeting at the large conference room, he and his colleagues learn that the vice president of human resources is using that room, having been asked to participate in an impromptu video-conference with the firm's office in Munich. The finance department shares a number of resources with the other support functions at the U.S. headquarters: human resources, accounting, marketing, and facilities. The CFO smiles and quickly suggests to her team that they grab a mobile whiteboard and head to the atrium to hold their meeting. Jon has noticed an absence of territorialism surrounding shared resources. He's heard about other organizations where there is a culture of resentment, but he has no problem making compromises. After all, a significant percentage of his annual compensation is tied to the productivity of the entire firm.

The agenda of the finance department's monthly staff meeting always includes a period during which to entertain suggestions from the group for process improvement. The team then selects one workflow from the numerous ideas shared and brainstorms the one improvement that will most positively impact the department. Jon is excited when he shares his recent discovery for reducing the time spent on a specific workflow, and his peers select it as the subject for the brainstorming exercise. Using convergent thinking, the group validates Jon's alternative method and is able to refine the process a bit further. The CFO credits Jon Matthews for a job well done. In wrapping up the meeting, she asks her staff to use Jon's new method, as appropriate, over the next 30 days and be prepared to share feedback at the next monthly meeting.

Organizational Innovation

The top right quadrant, Organizational Innovation, reflects the highest degrees of workplace variation and behavioral variation. It is in this context, where divergent thinking is combined with a diverse choice of work settings, that innovative outputs are most effectively enabled, if properly aligned with the various components of the Critical Influence System.

Continuing with our example of Jon Matthew's experience in the finance department of an international law firm, we'll now move to an example articulating the interdependence of the variance of employee behaviors with the diversity of physical work settings available for the workforce. It is November, and the partners of the practice are focused on innovative ways to grow the number of clients, as well as the profitability per client case in the coming year. As with many other fields, the legal profession has become increasingly competitive. Firms compete for high-visibility cases to build their reputation. With the recognition of the positive impact of branding to potential clients, marketing and business development are growing in importance as a support for legal firms. Human resources departments strategize more and more with the partners in an effort to attract and retain talent in both the legal practice (partners, attorneys and other legal professionals with direct involvement in client casework) and the business practice (finance, human resources, accounting, marketing, business development, facilities and other operations professionals) roles. Dialogue is ongoing on emerging areas of specialization, and whether expertise should be acquired by attracting new hires or developed within the firm.

The partners have requested that each department executive participate in the firm's annual two-and-a-half-day strategic planning session. In addition, the heads of these functional areas have been asked to select three people from their teams to join in the event to address the goals of determining innovative ways to grow the client base and the profitability per case. The individuals to be selected, in the words of the partners, should be "the best and the brightest, proactive, forward-thinking professionals, willing to take risks and speak out for change, and who represent our growing multigenerational workforce."

Jon is called into the project room in the business practice office the next morning, where he learns of his appointment to this exciting initiative. He spends the morning there with the chief financial officer and two departmental peers also selected to participate in the partners' strategy session, chatting about how they can best contribute to the opportunity at hand. After the CFO leaves to catch a flight, the three colleagues have a full afternoon ahead of them, as they have identified a number of potential ideas to discuss relative to the upcoming session. They decide to go for a takeout lunch and bring it back to the "war room" to have a solid hour behind closed doors to continue their dialogue.

The day arrives for the kickoff of the strategic planning session. Each participant is provided a well-designed agenda that combines enough structure and direction to keep things flowing, yet much flexibility to enable innovative outcomes by the end of the session: develop a strategy for the new year that will grow the number of clients, as well as the profitability per client case. The partners have designated a multitude of areas within the facility to accommodate the entire group, departmental break-out sessions, and cross-functional and cross-generational round table discussions. Jon makes a mental note that the firm not only is leveraging its diverse workforce, but also the diversity of the firm's entire office environment to come up with the best ideas for the new year. He loves the culture—what a great place to work!

LESSONS LEARNED IN THE DESIGN OF INNOVATION-FRIENDLY WORKPLACES

In collecting my thoughts to share lessons learned in the design of innovation-friendly workplaces, an experience came to mind. I was invited to speak at a CoreNet Global Summit in Denver on the topic "Preventing Workplace Strategy Failure," and was strategizing over the phone with Amanda Brooks, director, Summit Education Programs, and Eric Bowles, director of Global Research, to determine the specific business issues to address and the appropriate level of knowledge to share with the participants of my educational session.[18] I was told that CoreNet Global members are sophisticated, highly experienced professionals who enthusiastically further their education on the workplace. The challenge? They've already been exposed to a great deal of research on increasing employee satisfaction, enhancing collaboration, and improving productivity. They want to hear the war stories, the "aha!" moments that have caught workplace professionals off-guard.

As we develop a set of conditions that support innovation, creativity is definitely a necessary ingredient for inclusion; creativity, however, is not alone sufficient to produce innovative outputs. What true lessons have been learned from office design projects where innovation is a mission-critical requirement of the client organization? What are the essential components of an innovation-friendly workplace?

Many workplace environments designed for innovation make the mistake of downplaying, or even ignoring, the importance of performance maximization.

The innovation-friendly workplace must also be designed to support performance maximization through alternative choices of work settings, where individuals or groups can analyze and improve existing tasks and processes. An excellent example of a design that enables both performance maximization and innovation was created by Robert Luchetti Associates for Boston Consulting Group's International Business Services Headquarters, shown in Figures 3-9, 3-10, and Figure 32 in the color insert. A corner meeting room offers a clear view into team "neighborhoods." Different types of thought processes are enabled through Luchetti's interpretations of an 8 foot by 8 foot footprint: one as a private home base, and the other as an adjacent team "huddle" room.

The physical workplace needs to be fluid, or elastic, to provide work settings that accommodate both

Figure 3-9: The Boston Consulting Group's International Business Services headquarters, designed by Robert Luchetti Associates of Cambridge, Massachusetts, emphasizes both the individual and group work that need to be supported in the workplace. Strategically placed in the corner where paths cross, the glass-walled meeting room shown here is also close to activities taking place in the team neighborhoods.

Planning and Design: Robert Luchetti Associates; photographer and photo copyright 1998, Paul Warchol.

Figure 3-10: Robert Luchetti Associates designed flexibility into the workplace for Boston Consulting Group. Dependent on changing work styles and business needs, an 8 foot by 8 foot space can be an individual touchdown area one day and a small team room the next.

Planning and Design: Robert Luchetti Associates; photographer and photo copyright 1998, Paul Warchol.

divergent and convergent thinking in a dynamic, ever-changing way.

The overall office design must morph to the diverse needs of individuals, small teams, large work groups, and others, by offering a variety of workplace settings in which employees can work based on the type of activities to be performed (see Figures 3-11, 3-12, and 3-13).

An independent "kit of parts" approach to furniture components remains valid, regardless of private offices, dedicated workstations, totally unassigned work environment, or a combination of these.

Rather than a planning methodology based on "six-packs" or "eight-packs" of workstations,

increase the adaptability of the physical space by designing bays. This approach allows the designer to create bays of diverse sizes, and cluster them in different ways to allow the space to define a certain type of behavior, such as encouraging employees to make use of a collaborative area, or drawing individuals into an oasis established for quiet thought.

The choice of adopting either a fixed-point system or a spine system for housing utilities should be expanded to the consideration of a wireless workplace, which can improve workforce flexibility by better utilization and deployment of the furniture kit of parts (see Figures 3-14a, 3-14b, and 3-15).

Figure 3-11: A variety of workplace settings from which employees can choose to work is an important concept of the innovation-friendly workplace, as shown here in the offices of Hanon McKendry, a public relations/ad agency in Grand Rapids, Michigan.

Rockford Construction Company, © 2005 Kevin Beswick, People Places & Things Photographics.

Figure 3-12: Hanon McKendry's space in downtown Grand Rapids' Arena Station includes mobile furniture components and lightweight storage towers to allow the space to morph to changing business needs and work styles.

Rockford Construction Company, © 2005 Kevin Beswick, People Places & Things Photographics.

Figure 3-13: A variety of casual meeting areas in Synovate's Chicago facility from which employees may choose to work fosters the generation of new ideas and social connections between colleagues.

© 2007 Whitney, Inc.

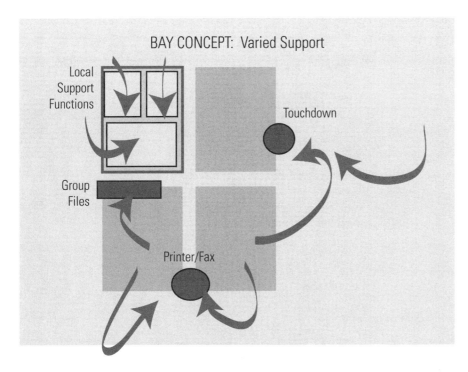

BAY CONCEPT: Varied Support

Local Support Functions

Touchdown

Group Files

Printer/Fax

Figure 3-14a: The bay concept depicted here provides varied support for employees using a fixed-point system.

© 2001 STUDIOS Architecture.

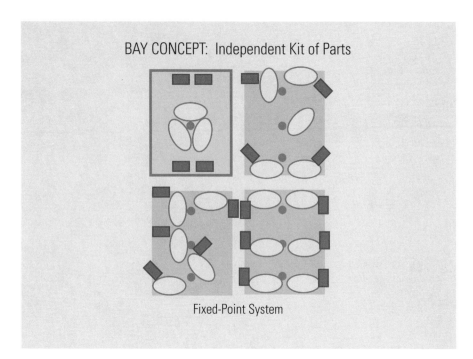

Figure 3-14b: The bay approach, employing an independent kit of parts, enables flexibility of a fixed-point system.

© 2001 STUDIOS Architecture.

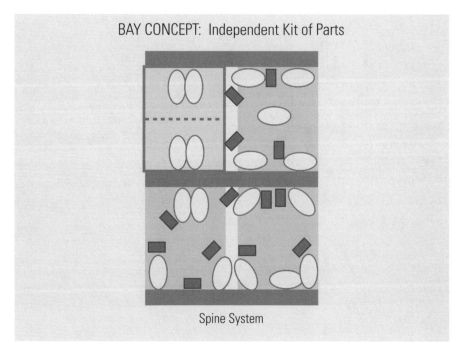

Figure 3-15: In this example, the bay concept applies the independent "kit of parts" to a spine system.

© 2001 STUDIOS Architecture.

BENEFITS OF COLLABORATION TO INNOVATION

I want to close this chapter by reinforcing the benefits of collaboration to organizations that are seriously committed to improving innovative outputs. Certainly, individuals within the same enterprise may operate as intrapreneurs, developing new concepts within self-imposed silos. However, there is much more to be gained by strategically combining forward-thinking professionals, a physical work environment that enables end users to define their work spaces for the tasks at hand, and a culture that encourages taking educated risks. By creating a trusting environment where individuals look forward to sharing their ideas with others, organizations can avoid the redundancy that may result from two intrapreneurs pursuing similar concepts, yet fiercely protecting their projects as if their own personal finances were at stake. In a circumstance such as this, a team of two or more employees sharing a passion for the same type of improvement could generate far more alternatives to explore, most likely resulting in a richer outcome. Emphasizing collaboration can increase employee engagement, which is an essential ingredient to attracting and retaining talent from each generation. And last, driving innovation through collaboration can result in improved productivity and, subsequently, a reduction in the time to commercialize the concept.

NOTES

[1] Roberts, Royston M., *Serendipity: Accidental Discoveries in Science*, New York: John Wiley & Sons, Inc., 1989.

[2] CREATE Conference, Creative Processes for Enterprise Innovation, Udine, Italy, March 2005.

[3] Andriopoulos, C., "Determinants of organizational creativity: a literature review," *Management Decision*, 2001.

[4] Vicari, S., *La creatività dell'impresa. Tra caso e necessità*, Milano, Etas Libri, 1998.

[5] De Toni, A.F., Sanfilippo, M., CREATE Project Conference, March 2005, adapted from E. de Bono, Serious Creativity, 1996.

[6] Von Stamm, 2003.

[7] De Toni, A.F., De Santi, D., *Handbook for Creativity Management*, CREATE Project Conference, March 2005, adapted from Kletke, M.G. et al, "Creativity in the Organization: The Role of Individual Creative Problem Solving and Computer Support," 2001.

[8] Gurteen, D., "Knowledge, Creativity and Innovation," *Journal of Knowledge Management*, Vol. 2, n. 1, September 1998, pp. 5–13.

[9] Gardner, Howard, *Frames of Mind: The Theory of Multiple Intelligences*, 2nd ed., Cambridge, MA: BASIC BOOKS, a member of Perseus Books Group, 1983.

[10] "Multiple Intelligences Self-Inventory, Concept to Classroom," produced by Thirteen/WNET New York. http://www.thirteen.org/edonline/concept2class/mi/index.html (accessed January 9, 2007).

[11] IDEO, Palo Alto, California, www.ideo.com;, visit by the author, May 2001.

[12] Roberts, Sherman D., "Promoting Innovation & Organizational Change," executive eduation program, Harvard University, Cambridge, MA, 2001. An updated framework, "Optimal Performance and Leadership: The Five Process Model," has been released, based on further research conducted by Roberts, *Ivy Faculty Reports*, Number 07–3, www.ivyfaculty.org, 2007.

[13] Employee Involvement Association, www.eianet.org.

[14] Savageau, John, "World Class Suggestion Systems Still Work Well," *The Journal for Quality and Participation*, Vol. 19, No. 2, March 1996, pp. 86–90.

[15] *Handbook for Creativity Management*, CREATE Conference, March 30, 2005.

[16] Kepner, Charles, and Benjamin Tregoe, *The New Rational Manager*, Princeton, NJ: Princeton Research Press, 1996.

[17] Jagger, Mick, *Gimme Shelter*, 1969.

[18] Stegmeier, Diane, "Preventing Workplace Strategy Failure: Critical Influence Design," CoreNet Global Summit, Denver, April 30, 2007, www.corenetglobal.org.

> "What is important is not the quantity of creativity in an organization, but the relational and social context where individuals work."
>
> —S. VICARI

CHAPTER 4
UNDER THE INFLUENCE

© Frank Tielemans Fotografie BV.

© Frank Tielemans Fotografie BV.

WORKPLACE TRANSFORMATION AND THE CRITICAL INFLUENCE SYSTEM

When are workplace transformation projects most susceptible to the Critical Influence System? Under which circumstances should you prepare yourself for the greatest resistance from the workforce? In which organizational initiatives is the physical workplace—one of the 15 Critical Influences—typically underutilized as a positive force to drive change?

Professionals in the fields of architecture, interior design, facilities management, and corporate real estate have experienced dramatic changes over the past decade. Their roles have never been static, yet the pace of physical property change is ever increasing, with activities such as reducing real estate holdings, closing unprofitable facilities, and consolidating locations. As it relates to the interiors of buildings, the tasks include moving managers from private offices to the open plan, reducing the square footage of individual workstations, and switching from dedicated to shared workspaces or unassigned space.

None of these situations is easy, to be sure, yet the fact that the physical workplace is just one of 15 elements comprising the Critical Influence System challenges workplace professionals to continuously take a higher view of organizational dynamics. Let's take a look at a number of situations where the physical workplace is most "under the influence."

Restructuring, Mergers, and Acquisitions

According to a special issue of the *British Journal of Management* edited by Susan Cartwright and Richard Schoenberg, "Thirty Years of Mergers and Acquisitions Research: Recent Advances and Future Opportunities," published in 2006, there were 30,000 acquisitions completed globally in the year 2004, the equivalent to one transaction every 18 minutes.[1] Estimates by the McKinsey organization put the value of merger and acquisition activity for that same year to be $2.0 trillion. And for the first 11 months of 2006, McKinsey reported the annual volume of announced M&A activity at nearly $4 trillion globally, surpassing the record levels hit in 2000.[2]

Gensler's Brian Ferguson has worked with numerous clients who want to leverage their organizations' physical space to support diverse changes. In an interview with me, he stated that significant changes—such as a corporate merger—often cause a client to rethink the work environment—for example, "We'll never have this merger again. It's an opportunity to look at what's working and what's not, and develop a common physical environment where two distinct cultures and sets of processes can be brought together." In the early stages of developing a workplace design for a client that is acquiring another firm, the dialogue is typically centered on, and can easily get stuck on, what currently is not working well. Clients may not know specifically where they should be headed as it relates to the physical work environment, but they're typically sure what's wrong. The challenge is the unknown, developing and designing to where the organization needs to be. Ferguson uses a football analogy to explain: "When you throw a pass to someone, you don't throw to where they are, but rather to where they're running."[3]

With the increasing rate of mergers, acquisitions, and restructuring that range from the merger of two Fortune 500 companies to the blending of two divisions of a single entity, it's interesting to note the commonalities of clients, whether they are manufacturing firms, service providers, not-for-profit organizations, or agencies of the federal government. Let's look at various goals and challenges of some of them, at how the workplace was designed to influence behavior and enable the future vision, and the lessons learned along the way.

Challenges

The initial challenge often surfaces with the realization that two distinctly different cultures exist in an organization, followed by the desire to develop a common platform to enable a single, shared culture moving forward. Early dialogues on creating a workplace strategy are driven more by what the organization doesn't know about the future than what it does know. Designing a work environment that is acceptable for the way people work today, with the intention of maintaining that same workplace configuration until the furniture has worn out and the lease on the building is ready to expire, is directly opposed to creating a flexible, adaptive workplace to lead the workforce on a journey to an unpredictable future. It's the difference between an environment that is simply "not in people's way" and one that truly guides the desired human behaviors to help the organization strategically carry out its mission and meet its business goals.

Workplace Priorities

Two of the top priorities of workplace strategies that support mergers and acquisitions are to:

- Diminish the loss of staff to competition (which is interesting considering that the two firms may previously have been tough competitors).
- Decide the level of attrition the organization is willing to accept. Do the people who would

potentially leave the firm match the profile of an adaptable, change-ready employee, identified as a good fit for the evolving enterprise?

When organizations restructure, merge with other entities, or are in an acquisition mode, changes in the physical workplace are typically taken very personally by members of the workforce. Employee productivity plummets as the workday is interrupted with rumors of mass downsizing due to potential redundancy of roles or elimination of once-critical positions that will no longer be needed due to an evolving corporate direction. Some of the seemingly small issues result in the loudest uproars among the troops. For example, in the case of more than one of my clients, the major issue on the minds of the workforce has been the geographic distance from their homes to the new office location. The threat of an additional 12-minute drive time to and from work has resulted in hours and hours of lost productivity per affected employee throughout the time period leading up to the move to the new workplace.

High-Velocity Environments

A high-velocity environment is associated with an organization experiencing sustained, accelerated growth. In many cases, this growth is organic (rather than a result of acquisitions), with surges of greatly increased business activity and staffing requirements occurring as a result of market acceptance of the firm's products or services offered. Arnold Levin, former director of

Mancini Duffy's Center for Workplace Innovation, offered an example of a client on just such a fast track, in terms of market share, revenue stream, and size of the workforce. Two years after moving into a new headquarters building designed by another architectural firm, Mancini Duffy was called in to support an already large institution that was growing more quickly than anticipated.

The client's original business focus was evolving, and what seemed like an appropriate workplace solution for the firm's 14-story building two years earlier was recognized as being misaligned with the vision and goals of the organization. The building did not reflect the brand nor the work processes within the company. The executives felt the interior looked cold and austere; but because this was the headquarters location, they wondered how to develop a sophisticated, high-velocity environment without looking like a start-up company. The culture of the organization reflected collaboration, yet the physical surroundings did not. Collaboration was a top priority for the client, and it was crystal clear to the executive leaders that mobility was the way to enable that collaboration. The project evolved into an exploration of the future of work at the organization. With an ever-present focus on creating a workplace with optimal flexibility to morph in response to the organization's fluid business conditions, the emphasis centered on technology, collaboration, and mobility.[4]

Levin had been brought in to assist in the development of a solution for this fast-paced client. I met Levin in Chicago, in 2002, behind the scenes of NeoCon, where we were both presenters. He was sharing the results of his studies on the relationships between the organizational strategies of a business and the design of the workplace; I was introducing my research in a talk entitled "Enabling Innovation in the Workplace: How Can an Organization Create an Environmental Context in Which Innovative Human Behavior Occurs?"[5] Early in our conversation, we discovered we had both pursued our MBAs around the same time and shared a passion for applying the business and organizational theories of experts such as Henry Mintzberg, Michael Porter, David Nadler and Michael Tushman, Jay Galbraith, and Robert Kaplan and David Norton to the challenges of creating effective office design. I found Levin's approach refreshing, in particular his comparison of workplace design to the doctrines of Nadler and Tushman that speak of a new architectural design, one that addresses business design and business architecture rather than the development of physical space. Their message can also be applied to workplace design: "As constant redesign becomes a fact of life, successful organizations will learn to create flexible architectures that can accommodate constant change."[6] In contrast, Levin points out that the successful organization is one that has established a flexible workplace that can keep up with the changes being imposed. According to Levin, "Parallels between organizational design and workplace design suggest that there is a framework for positioning workplace design in the context of strategy that has been accepted in the world of business."[7]

Physical Space as Currency

Recall Brian Ferguson's football analogy earlier, on throwing a pass to where the player is running. It brings to mind the philosophies of Christopher Budd, of STUDIOS Architecture. Budd has commented on the broken processes he witnesses frequently in his role as a principal of his firm. More often than not, he says, the questions asked of clients early in an office design project are not focused on how people *should be* working but on how they currently are working. This self-reporting results in a snapshot of where clients are today, rather than where they're headed. Unfortunately, in too many companies, physical space has become a form of currency used to reward status. When architects and interior designers question midlevel staff members in a client organization where such a mind-set exists, the responses are typically centered on how individuals will be affected, not how the overall group can be more effective.

According to Budd, the preferred approach needs to include an examination of the current state of the organization, as well as the identification of the barriers to staff members working the way they should. The architectural or design firm thus needs to guide the client leadership group to setting the direction, and link what the organization has to do to meet its goals.[8]

One of the greatest risks workplace professionals face is what I call "silent sabotage." Here's how it manifests: Initially, managers nod their heads in agreement with the new corporate direction, and echo the importance of collaborative behavior in supporting business innovation. But all the while their mental wheels are spinning to find ways to justify why things should stay the same. "I need my private office because I deal with confidential information regarding our competitors." "I have to keep my hard-walled office with a door because I conduct annual performance reviews with my direct reports." Rationalization regarding privacy requirements cannot disguise the psychological issues underlying the surface. "I've worked my way up through the ranks and I have earned a private office." "My staff will think less of me if my workspace looks the same as theirs." They dig in their heels to maintain the status quo of the physical environment. And sometimes, they win. When that happens, the newly planned office environment is not much different than before, possibly with the exception of an updated color palette and more ergonomically advanced seating— and, of course, a cool coffee bar. What hasn't changed is that physical space remains a currency, to reward time or performance in the company; a symbolic tribute to the executive's title and power. You can peek into any private office and, by counting the number of ceiling tiles, accurately guess the occupant's status in the organizational hierarchy.

Competitive Office versus Collaborative Workplace

STUDIOS Architecture's Christopher Budd often hears clients say such things as, "I wish we were more like a family, not individuals positioned as competitors." He believes this perception of internal competition erodes the potential for maximum productivity.

> "The uncreative mind can spot wrong answers, but it takes a very creative mind to spot wrong questions."
>
> —ANTHONY JAY

> "You have not converted a man because you have silenced him."
>
> —JOHN VISCOUNT MORLEY, BRITISH STATESMAN AND JOURNALIST, 1838–1923

> "Change motivates ancient drives that evolved to aid survival and access to resources."
>
> —PAUL LAWRENCE AND NITIN NOHRIA, *DRIVEN: HOW HUMAN NATURE SHAPES OUR CHOICES*, 2002.

In client interviews focused on gathering feedback on barriers to collaboration in the workplace, I've heard similar concerns voiced. Stegmeier Consulting's workplace research has revealed four primary sources of conflict in the workplace that result in a competitive work environment:

- Misunderstanding or misinterpretation of facts
- Use, or limited use, of any given resource
- Different values, opinions, and/or beliefs
- Different perceptions of a situation

As organizations attempt to transform their offices to increase collaboration, there has to be a heightened awareness of internal competition for shared resources, such as conference rooms, mobile whiteboards, and other tools. (You'll read more about internal competition in Chapter 7, on the Collaborative Principle Index.)

Although the typical midlevel manager in corporate America may not have the deep understanding of how physical space impacts behavior in the workplace necessary to articulate office design criteria, he or she can quickly recognize the difference between a competitive office and a collaborative workplace. An architectural or design firm that attempts to create a collaborative work environment without first addressing the internal competitive culture resulting from the four primary sources of conflict in the workplace should be prepared for a mediocre outcome, at best.

Multigenerational Workforce

Figuring out how to create an appropriate physical work environment to accommodate the four generations in today's workforce is a growing concern to many workplace professionals. Add to that the desire to support an increase in collaboration to produce greater innovative outputs and you've just identified a baffling problem with no simple solution.

In many organizations today, members of the two youngest groups in the workforce, the millennial generation (born 1975 and after) and Generation Xers (born between 1961 and 1974) are not in significant positions of power and so have to play by the rules created by the veteran generation (born before 1946) and being enforced by the baby boomers (born between 1946 and 1964).[9] Many members of the millennial generation and Gen Xers may not yet be in supervisory or management positions, but they will be soon. As they gain work experiences to help them advance in their careers, many business leaders wonder whether these workers' social skills and approach to human interaction in the workplace will be adequate to drive organizational success.

To illustrate this issue, here's an example related to one Critical Influence on collaborative behavior—communications. A 50-year-old individual working in a particular office building may prefer to contact a colleague to compare calendars and schedule a meeting electronically to be held in his or her private office, attaching an agenda to efficiently discuss a topic of medium-range importance. Elsewhere in that same office is a 20-something member of the workforce, who makes a critical career decision on the spot and submits his or her resignation with no advanced notice via a text message to the manager, who happens to be sitting six feet away. While the more mature generations may employ technology to orchestrate human interactions, I often hear clients express concerns that younger workers may be relying too heavily on technology to compensate for their less-developed social skills. For Stegmeier Consulting Group's clients, strengthening internal communications is consistently an area targeted for improvement. Workshops such as our Business Communications Boot Camp (BC²)[10] have evolved over time and now place significant emphasis on the diversity of communication styles in multigenerational work environments.

In general, the pendulum is swinging away from work environments where managers strive to earn the right to physical spaces that symbolize prestigious titles and the associated authority. Both highly defined dress codes and protocols for addressing authority figures are today being challenged and, as a result, are becoming less rigid. The pendulum is moving toward environments where staff members expect to be engaged every day in work that is important, to be given opportunities to make an impact today, and to be offered growth potential in the future. These organizations encourage managing, coaching, and development among staff levels. A growing emphasis is on serving the people at lower levels of the organization—the next generation of leaders.

Many young people today do not regard a private office as a reward or as having any true value. They have witnessed their parents give everything to their careers, only to be downsized one or more times,

and have come to value a different kind of reward. According to Arnold Levin, although in most conventional organizations the private office is perceived to be part of a manager's compensation, more forward-looking clients, strategically setting out to hire the best and the brightest college graduates, are appealing to the desired rewards of this demographic group by providing state-of-the-art technology and a workplace design that allows mobility.

On the surface, it is tempting to believe that the generations have nothing in common; but, in fact, there is a growing desire shared by all—to achieve a better balance between work and personal life. A significant finding of a life's work study of 1,008 adults aged 21 and over, conducted by the former Radcliffe Public Policy Center at Harvard University, revealed the high value young men, aged 20 to 39, place on flexibility at work, so that they may spend more time with their families.[11] The fathers or grandfathers of these young men would not have dared to express the desire to work less in order to nurture better relationships with their spouses and/or children. Today, both genders can talk more openly about personal demands, ranging from childcare to assisting with elderly parents, without fearing the stigmas of the past. Workers of all ages have become more vocal in demanding a work/life balance, asking their employers to support flexible work conditions. Wise decision makers within the business world are taking the time to evaluate these requests and develop the appropriate policies and options in response to them.

Shifting generational attitudes can be manifested in the physical space.

A workplace strategy that includes flexible scheduling and options such as working from satellite offices or telecommuting can contribute to meeting the widespread desire for an improved quality of life for the entire workforce. The notion of providing a dedicated workspace for each employee is costly in terms of real estate, furniture, and work tools, and long outdated. In Chapter 5, we'll look at some very impressive quantitative results realized by enterprises that have adopted new approaches to allocating their physical office space. In particular, Cisco has documented some formidable results that will get the attention of the most skeptical reader.

Telework

The Case for (and Against) Telework

Much of the push for telework in the early years of its existence focused heavily on the financial benefits to the organization. The business case for employees working out of their homes was driven largely by the desire to reduce aggregate corporate real estate holdings, as well as the associated utilities to maintain them. Environmental benefits included a reduction in pollution caused by the growing number of vehicles transporting individuals to and from work each day.

Toni Kistner, managing editor of *Network World*, interviewed me for the March 31, 2003 issue, for an article titled, "Time for a Change." It highlighted a number of key areas of resistance to implementing a successful telework program, along with suggestions on how to better involve and engage middle management

in the organization early in the process. One of the highest barriers to success is the lack of trust managers place in their staff members. Kistner captured the predominant issue: "If the company values visibility over results, that behavior needs to change."[12] The behavior to which I was referring was that of the manager, and while lack of trust may be attributed to the characteristics of individual personalities, the organization may be to blame for not preparing its supervisory staff members for results-based operations. Trust, of course, works both ways, and a less recognized issue related to telework initiatives is that some employees are not cut out for telework, and know it. They fear reduced productivity, caused by the distractions of young children, for example. In such cases, declining an offer to work remotely may be an easy conversation to have with one's manager—after all, they are looking out for the best interest of the company. More difficult is when individuals know they will not be productive in a home office environment because they need the constant motivation of a supervisor to work effectively. But unlike citing the distraction of children under foot, admitting to your boss that you are not self-directed may not be a wise career move.

Positive Impact of Telework on Productivity

In addressing the issue of trust when considering telework initiatives, business leaders would be wise to reflect on the statistics available regarding the impact of telework on productivity. The Future Foundation conducted research for Brother Industries, Ltd. focused on maximizing the benefits of telework. The project examined telework as it is in practice today in the United Kingdom, France, and Germany. As part of the study, the research group predicted the future of teleworking to the year 2020.[13] The findings revealed that telework often results in employees working more hours, rather than fewer, indicating that telework has a positive influence on worker productivity. Surveys of teleworkers provide evidence to the greater investment of time devoted to their jobs. Of the total surveyed:

- Forty-two to 81 percent say they begin working earlier in the day.
- Thirty-four to 91 percent work more in the evenings.
- Fifteen to 82 percent work more on weekends.

Of course, supervisors and managers who lack trust in their direct reports could read these statistics and argue that putting in more hours does not guarantee improvement in productivity. The important point, however, is that there are additional hours spent working that can potentially contribute to productivity. Aligning with the various elements of the Critical Influence System—in particular performance management, rewards and consequences, technology, and communications—will help build the strongest foundation for achieving the most productive results.

Another positive aspect of telework pointed out by the Future Foundation study is the time employees begin working on an average day. Often, they say they begin working at the same time they typically would be walking out the door to travel to their office. That travel time becomes valuable work time for those teleworking. Here are the statistics:

- In the United Kingdom, 41.8 percent of teleworkers saved between 6 and 10 hours weekly.
- In Germany, 37.9 percent of teleworkers saved between 3 and 5 hours per week

Let's do a bit of calculating based on these statistics. In the United States, assume an employee earns 15 days of vacation per year and is given 10 days off for holidays. This individual has 47 workweeks per year. If this staff member is a teleworker, statistics reveal that he or she could perhaps save six hours per week just by not commuting to a conventional office. That one person has gained 282 hours over the course of a year, or approximately seven weeks. You may want to do the math for your own organization. Using even conservative estimates, you might be pleasantly surprised by the amount of time you would gain, even if the percentage of employees who telework is small relative to the entire workforce.

Key Stakeholder Issues on Telework

The decision for an organization to offer telework arrangements to its employees is not an easy one. For example, the senior leaders of a company may want to offer the option to its front-line staff members; but the resistance by supervisors and managers, concerned that their direct report may not put in a full day's work, may raise a major barrier to moving forward. Or, those employees whose requests to telework are denied may feel they are not trusted. The following lists comprise a compilation of key stakeholder issues surrounding the impact of telework on human capital. Ask yourself whether any of the concerns ring true for your own organization.

Key Issues of Organizational Leaders

- Concern that the profiles of employees do not match the ideal profile of a teleworker (self-motivated, able to deal with ambiguity, highly focused, energetic, etc.).
- Concern that the organization will lose the managers who are currently overseeing the employees due to their perception of lost power.
- Can the organization eliminate a layer of management? Should it?
- How can the organization sustain its corporate culture?
- Which jobs are most appropriate for telework?
- How can the organization quantify the risks and rewards of telework?

Key Issues of Organizational Managers

- Perception that the manager's value to the organization is measured by the number of people surrounding him or her in the workplace (i.e., less physical evidence of direct reports, resulting in an interpretation of lower managerial value).
- Should the manager be a teleworker as well?
- How can new hires be trained on best practices of telework?
- How will the manager monitor his or her people?
- Should staff meetings be scheduled more frequently to keep in touch?
- How will the manager measure the productivity and effectiveness of teleworkers?

Key Issues of Facilities Managers

- How much space should we allow in our facility to accommodate teleworkers when they work on-site rather than at home?
- What would happen if all of the teleworkers showed up at the office to work on a given day, rather than working remotely?
- Is there a "paint-by-number" plan to make this work (a step-by-step process proven to be successful)?
- What type of furniture is best suited for a home office? Can we provide a lesser quality, since it will be used only by one person?
- How much does the company need to provide versus what employees may already have in their homes (second phone line, high-speed Internet service, suitable lighting)?
- Do I need to grow my facilities staff to respond to the needs of teleworkers?
- Does the company need to invest in fleet vehicles for facilities and information technology specialists to make "house calls" to teleworkers' homes?
- What if the organization finds it necessary to return to the current way of working after excess real estate has been sold off?

Key Issues of Employees Asked to Telework

- Concern about damage to their professional image.
- Concern that fewer opportunities for visibility within the organization will result in a reduction in career opportunities.
- Will the company grapevine cease to exist?
- Feelings of isolation.

- Reluctance of teleworkers to admit to the employer that they are not self-disciplined enough to perform well without supervision.
- Is the organization going to pay for the needed support (furniture, phone lines, fax machine, printer, storage)?
- If the company will not pay for needed support, should employees consider going to work elsewhere, or perhaps start their own firm?
- What are the personal tax implications for employees?
- What if the employee gets injured at home while working? Who is liable?
- Is the company going to pay for cleaning services, as well as the wear and tear on the employee's home?
- What if the employee's spouse also teleworks? How can they coordinate their needs for equipment, physical space, acoustics, and so on?
- How will the employee get technical support as quickly as needed?

Key Issues of Employees Not Eligible for Telework
- Feeling that they are not trusted by management to work at home.
- Misconception that their roles can be performed anywhere (e.g. receptionist charged with greeting customers).
- Anger that all employees are not treated equally.

Common threads surface when looking at the stakeholder issues side by side, and you will notice that many of the concerns have to do with behavioral change. In addition, note that the issues fall into three general categories:

- *Cultural*, such as the business leader wondering how to sustain the organizational culture, or the teleworker's concern about fewer opportunities for visibility within the organization, resulting in the reduction of career opportunities.
- *Operational*, such as the tax implications for the individual teleworker, the organizational leader's question on how to quantify the risks and rewards, or the facilities manager wanting a paint-by-number plan to implement telework.
- *Environmental*, such as a teleworker whose spouse also works at home anticipating acoustical distractions, or the quandary of the facilities manager in determining how much space to allow in the conventional work environment for teleworkers spending time on-site.

Categorizing issues into cultural, operational, or environmental elements is helpful in ultimately developing solutions to barriers you uncover that negatively influence behavior in the workplace. As we continue, you'll learn that this segmentation can be applied to leverage that which is working well, by including those favorable influences in your workplace design solution. In Chapters 6 and 7, we'll look in depth at the cultural, operational, and environmental elements influencing innovative behavior.

Emphasis on Work/Life Balance

As mentioned earlier in the section on the multigenerational workplace, the issue of work/life balance is taking on greater importance among all age groups in the workforce. Telework is certainly one method of improving their quality of life, by reducing long commutes to and from a more conventional work environment. In my work, I interact frequently with human resource executives, and hear repeatedly that what keeps them awake at night is their concern about the increasing shortage of talent to fuel human capital, resulting from the waves of retirement by the aging workforce. To improve the retention rate of existing, mature staff members, as well as to attract new talent, whether recent college graduates or individuals in early to midpoints in their careers, these professionals are developing strategies to increase employee satisfaction. However, although there is increased awareness within the human resources community of the "power of place," the physical work environment remains underrecognized as a significant factor in attraction and retention strategies in organizations where functional executives operate independent of each other. These leaders advocate and expect collaboration and teamwork of all levels working under them in order to meet their business group's objectives. Yet time and again, in conducting diagnostics of clients' Critical Influence System, the results reveal organizations where functional silos exist and interdepartmental alignment with the enterprise's overall goals is in need of much improvement.

The recommendation to principals committed to positioning their independent architectural or interior design firms as credible in delivering a workplace solution capable of achieving their clients' holistic business strategy is to become better educated on human resources issues. Specifically, subscribe to an online publication devoted to human performance optimization, talent management, or any number of people-related e-zines. Recommend that a staff member in your firm, who is responsible for business development, join and actively participate in the local chapter of the Society for Human Resource Management[14] (reference www.shrm.org).

For those directly employed in corporate real estate or facilities management—and in enterprises large enough to employ their own architects, interior designers, or workplace strategists—the suggestion is to forge an internal business alliance with the human resources group. Understand that department's challenges. Learn about its initiatives, and determine how the physical work environment can support its objectives. Don't wait for your employer to "connect the dots" and ask your teams to collaborate. This relationship can enhance the credibility of your role within the company—and theirs.

Flexibility to Enable Work/Life Balance

Flexibility is an essential component in enabling a work/life balance. What characterizes flexibility in the organization? To workplace professionals, the concept may be manifested in tangible elements such as mobile furniture and work tools, portable electronic devices, demountable walls, and raised flooring. To other functional groups, flexibility is underscored in its company policies. To employees, it may be manifested in leaders "walking the talk," helping them to use the tangible tools and the policies. In other words, it's not just having the rules in place; it's the organizational attitude toward their use, whether the policies, work tools, or choice of physical spaces. Many members of the workforce feel their employers have put the mechanisms in place for flexibility, yet maintain a culture that stifles the advancement of those who actually use the flexible arrangements offered. It is in the integration of a flexible physical work environment, tools, policies, and an appropriate culture that will raise the chances of success of such an important approach to better supporting the workforce.

Workplacelessness

In "Workplacelessness: The Advent of the Digital Nomad," a white paper presented at the Futures in Property and Facilities Management II Conference in London, Bob Grimshaw, of the University of the West of England, and Peter McLennan, of the University College London, warned that new ways of working could have the same effect on people as homelessness. Spaces such as a home office that is nothing more than a kitchen table, or "nonplaces" such as hotel rooms, subways, or airport lounges, represent none of the meaning nor symbolism of conventional work environments, and, as such, are placeless. The authors define *workplacelessness* as "mobile working, without a territorial space, and in spaces that lack the symbolic characteristics to make them places." These digital nomads move from nonplace to nonplace, relying on technology for communication. The lack of cultural symbols found in the typical workplace has a negative impact on an increasing number of employees, hence can

BEST BUY'S APPROACH TO WORK/LIFE BALANCE

An example of an organization that walks the talk when it comes to work/life balance is Best Buy, and it has done so by creating a culture that emphasizes employee results rather than a specific number of hours working on-site. Headquartered in Richfield, Minnesota, Best Buy operates a chain of more than 780 electronics stores in North America. In 2002, the company began a program called the Results-Only Work Environment (ROWE) at its headquarters campus. ROWE challenged outdated management styles centered on judging employees by the amount of time they spent at the office, and encouraged supervisors and managers to focus on the achieved results of their staff members.

With a goal of offering employees optimal work/life balance, Best Buy's ROWE initiative provides its salaried workforce maximum flexibility in how, where, and when they work, as long as they meet their individual productivity goals.

Although ROWE has a way to go before reaching full implementation among the various departments on its headquarters campus, it has already achieved significant quantitative results. According to the company, employees in departments that have converted to a Results-Only Work Environment have realized a 35 percent increase in productivity. In addition, ROWE teams have a 3.2 percent lower voluntary turnover rate than teams that have not transitioned to the new performance system.[15, 16, 17, 18]

result in many of concerns identified in the key stakeholder issues regarding telework, identified previously. Grimshaw and McLennan's research results revealed that, "It is clear that the role of the physical environment in conveying messages about culture, relationships, and power are missing from workplaceless space and need to be re-created in some form if lack of connectivity on all levels is to be avoided."[19]

That said, researchers anticipate that telework and other alternative work arrangements will increase markedly in the future. It is interesting to note that the very concept of work as a "place" has evolved dramatically. The research findings of the Future Foundation support this shift in our perception of work and where it is conducted.

According to the foundation, the original notion of teleworking was based on "an Industrial Age conception of work and home as two distinct places."[20] I see these blurred boundaries between the residence and office when consulting clients on barriers to workplace effectiveness. Many homes today are equipped with wireless technology, a printer and fax machine, and a comfortable, albeit small, space to work on a PC or laptop. These are not necessarily houses where an employer has provided the tools and technology for an employee to work remotely. What I've described is Any House, U.S.A. In contrast, the employer has increased the amenities in the office environment to increase employee productivity using elements that were once comforts only found in the home. Collaboration areas include lounge seating and flat-screen televisions. Concierge services take care of staff members' dry cleaning or car maintenance. The home has become as efficient as the office. Conversely, the office has become as comfortable as the home. Remember, work is not about where we go; it is about what we accomplish.

The following gives further details of the research conducted by the Future Foundation for Brother Industries, and indicates a shift in the reasons why an individual, given the choice, would rather go to the workplace than work from a remote office located in their home.

Workplaces themselves will change, becoming more a site for collaborative and social interactions than for work activity itself. Remote working and devolved responsibility will influence the relationship between employer and employee. Paradoxically, there will be a greater emphasis placed on performance measurement, particularly of outputs, while at the same time leading edge employers will recognise the importance of trust and social networks in employee relationships. Underpinning this shift to more flexible and fluid patterns of working will be communication. More than ever before, we will spend large parts of our working days keeping in touch, maintaining relationships, finding new connections. New technologies will enable this to happen in ever more complex and subtle ways.

One of the most interesting themes is how all the above trends will influence the way we think about work and our private lives. Work will be less a place we go to and more how we use our time: we won't *go to* work in 2020. We will just *do* work.[21]

The point of this section is neither to advocate a position for or against organizations offering employees alternatives to working in the conventional office environment. It is to illustrate the impact of the physical workplace—whether a private office, open workspace, airport lounge, or kitchen table—on employee behavior. It is also to offer insight on the interdependency of other influences on the success of the workplace alternatives determined appropriate by the enterprise.

Attraction and Retention Strategies

At a kickoff session for the Best Places to Work competition, I had the opportunity to hear a talk given by Richard Hadden, coauthor of the book *Contented Cows Give Better Milk: The Plain Truth about Employee Relations and Your Bottom Line.*[22] This was one of 23 regional kickoffs, and the ballroom at the Marriott Hotel was overflowing with enthusiastic business leaders. Hadden compared

"The most visible differences between the corporation of the future and its present-day counterpart will not be the products they make or the equipment they use—but who will be working, why they will be working, and what work will mean to them."

—ROBERT HAAS, CHAIRMAN OF THE BOARD, LEVI STRAUSS & COMPANY

"contented cow companies," organizations recognized as being employers of choice, with happy, productive employees, with "common cow companies," comparable companies in the same business or industry that compete in a significant way with contented cow companies, against which benchmarking was conducted. Contented cow companies substantially outperformed their competitors. They outgrew common cows by a margin of approximately four to one, created 16 times more wealth, and tripled the net income per employee.

During the event, I chatted with a myriad of participants, as well as with staff of the *Business Courier* and other host sponsors. It struck me that not one individual I spoke with had considered developing a strategy to leverage physical space to assist his or her organization in earning the status of a best place to work. Clearly, the establishment committed to improving each of the categories of this competition—as well as to integrating a strong workplace strategy—will win a competitive advantage in the War for Talent against employers in the same industry or other companies hiring in the same geographic region.[23]

The Great Places to Work® Institute, founded in 1991, evolved from research initiated in 1980 by Robert Levering and Milton Moskowitz. In the early nineties, when I was considering joining Steelcase Inc., Levering and Moskowitz's book, *The 100 Best Companies to Work for in America*, served as my road map to compare and contrast the firm with 99 other establishments recognized as employers-of-choice.[24] Today,

diverse organizations throughout the world seek to become Great Places to Work, recognizing that in improving their workplace environments, they can also enhance their image and positively impact their financial performance.

In an interview with Hal Adler, president of Great Places to Work, I gained insight on the benefits organizations can realize from placing emphasis on the trust, pride, and camaraderie employees experience in the workplace. The institute's data reveals the ROI on shareholder value for Great Places organizations outperforms that of their industry peers by three to one. The employee turnover rates for Great Places are half that of their less effective counterparts. According to Adler, the institute has been measuring companies competing for annual Great Places status since 1980. The employee perspective is quantified via a survey, examining the degree to which they perceive credibility, respect, and fairness as a function of trust, as well as the level of pride and camaraderie they experience in their workplaces. The organizational leaders of competing companies also participate in a Culture Audit, which looks at specific things the company does to support an environment centered on these principles.[25]

In my interactions with clients driving physical workplace changes, initially they are surprised that there are ways to quantify improvements related to behavioral change. Whereas the task of developing metrics surrounding cost savings, such as a reduction in square footage, is generally approached without much trepidation, managers are less comfortable when they are asked to quantify improvements related to behavioral change. Quantifying the level of employee commitment or engagement can be tied to indicators such as turnover rates, average length of time in the organization, number of volunteers for community projects, the company's success rates in college recruitment, or the percentage of candidates who accept offers made for employment.

Surprisingly, even among Great Places organizations, examples are relatively few of those that strategically and proactively leverage the physical work environment. Adler did share one example, however, of a Great Places enterprise that constructed its office and conference room walls out of glass to reflect its core values of openness, transparency, and communication. Another of the institute's award winners, for which environmental sensitivity is a priority of their value system, became one of the first LEED facilities in the United States. The elements included in its offices reflected a commitment to renewable energy. According to Adler, these "subtle decisions play to the reinforcement of who they are"; and by and large, the expectation is that the work environment is a safe place, has the tools and information employees need, and contributes to the employees' ability to get their work done, by staying out of their way.

For those of us making our living as an architect, interior designer, or professional supporting the workplace design field, we know how important "power of place" is in contributing to a positive employee experience. Perhaps the burden is on us to be proactive in sharing our research with new audiences to heighten the awareness of the role that physical space can play in supporting attraction and retention strategies. We have a major opportunity to carve a niche and market ourselves to enterprises that are working diligently to create positive places to work, for the purpose of attracting, inspiring, and retaining talented employees. Two of the goals I've established for Stegmeier Consulting Group are: to apply the research findings of the Critical Influence System to support client organizations focused on achieving measurable improvements in their attraction and retention efforts, and to develop strategic alliances with those architectural and design firms targeting the same niche.

How can architectural and design firms contribute to the success of their clients' strategies centered on attraction, enabling, and retaining top talent? Don Crichton, HOK's vice president, Workplace Solutions Canada, shared his insight while discussing several of his firm's projects. In Crichton's words, "Over the past three years, we have taken numerous clients through HOK's visioning process to identify their key issues and priorities. They have all indicated that attraction and retention is a major challenge."[26]

Case in point is Warner Music Canada, a project that earned HOK an Award of Merit from the Association of Registered Interior Designers of Ontario (ARIDO). Warner Music Canada had been located on two floors of another building, with one floor housing the distinctly creative teams and the other level home to the organization's accounting and other business function teams. Prior to HOK's involvement, this client location was a distribution arm of Warner Music Group in New York, where activities included processing orders, fulfilling the accounting needs of the organization, and providing information technology support. To the outsider, the space Warner was occupying might just as well have been an insurance company or other conventional business workplace. The offices looked anything but an enterprise operating in the entertainment industry. The physical space did not reflect the energy or excitement of a business focused on capturing the essence of an artist's live or studio performance.

In contrast, the new 25,000-square-foot facility was designed to play a major role in attracting talented employees. The company wanted much more than to simply retain existing staff. The goal was to bring the different groups together, to create a sense of community, and to return to the roots of the business—musical artists and their works. An emphasis on leveraging the physical space to reflect the branding of the organization would ensure the workplace did not look like the average insurance claims office.

As described in Chapter 3, designing an environment that will inspire creativity must also balance performance maximization requirements. The Warner Music project corroborates the importance of mastering this balancing act, and doing so challenged Crichton and the HOK team. Their physical space solution had to support the "heads-down" business teams as well as the "volume-up" groups involved in promoting artists and their music. In these dichotomous requirements was a very strong, common desire for an overall workplace that would inspire each

employee to perform well in his or her chosen profession, whether he or she was developing a marketing campaign for an emerging rock star or compiling the monthly profit and loss statement.

The design intent for the reception space was to create the experience of entering a nightclub, instead of a typical office reception area. The contrast of materials provides visual interest by the use of laser-cut, brushed stainless steel; the warmth of raw, Douglas fir beams; polished concrete flooring and eye-catching, billowy lighting (see Figure 4-3).

Figure 4-3: HOK captured the boldness of the music industry in the design of Warner Music Canada's reception area. Larger-than-life photographs of Warner artists welcome guests entering the space.

Courtesy Ben Rahn/A-Frame.

Larger-than-life photographs of Warner artists are placed strategically in the reception area and throughout the entire office environment, to reflect the "in your face" boldness of the music industry.

The workplace design created by HOK employed a neighborhood concept, wherein workgroups could maintain their unique distinction while clustered around a community square that encourages interface not only between diverse employees but also with Warner Music's visiting customers and musical artists (see Figure 4-4). Crichton and the HOK team planned a circulation path along the perimeter of the office space where nearly full-height windows enable all employees to enjoy natural light from all four exposures (see Figure 4-5).

Workstations are crisp and professional-looking, to reinforce the importance of the business side of the music industry. The design of the individual workspace extends an invitation for employee interaction by including a fun-shaped, lightweight table that encourages team members to pull up a chair to discuss the business at hand—or their favorite artist's latest musical release (see Figure 4-6).

HOK Canada's workplace design for Warner Music includes a common-sense solution to address meeting space that could be applied to most any industry client. How often do you try to spontaneously pull together a small number of peers to quickly discuss an issue that needs immediate attention? You and your teammates head toward a large

Figure 4-4: In the open, interactive area designed by HOK for Warner Music Canada, employees may run into a colleague—or a favorite musical artist who happens to be on-site that day.

Ben Rahn/A-Frame.

Figure 4-5: HOK designed a circulation path along the perimeter of the Warner Music space to take advantage of natural light streaming in from all four exposures.

Ben Rahn/A-Frame.

Figure 4-6: In the music industry, not all work is performed on stage. Warner Music Canada also includes the furniture, technology, and work tools necessary to get down to the business at hand.

Ben Rahn/A-Frame.

conference room, only to find it occupied. But your group really doesn't need that large a meeting space—you just need a space. Now. To meet such a need at Warner Music, just outside the spacious meeting room capable of holding large groups, HOK has installed a small, but comfortable table and chairs ideal for expediting business decisions (see Figure 4-7). Large, sliding wood doors ensure acoustical privacy for users of either the formal or informal meeting spaces, and include slats of glass to give a subtle sense of a meeting in progress.

Another excellent example of clustering areas that inspire interaction, exchange of information, and the generation of new ideas can be found in the spaces designed by Shepley Bulfinch Richardson & Abbott for their own offices in Boston. Staff members crossing paths while arriving for a scheduled project meeting, an impromptu team brainstorming session, or a casual one-on-one dialogue are given the opportunity to make further connections with peers, thanks to the use of diverse spaces (see Figures 4-8 and 4-9).

You'll see an aggressive pursuit of the brightest candidates in the labor pool reflected throughout the case studies in Chapter 5. Enterprises that have been successful in achieving their goals of recruiting and keeping talent have adopted a two-prong approach. First, a strategy to build an infrastructure that leads to the reputation as an employer of choice in a particular industry can result in attracting mid- to senior-level talent who may be willing to relocate for the opportunities for upward mobility. In addition, this industry reputation can be leveraged during college recruitment campaigns. Second, by achieving the status and brand recognition of an employer of choice in its geographic regions of operation, the competitive pressures of hiring in tighter labor markets can be reduced. In the words of Hal Adler of the Great Places to Work® Institute, organizations recognized as being positive work environments for employees don't simply receive more resumes, "they get a better quality of resumes."

Figure 4-7: The Warner Music Canada facility offers numerous areas where either meetings or informal dialogue can take place.

Ben Rahn/A-Frame.

Figure 4-8: Shepley Bulfinch Richardson & Abbott's own space in Boston is designed for interaction, whether scheduled or spontaneous.
© Anton Grassl/Esto.

Figure 4-9: Staff members of Shepley Bulfinch Richardson & Abbott can easily leverage the creativity and insight of colleagues in their work environment, which fosters collaboration.
© Anton Grassl/Esto.

SUMMARY

The accelerated pace of change in the business environment presents new challenges to workplace professionals. An organization may be growing organically because of sustained, positive customer response to a new business direction, or be increasing in size due to a merger or acquisition. Employee expectations linked to a culture where physical space is treated as a currency to reward managers with private offices need to be balanced with new organizational expectations where everyone interacts collaboratively—perhaps in an open office environment, despite the fact that there will always be internal competition for limited resources. The physical work environment needs to attract future business leaders today, without causing a mass exodus of experienced, high-level managers in the process.

The organization dedicated to doing what is necessary to support a new strategic direction must make tough decisions when creating the appropriate work environment—regardless of intense overt resistance and silent sabotage working covertly to undermine all good intentions. The welcome news is that workplace professionals don't have to go it alone, if their senior leaders understand the Critical Influence System and the power physical space has on behavior. The workplace should never bear 100 percent of the burden of transforming the way people work.

In Chapter 5, I'll introduce you to organizations in the financial, high-technology, pharmaceutical, manufacturing, telecommunications, and professional services, as well as the U.S. federal government. We'll take a look at a number of winners of *Fortune Magazine's* Best Companies to Work for in America and the Great Places to Work Institute's Best Small and Best Medium Companies to Work for in America. You'll read about diverse approaches taken by the architectural and design communities in serving their clients. You'll find that though challenges and approaches may differ, there's a commonality in the emphasis placed on building flexibility into the workplace solution, to enable the physical space to morph in response to future changes in business direction.

NOTES

[1] Cartwright, S., and R. Schoenberg, "Thirty Years of Mergers and Acquisitions Research: Recent Advances and Future Opportunities," *British Journal of Management*, 2006 17, 1, pp. 1–5.

[2] Dobbs, Richard, Marc Goedhart, and Hannu Suonio, "Are Companies Getting Better at M&A?," *McKinsey Quarterly*, December 2006, http://www.mckinseyquarterly.com/article_page.aspx?ar=1886&L2=5&L3=4 (accessed March 12, 2007).

[3] Ferguson, Brian, Workplace Strategy, Gensler, interview with the author, August 15, 2006.

[4] Levin, Arnold, Cushman & Wakefield, interview with the author, July 21, 2006.

[5] Stegmeier, Diane, "Enabling Innovation in the Workplace: How Can an Organization Create an Environmental Context in Which Innovative Human Behavior Occurs?," white paper presented at NeoCon, June 2002.

[6] Nadler, David, and Michael Tushman, *Competing by Design: The Power of Organizational Architecture*, New York: Oxford University Press, 1997.

[7] Levin, Arnold C., *Workplace as Asset: The Unconventional Wisdom*, white paper presented at NeoCon, June 2002.

[8] Budd, Christopher, Principal, STUDIOS Architecture, interview with the author, July 28, 2006, www.studiosarch.com.

[9] Hillman, Rachel, *The Age Divide: Generations in the Workplace*, Department of Employment

and Economics Development, St. Paul, MN, April 2006. http://www.deed.state.mn.us/lmi/publications/trends/0406/age.htm (accessed November 25, 2006).

[10] Stegmeier, Diane, Business Communications Boot Camp Workshop (BC²), 2006, www.stegmeierconsulting.com.

[11] *Life's Work: Generational Attitudes toward Work and Life Integration*, Radcliffe Public Policy Center, Cambridge, MA: Harvard University, 2000.

[12] Kistner, Toni, "Time for a Change: Interview with Diane Stegmeier," *Network World*, March 31, 2003.

[13] "The Future of Teleworking: Maximising the Potential Benefits of Teleworking to 2020," Future Foundation, September 2005, www .futurefoundation.net.

[14] Society for Human Resource Management, www.shrm.org.

[15] Sridhar, Bindu, "Bye Bye Office Hours, Now Welcome ROWE," *The Hindu*, October 25, 2006. http://www.thehindu.com/thehindu/jobs/0610/2006102500340800.htm (accessed November 25, 2006).

[16] Thottam, Jyoti, "Reworking Work," adapted from *Time Magazine*, July 18, 2005 by Minnesota Work-Life Champions, www.worklifechampions.org (accessed October 7, 2006).

[17] Kiger, Patrick J., "ROWE's Adaptability Questioned," *Workforce Management Magazine*, October 7, 2006. http://www.workforce.com/archive (accessed November 11, 2006).

[18] Ibid., "Throwing Out the Rules of Work," *Workforce Management Magazine*, September 25, 2006. http://www.workforce.com/archive (accessed November 10, 2006).

[19] Grimshaw, Bob, and Peter McLennan, "Workplacelessness: The Advent of the Digital Nomad," white paper presented at the Futures in Property and Facilities Management II Conference, London, March 2004.

[20] "The Future of Teleworking: Maximising the Potential Benefits of Teleworking to 2020," Future Foundation, September 2005, www .futurefoundation.net.

[21] "The Future of Teleworking: Maximising the Potential Benefits of Teleworking to 2020," Future Foundation, September 2005, www .futurefoundation.net.

[22] Catlette, Bill, and Richard Hadden, *Contented Cows Give Better Milk: The Plain Truth about Employee Relations and Your Bottom Line*, Germantown, TN: Saltillo Press, 2001.

[23] "2006 Greater Cincinnati's Best Places to Work," Business Courier, Marriott Hotel, Hebron, Kentucky, June 16, 2006.

[24] Levering, Robert, and Milton Moskowitz, *The 100 Best Companies to Work for in America*, New York: Addison-Wesley, 1984.

[25] Adler, Hal, President, Great Place to Work, Institute, interview with the author, December 12, 2006, www.greatplacetowork.org.

[26] Crichton, Don, Vice President, Workplace Solutions Canada, HOK, communications with the author, September 6, 2006, www.hok.com.

CHAPTER 5
CASE STUDIES: COLLABORATIVE WORKPLACES THAT WORK

Examples of workplace designs to aid clients in their effort to increase collaborative behavior to produce more innovative results for their organizations are numerous, and as diverse as the clients and the design professionals hired to work with them. To a few, an effective workplace design to enhance collaboration requires little more than, for example, using brightly colored paint on the office walls and installing a surfboard as the surface for a boardroom conference table. Such "shock value" elements are reminiscent of the details added to dot-com-era office environments, which were intended more to make a statement to Wall Street, that the stock of these firms was a sound investment, than to integrate sound principles of behavioral psychology.

More successful, of course, are those organizations in which new workplace strategies evolved from a deep exploration of long-term goals, an evaluation of leaders' behaviors to drive the desired culture, and conscious commitments to identify and remove operational barriers to successful implementation of the enterprises' workplace strategies.

Before you read the case studies in this chapter, consider the following questions about workplace design as they relate to your clients' organizations or to your own:

- Should physical space be used as a currency to reward the rank and status of individuals within the organization, at the expense of functional support, team decision making, work process efficiency, and overall organizational effectiveness?
- Do workplace strategies need to adopt either a system based on entitlement or an approach centered on user need rather than status?
- Is it possible to select an appropriate point on a continuum from which to drive incremental change without disrupting the confidence and security of staff at all levels?

- Is incremental change even an option in the increasingly competitive global economy, where innovative product and service breakthroughs are quickly commoditized, thereby diluting competitive advantage?

CASE STUDY: ALCOA CORPORATE CENTER

I chose Alcoa as the first case study in this chapter for a reason. In 1996, I was an MBA graduate student at Kent State University, with Leading Organizational Change as my area of concentration. I had decided to focus my research on the role of leadership in driving change, and the impact of physical space on behavior in the workplace. At the time, I was employed by Steelcase Inc., trying to absorb every piece of research related to the influence of physical space on behavior, from inside and outside of the company. I read countless books and articles on successful leaders in the corporate world looking for the common threads among them. I wanted to know, how did they drive sustainable change? And, importantly, what was the link between leadership behavior and leveraging the physical workplace to transform an organization?

At about the same time, Martin Powell, AIA, NCARB, and principal of the Design Alliance Architects, was called to Alcoa's headquarters in Pittsburgh, Pennsylvania, to meet with Chairman Paul O'Neill.[1] Powell tells the story of a humbling—and a bit intimidating—journey that began upon his entering the old Alcoa building for that meeting. The trek led him past three different

security guard stations and a battery of administrative assistants before he was escorted into O'Neill's office. O'Neill, himself, was anything but intimidating—in fact, just the opposite. He could be described more accurately as an enabler of people's best performance, rather than one who drives results through fear and intimidation.

O'Neill explained to Powell that he was concerned that, internally, his employees weren't able to convene at a moment's notice or make important decisions fast enough to keep up with external changes in the global business environment. Rather, communications between Alcoa executives often took a circuitous route, not unlike the path Powell experienced in walking through the Alcoa building to meet with the chairman. It could take several days before leaders, their schedules, and the physical space to meet could be aligned. In O'Neill's words, "I have concluded that we were not going to be able to improve our pace with the existing structure, processes, people capability, and people involvement."[2]

Throughout the development of the new Alcoa Corporate Center, O'Neill stayed actively involved with Martin Powell and the Design Alliance team. Early in the process, nine design principles were identified to guide all decisions regarding the headquarters project (see Table 5-1).

With the emphasis Alcoa's most senior executive was placing on speed, flexibility, and adaptability of the organization itself, those same characteristics had to be translated into the physical space solution the Design Alliance would develop. There was an intense focus on the

TABLE 5-1 Alcoa Corporate Center Design Principles

Drive design by function and need rather than by status and hierarchy.
Encourage cross-functional collaboration, communication, and spontaneous contact.
Support organizational and process effectiveness and responsiveness.
Design the building to fit into and contribute to the neighborhood.
Make the building architecturally important, but not faddish or monumental.
Develop a safe, open, environmentally and ergonomically appropriate workplace.
Reflect Alcoa's values, and make employees proud.
Ensure that information systems and technologies meet Alcoa's effectiveness standards.
Make the building an innovative, flexible, and efficient workplace.

fact that the velocity of change in Alcoa's business would increase over time. Thus, the building needed to adapt to factors no one could predict. Workplace Design concepts surfaced as the project evolved, and reflected attributes critical to the long-term success of Alcoa (see Table 5-2).

The Design Alliance's solution for the Alcoa Corporate Center resulted in a 242,176 gross square-foot, six-story building, shown in Figures 5-1 and 5-2. Distinguishing features of the workplace include a truly open office environment where each employee—including Chairman Paul O'Neill—was provided a 9 foot by 9 foot workstation and flexible technology access via the raised flooring.

The open offices were positioned to follow the serpentine curve of the building, enabling staff members to enjoy views of Pittsburgh's three rivers and the network of bridges connecting its shorelines. The typical floor plan also incorporated team rooms, a large videoconferencing room, and a self-paced learning center (see Figure 5-3).

The workplace design concept that "a person's office is the entire facility" teaches a powerful lesson as to why the Alcoa Corporate Center is a collaborative workplace that works. The building was designed to offer numerous options from which a staff member can choose to work. Using the floor plan shown in Figure 5-4

TABLE 5-2 Alcoa Corporate Center Workplace Design Concepts

Create a people focus.
Encourage informal encounters.
Make people more visible and accessible.
Create a greater variety of collaborative spaces.
Fill the workspaces with natural light.
Have as many people per floor as possible.
Design workspace by need, not status.
Make offices comfortable, not permanent.
Design so people can modify their own workspaces.
Adhere to the philosophy that a person's office is the entire facility.

Figure 5-1: Entrance to the Alcoa Corporate Center in Pittsburgh, Pennsylvania.

© 1999 Steve Hall, Hedrick Blessing.

Figure 5-2: The Alcoa Corporate Center, designed by the Design Alliance Architects, lights up the night sky of Pittsburgh, the "three rivers" city.

© 1999 Steve Hall, Hedrick Blessing.

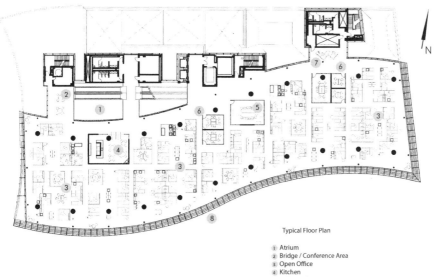

Typical Floor Plan

1. Atrium
2. Bridge / Conference Area
3. Open Office
4. Kitchen
5. Videoconference
6. Team Rooms
7. Self-paced Learning Center
8. Sunscreen

Figure 5-3: Typical floor plan of the Alcoa Corporate Center.

© 1999 The Design Alliance Architects.

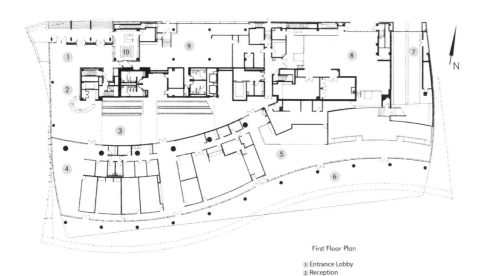

First Floor Plan

1. Entrance Lobby
2. Reception
3. Atrium
4. Conference Center
5. Employee Dining Room/Large Meeting Area
6. Outdoor Terrace
7. Entrance to Lower-Level Parking
8. Loading Dock
9. Public Restaurant
10. Public Newsstand

Figure 5-4: First floor plan developed for Alcoa by the Design Alliance Architects.

© 1999 The Design Alliance Architects.

Figure 5-5: In the dining area in the Alcoa Corporate Center, employees can enjoy a view of Pittsburgh's fabulous network of bridges.

© 1999 Steve Hall, Hedrick Blessing.

as an example, when an employee does not want to work in his or her open office space on the third floor, he or she can choose to go to the ground floor and work on the terrace or in the atrium. Two colleagues can arrange to meet on the employee dining terrace to exchange information while looking out at the Allegheny River (see Figure 5-5).

The Design Alliance applied the workplace design concepts "make people more visible and accessible" and "create a greater variety of collaborative spaces" to guide their creation of vertical movement throughout the building. The firm's use of escalators in the six-story atrium (Figure 5-6), with spacious landings designed as gathering spaces for interaction (Figure 5-7)

increased the opportunities for colleagues to run into each other more often and provided comfortable spots for spontaneous discussions.[3, 4, 5, 6]

As stressed throughout this book, a workplace strategy can easily fail if Critical Influences raise barriers to employee use of the space as the architectural and design firm intended. The strong leadership of Paul O'Neill, who insisted on an infrastructure designed for optimal performance and that workspaces would be designed by need not by status, contributed significantly to a culture that fosters collaboration.

People experience the movement of light and color when in the Alcoa Corporate Center. There is a sense of constant, dynamic motion, thanks to the movement of escalators, the view

Figure 5-6: Escalators provide vertical movement throughout the Alcoa Corporate Center.

© 1999 Steve Hall, Hedrick Blessing.

Figure 5-7: Landings in the Alcoa building were designed to encourage collaboration and knowledge exchange.

© 1999 Steve Hall, Hedrick Blessing.

of changing cloud patterns through the 11-foot–2-inch floor-to-ceiling windows, and the sight of the 22,500-square-foot park at the river's edge from the S-shaped exterior wall (see Figure 5-8 and Figure 2 in the color insert). Dynamic and in constant motion: perhaps the appropriate description of the Alcoa organization as well.

Figure 5-8: The Alcoa Corporate Center, designed by the Design Alliance Architects, is a 242,176 gross square-foot, six-story building in Pittsburgh, Pennsylvania. With its S-shaped curves, the exterior of the building suggests an organizational culture of both strength and flexibility.

© 1999 Steve Hall, Hedrick Blessing.

CASE STUDY: MARCONI COMMUNICATIONS

At the age of 21, in 1895, Guglielmo Marconi (1874–1937) transmitted the first wireless message. On April 15, 1912, his invention of wireless telegraphy was credited with saving 700 lives when the *Titanic* was sinking, as it enabled the transmission of distress calls.[7, 8]

One hundred and six years after that momentous first transmission of a wireless message, I had the pleasure of meeting Paul Harris, vice president, Estates, who worked out of Marconi Communication's United Kingdom-based headquarters. He shared with me the organization's Workplace Futures initiative. The Estates team, Marconi's corporate real estate staff, set out to create the concept for a physical workplace infrastructure that would support the company's aggressive pursuit to become the number-one choice of customers, as well as to earn the reputation of employer-of-choice in the telecommunications industry and its geographic regions of operation. The challenge was to determine how employees could collaborate as "one company," to be more responsive to customers, to better address customer business requirements, and to become more proactive in providing innovative solutions.

STUDIOS Architecture had a long-standing relationship with Marconi Communications, having completed master planning, architecture, and interiors for the company's campuses in Warrendale, Pennsylvania (see Figure 5-9 and Figures 3 and 4 in the color insert), and San Jose, California.[9] Although each location was unique, and made a statement on its own, a common design approach

Figure 5-9: On Marconi Communications' Warrendale, Pennsylvania, campus, the central circulation link becomes the main street where everyone meets.

© 1997 Richard Barnes.

was used where, in the words of Erik Sueberkrop, founding principal of STUDIOS Architecture, "regional history informs building and landscape architecture" (see Figure 5-10). The same design approach was taken by STUDIOS in developing the concept for Workplace Futures, where the design team was charged with establishing a common platform to be tested in a pilot program involving 10,050 people working in three sites in two countries, eventually to be applied to multiple locations globally.

For the two sites in England and the third site in Italy, the firm planned an integrated composition of multiple buildings, basing each campus on the organic development of European towns, as shown in Figures 5-11 and 5-12. Sueberkrop and the STUDIOS team were asked to create an infrastructure that would

provide sufficient variation in work settings, team organization, and work tools to fit the range of job profiles identified within the company. In addition, Workplace Futures had to enable connectivity: aligning the people, the workplace, and new ways of working with the new organizational direction.

The telecommunications industry has gone through a multitude of changes over the past several years, and Marconi Communications has not been immune to those changes. Its strategy for success in this highly competitive industry was to become a leader in innovation, creative thinking, new markets, and new technologies. Paul Harris's team was passionate about the power of place to drive the behavioral changes necessary for the company's success. In developing Workplace Futures, the

Figure 5-10: The phase one model of Marconi, Warrendale, shows a campus that is a series of different buildings "skewered" by a main street.

© 2000 Michael O'Callahan.

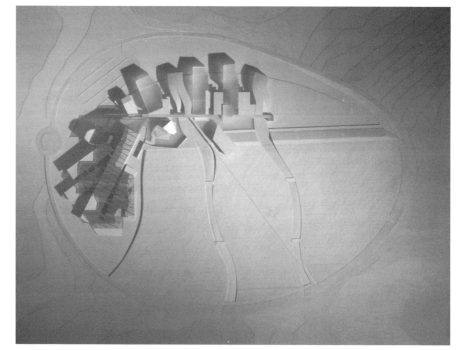

Figure 5-11: Site model for Marconi's Ansty campus in the United Kingdom derives from prehistoric hill forts. All roof and surface water is treated on-site by sand filtration before it enters local streams. The architect maximized light and air by composing a series of "finger" buildings, many of which have turf roofs to provide more sustainable horizontal surfaces.

© 2001 Gerald Ratto.

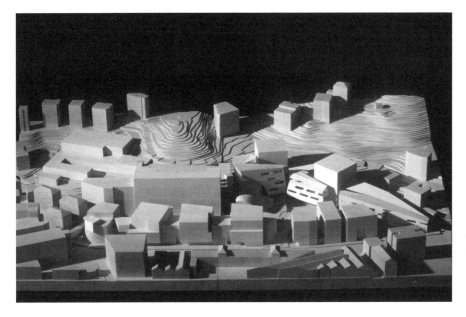

Figure 5-12: The Marconi campus in Genoa, Italy, knits together century-old buildings with new infill components, to create a rich-textured, urban landscape.

© 2001 Michael O'Callahan.

prime drivers of change were identified first. New employee behaviors—39 of them—were profiled in support of the ideal work culture the company required for success in the future. Those behaviors were divided into four core value categories, which came to be known as the Marconi Way. Finally, the physical space would

be designed using specific workplace inspirations as the common denominator for any Marconi facility throughout the world, with appropriate accommodations made for unique processes and cultural variations (see Table 5-3).

Drawing inspiration from prehistoric hill forts in the flat English

TABLE 5-3 Workplace Futures: Driving Change at Marconi

Prime Drivers	Business driver: Increase profitability and efficiency.
	Resource driver: Win the war on talent.
	Client driver: Increase client perception of Marconi.
	Value driver: Enable the Marconi Way.
The Marconi Way	Passion and pride behaviors
	Real-people behaviors
	Radical outlook behaviors
	High-velocity behaviors
Workplace Inspirations	Leave home to come home
	Employer of choice
	Social heartbeat
	Learning
	Connectivity
	Customer confidence

countryside, which create a sense of place, STUDIOS Architecture translated the client's vision and requirements into a scheme of finger buildings organized along an internal pedestrian spine (see Figure 5-13). A typical section illustrates the use of photovoltaic cells along the south window-wall in the primary pedestrian spine, providing heating and cooling for employees and guests without blocking views of the scenery (see Figure 5-14). The underfloor air distribution system integrates structural slab as a thermal mass. The conceptual floor plan emphasizes user comfort by implementing operable windows for natural ventilation and by placing enclosed spaces at the center of the work environment, for optimal natural air circulation (see Figure 5-15). STUDIOS' furniture plan for the workplace employed a kit-of-parts, tethered to a data and electrical point. The kit was composed of components flexible enough to be moved as necessary by the end-users (see Figure 5-16).

Lessons learned from Workplace Futures could fill this entire chapter, but space restrictions require me to focus on one concept, about which the Estates team was adamant: The entire workplace had to reflect a "social heartbeat." What did Marconi mean by that? It was defined as "a center of energy and excitement that radiates to all parts of the facility." Certainly, energy and excitement naturally come to mind when thinking of such public spaces as the reception area or the employee cafeteria, because in those spaces, you find the most diverse groups of people

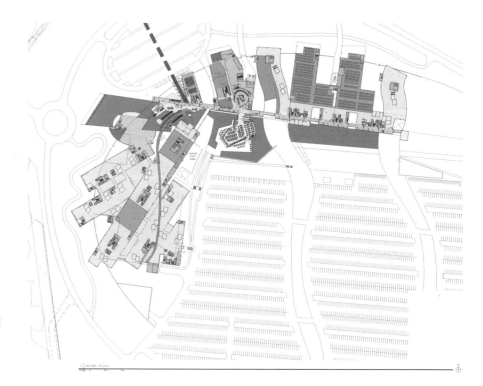

Figure 5-13: The plan for Marconi's Ansty, England, ground floor, shows how the various finger buildings of the scheme are organized along an internal pedestrian spine.

Courtesy STUDIOS Architecture.

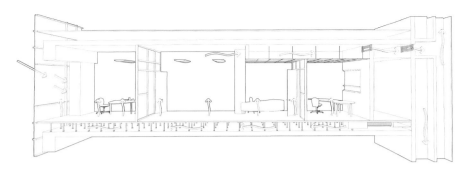

at any given time. Conversations are typically warm and friendly in environments that are generally free from stress. But the organization's desire was to extend the positive aspects of social interaction occurring in public spaces into the diverse work areas of the entire facility.

How did STUDIOS Architecture translate the social heartbeat concept into the physical space plan? The firm did so by developing a plan to enable informality and spontaneity. They designed a dynamic hub as the center, then "guided" the social energy into work neighborhoods, where the "heartbeat" served as a magnet to draw people in and foster interaction. Neighborhoods were varied, to support the specific requirements of each workgroup. For example, it was particularly important to Marconi that its R&D staff members have a social spot where they could "blow off steam" as a respite from periods of intense concentration. For the design firm, this outcome could not be achieved simply by designing cappuccino bars, soft seating areas, and huddle rooms into the plan. It required defining an entirely new spatial model in order to transform the old workplace attributes and culture (see Table 5-4). In moving forward, "space as a right" became

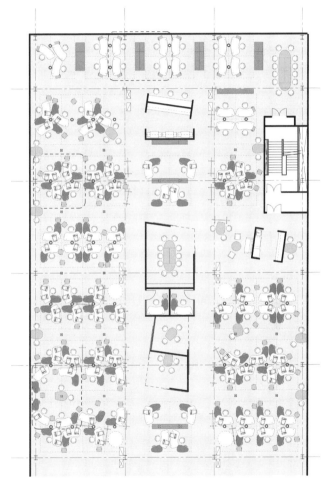

Figure 5-15: The concept for Marconi's Ansty workplace allows for natural ventilation provided by both operable windows and underfloor forced air. This design approach suggests that floorplates should not be wider than 30 meters and that open offices should be generally distributed to the perimeter. By locating enclosed areas at the center, maximum natural air circulation is provided for the majority of the space.

Courtesy STUDIOS Architecture.

Figure 5-16: The kit-of-parts furniture system STUDIOS Architecture planned for the Marconi workplace offered a variety of placement options for maximum flexibility.

Courtesy STUDIOS Architecture.

"space as a tool"; "information comes to me" was transformed into "I go to information"; "invisible architecture" became "messaging architecture"; and "management by control" was converted to "facilitated management."

The influence of the social heartbeat designed into Marconi's Workplace Futures initiative could easily have been ineffective had the organization not supported a culture centered on spontaneous interaction and group problem solving. It could have quickly failed had the organization been unwilling to address informal rewards and recognition, as well as a formal compensation structure focused on the team environment it

TABLE 5-4 New Spatial Model

Old Workplace Attributes	New Spatial Model
Space as a right	Space as a tool
Information comes to me	I go to information
Invisible architecture	Messaging architecture
Management by control	Facilitated management
Nonnegotiable	User-defined
Stored information	Active, displayed situation
Corporate sameness	Group identity
Social prescription	Social awareness and sensitivity
Sedentary	Mobile
Synchronous	Asynchronous

so clearly recognized as essential to the company's innovative outputs.

On January 24, 2006, Marconi Corporation plc announced it was changing its name to telent plc. That first wireless message transmitted by Guglielmo Marconi in 1895 was just the beginning of a rich history of innovation that continues today in telent plc. With alignment of the Critical Influence System, Workplace Futures is poised to guide the company to its future successes.

CASE STUDY: SEI INVESTMENTS

A client invited me to join him in a visit to SEI Investments in Oaks, Pennsylvania, so that I could witness firsthand the physical space changes his organization wanted to drive in its new headquarters building.[10]

SEI, founded in 1968 by Alfred P. West, Jr., is a leading provider of investment accounting and administrative services. The firm processes investment transactions exceeding $50 trillion each year, administers $320 billion in mutual fund and pooled assets, and manages investments totaling more than $135 billion. In April 2006, the company was named to the Global Outsourcing 100 by the International Association of Outsourcing Professionals (IAOP). SEI is also included consistently on *Fortune Magazine's* list of "Best Companies to Work for in America."[11, 12]

Prior to moving to the current Oaks location (phases I through III were completed from 1996 to 2001), the company decided to reinvent itself as part of a "prevention program" to avoid hindering the discovery of changes in the external environment that either enable opportunities or present threats. It was determined that the appropriate workplace design would foster a mind-set for transformation, enable the free flow of ideas, place emphasis on teams, spark creativity, and execute innovations. According to West, "Values encapsulated in words are just not as clear and concrete as those embodied in the office itself." The challenge was identified as "giving a physical presence to values." The successful outcome at SEI is as much a result of strong leadership, driving change through sound behavioral principles, as it is of the well-designed physical space created by Meyer, Scherer & Rockcastle, Ltd.

SEI's physical workplace clearly articulates the culture of the organization: nonhierarchical, entrepreneurial, innovative, inquisitive, collaborative, and focused. There are no private offices (Chairman and CEO West sits in the open environment just like everyone else), and no one has secretaries. If this sounds chaotic and distracting, I can assure you it's anything but. On my visit, I saw colleagues chatting in corridors, close to where others were engaged in phone conversations or individuals were working in their open workspaces. I saw a group of executives having a meeting in the open, seated on soft lounge chairs.

Sound absorption is enhanced by rubber flooring made of recycled tires—which, I noticed, also provides a very energizing feel as I walked throughout the headquarters. During my tour, I learned that staff members had to modify their behaviors in this new, open environment, becoming more sensitive to how voices carry in the space, as opposed to in private offices or paneled workstations.

The calm work environment at SEI is very well balanced, with strong, visual stimulation, the highlight of which is the West family's incredible private art collection displayed throughout the SEI facility. This was of particular interest to me, as I spent the early years of my career working as an artist, and then as a corporate art consultant for Fortune 500 clients (e.g., TRW, IBM, Procter & Gamble, Johnson & Johnson, PPG Industries, Allied Signal Aerospace, and Allnet Communication Services, Inc.), so I knew the positive impact art can have in the work environment to influence behavior. The ever-changing displays of contemporary art at SEI support a culture of diverse opinions and debate. To that end, employees are permitted to ask that an artwork they find objectionable be removed from the workspace and rehung in a corridor called the Hot Hall, where further dialogue is encouraged. A computer in the Hot Hall invites people to comment anonymously on the artwork, and feedback is posted for passersby so that they may learn from other interpretations of the works.

West's philosophy that workplace design and art are drivers of growth and innovation is reflected in all areas of the facility. The values of the organization are reflected in the workplace design, and the culture of the firm in the artwork.[13] Together, they encourage growth and innovation by:

- Attracting and retaining the right people
- Encouraging teamwork and interaction
- Facilitating communication and transparency
- Encouraging creativity
- Sending to all stakeholders a message of innovation and fiscal responsibility

As a result, SEI Investments produces continuous innovation and growth and achieves its corporate objectives.

And in regard to technology, which you know by now is a Critical Influence on behavior in the workplace, the SEI workplace design supports this requirement admirably, as well. To enable a truly flexible work environment, it incorporates "pythons," thick, red, spiral cables that contain electrical power, LAN, and telephone connectivity. They snake down from the ceiling and provide an 18-foot-diameter range of motion. End users can take their mobile desks on casters and select where on the SEI campus they can best do the work they need to complete for that day, that week, or any period of time. Employees simply arrive, set up, and get down to business. Once plugged into the "python," the SEI computer recognizes the employee and automatically routes e-mails, phone calls, faxes, or visitors to that specific location. Moreover, the plug-and-play technology compensates for the $1,400 in reconstruction costs and lost productivity of each employee who would have to move from one team to another in the old workplace.

SEI also has discovered the power of place as a tool to attract and retain talented employees. In addition, the office environment can be considered a competitive advantage for the company's sales force. SEI has increased its customer referral rate to

100 percent, from earlier rates ranging between 20 and 80 percent; and one of its business divisions has realized a 90 percent close rate when prospective clients make an on-site visit.

The financial performance is impressive, as well. Since its move to the new office environment, earnings growth reached 40 percent per year from 1996 to 2001. The average annual return was 28 percent. In the words of Al West and coauthor Yoram (Jerry) Wind, in *Putting the Organization on Wheels: Workplace Design at SEI*, "The environment has affected the business in many ways . . . With greater interaction of employees, decisions can be made more quickly, which increases efficiency and effectiveness. These offices, and the culture they reflect, have helped the company grow to become a leader in its market and to be consistently recognized by *Fortune* as one of the best places to work in America."[14]

CASE STUDY: GSA WORKPLACE 20\20

The changing nature of organizations, work practices, and the workforce led to an exciting initiative launched by the U.S. federal government called WorkPlace 20\20. In the words of Kevin Kampschroer, GSA's director of Research and Expert Services, "The challenges we faced were the classic challenges not just of the government but of corporate America: having less money, constant pressure for more efficiency, the need to do more with less, and get more effectiveness out of the same resources."[15] Increasingly, according to Kampschroer, one of the major issues is generational, resulting in cultural constraints. Managers today are not prepared to deal with four generations in the workplace at the same time. Indeed the government, as a business organization, saw strong similarities

Figure 5-17: The GSA Mid-Atlantic Regional Office in Philadelphia, Pennsylvania, was once the Strawbridge Building, a department store built in 1931. A historic auditorium was transformed into GSA's Data Network Access Center (DNA), combining a library, centralized records management, and informal meeting areas.

© 2006 Tom Crane.

to the evolution of the work world witnessed by Fortune 500 corporations. Work was increasingly more team-based and collaborative, and its workforce more mobile and less dependent on geography.

Not unlike the typical conglomerate with multiple divisions, product offerings, and geographic locations, the U.S. government had found itself reorganizing on an ongoing basis, bringing decision making closer to front-line staff members, and reducing the levels of hierarchical structure, all to provide higher value and more innovative solutions from the perspective of its customers.

This high demand on innovation within the federal government did not appear overnight. The last three administrations have pressured agencies to closely analyze what they were trying to achieve and how they could excel by improving business processes and adopting modern technology and communication methods to impact organizational performance. WorkPlace 20\20, established in 2002, led the charge for innovation as it related to physical space. "Experts told us we should look at improving human productivity," said Kampschroer, but he and his team came to understand that productivity was the wrong focus. The emphasis needed to shift to a more holistic perspective—at overall organizational effectiveness. Elaborating, Kampschroer posed this question: "What if I am more productive at the expense of others around me?" Imagine the difference between taking a microscope to examine one's individual productivity versus using a telescope to view the entire organization as if it were a constellation. An enterprise needs to focus on improving overall productivity in order to achieve its long-term goals.

Kevin Powell, director of research of the 20\20 initiative provided additional insights.[16] In studying applications of the open environment used by various organizations, the 20\20 professionals challenged the negative aspects of working in the open plan: visual and acoustical distractions, as well as an increase in interruptions. To address the complexity of decision making, necessitating team interactions, the WorkPlace 20\20 group learned that what's best for the entire organization is for individuals to be accessible to their teammates. But being able to more readily interact with managers, direct reports, or peers, to optimize the aggregate performance of the organization would, at times, reduce the output or productivity of each individual. Obviously, there had to be a balance between the effectiveness of the organization and that of the individual; but in general, each individual worker—regardless of title or responsibilities—needed to understand how his or her role supported the achievement of organizational goals. A strong communication strategy had to reinforce the message that in a collaborative work environment "the fate of individuals is inextricably bound to collective success."[17]

Shifting the emphasis from individual achievement to aggregate group performance also reinforces the importance of keeping the Critical Influence System in mind, especially as it relates to organizational structure, business processes, compensation, performance management, knowledge management, and rewards and consequences.

In sum, WorkPlace 20\20 is a new approach to viewing the workplace "as a strategic organizational tool rather than a physical container for work."[18] With strong emphasis on the four key elements of Robert Kaplan and David Norton's Balanced Scorecard (BSC)—financial, customer, human capital, and business process—the procedure includes testing each workplace design to ensure the solution addresses the BSC factors.[19] The WorkPlace 20\20 methodology is centered on three critical activities:

- *Organizational analysis.* In this set of activities, the federal government client's business goals and requirements, constraints, and vision for the future are translated into workplace themes, issues, and concepts.
- *Design charrette.* The information uncovered in the client's organizational analysis is used to develop a design direction to support the goals of the enterprise.
- *Workplace evaluation.* An evaluation of metrics is conducted prior to workplace changes being made, as well as postoccupancy, to quantify how well the workplace has supported the organizational goals of the client.

GSA Senior Leadership Space, Auburn, Washington

The first example of a GSA workplace project is the Senior Leadership Space (SLS), a living laboratory in Auburn, Washington, focused on creating a new business model for government work that is egalitarian, spontaneous, interactive, and innovative in changing not only ways of working but in thinking

as well. Drivers of this change included an increased concern about how to compete successfully with the private sector in satisfying federal client requirements and the One GSA initiative being led by the Central Office in Washington, DC, to implement a unified approach to serving customers. One of the aims of the Senior Leadership Space was to improve collaboration, communication, and strategic focus between three separate GSA branches through colocation in the laboratory's open office environment.

Goals for the SLS were focused on providing space for informal meetings as well as structured interactions, and on ensuring individuals and small groups could have privacy when needed. Workplace solutions for the Senior Leadership Space included 80-square-foot open plan workstations for occupants, who previously worked in 180- to 500-square-foot private offices. Open and enclosed spaces included a Village Green (see Figure 5-18) and conference rooms of various sizes. To accommodate privacy requirements, enclosed Focus Booths provided space for individual concentration and confidential conversations.

In touring the Auburn facility, I was most impressed with these Focus Booths—or "dens," as the workforce refers to them. Each offers solitude in a unique way. My favorite featured a corner sitting area wrapped with a simple, padded bench and an array of soft pillows. A small work surface supports the user's laptop and reference materials. The textured wall covering and soft lighting immediately create a sense of escape from the stress so common in the typical office environment (see Figure 5-19).[20]

Figure 5-18: The Senior Leadership Space in Auburn, Washington, was designed to colocate three separate GSA branches in an open office laboratory centered on enhancing communications, improving collaboration, and sharpening the strategic alignment of the three groups.

© 2006 Swimmer Photography.

Figure 5-19: The GSA Senior Leadership Space incorporated enclosed Focus Booths to enable individual concentration and privacy when needed by staff members. Each booth is unique; shown here is the author's favorite, a dimly lit space for relief from stress.

© 2006 Lara Swimmer Photography.

Upon entering the Senior Leadership Space, visitors are drawn to a prominent visual display titled "The History of the Office: A Study in Communication," shown in Figure 5-20 and expanded in the sidebar on page 149. Describing how the workplace has dramatically changed throughout time, it serves as introduction to what guests might

Figure 5-20: Visitors entering the Senior Leadership Space are reminded of the significant changes in the workplace environment throughout time through the display "The History of the Office: A Study in Communication."

© 2006 Lara Swimmer Photography.

see while in the facility. As important, the display clearly sets the tone for employees working in the space, expressing that offices—both physical and virtual—will continue to evolve in response to emerging technologies, innovative tools, and the changing preferences of the workforce.

The GSA WorkPlace 20\20 team describes the Senior Leadership Space as representing "a dramatic shift in workspace allocation and expectations on how leaders should work in the future." The federal government team emphasizes the importance of an organization taking a holistic approach to driving change by leveraging the workplace, yet not setting false expectations that it can take the place of other areas of expertise needed to develop a sustainable framework for behavioral change. Businesses serious about transforming the way people work can avoid costly mistakes by benchmarking

THE HISTORY OF THE OFFICE: A STUDY IN COMMUNICATION

From the first group of chairs pushed together in a circle to the latest high-tech office furniture, offices have always been about communication. How we interact, exchange information, make alliances, and produce whatever our mission requires of us.

- During the early part of the twentieth century, the mission of the war effort brought everyone together. The office was wherever the action was. But lack of privacy, poor equipment, and slow communication made life difficult.
- The prosperity of the '50s and '60s gave corporations new courage to build facilities and experiment with different styles of working and communicating.
- The ingenuity of the '70s and '80s offered many new storage, lighting, and seating variations. Open office styles and "landscapes" promised better connections with management and more efficient use of shared equipment.
- In the '90s, and in the future, distance learning, PDAs, cell phones, and e-mail link us in ways that offer access to part-time workers and a more satisfying work environment. The office workplace now is a time as well as a space.

GSA SENIOR LEADERSHIP SPACE,
AUBURN, WASHINGTON

what the GSA team learned from the Senior Leadership Space and other projects. According to Judith Heerwagen, Ph.D., a psychologist who supported this project, "The physical environment alone cannot be expected to carry the burden of change. In projects such as this, experts in organizational effectiveness and change management should be engaged to help build internal support structures that reward, model, and encourage changes in behaviors, values, and relationships."[21]

And Kevin Kampschroer explained the quantitative results realized from the Senior Leadership Space. "This space is interesting in that we took measurements after one and a half to two years and got middling results. Things were a little better, but not a lot. The team went back four years after move-in and the results were off the scale. I believe that it takes a lot longer to adapt to a new way of working than many businesses are willing to invest."

Public Buildings Service Adaptable Workplace Laboratory, Washington, DC

The second 20\20 project example is the Adaptable Workplace Lab (AWL) in Washington, DC, designed for the National Office of Real Estate Portfolio Management located in the GSA headquarters building. With a primary goal of establishing a collaborative, open environment to enable organizational agility, the importance of accessibility to colleagues was reflected in over 30 percent of the 10,000-square-foot space being designed as collaborative and shared spaces. A secondary objective was to test a variety of technologies supporting adaptability, including HVAC, lighting, connectivity, and interior systems.

The first goal, increasing accessibility of colleagues, was achieved through the design of an open environment featuring a variety of conference room configurations, informal team spaces, and project rooms. A major emphasis of the lab was to create a high level of user control over the configuration of the space. Plug-and-play capability was enabled by a raised-access floor housing a grid framework for voice, data, and electricity. Individual user control of thermal comfort was accomplished through thermal zone conditioning independent of ventilation.[22]

Public Buildings Service Rocky Mountain Regional Office, Denver, Colorado

Take a former World War II munitions factory whose interior offers little access to windows or daylight, convert it into offices in the 1950s, then add 50 years' worth of incremental "improvements," and what you end up with is a sense of randomness. But then apply the sound principles of the GSA WorkPlace 20\20 approach, as implemented by the talented members of Gensler's Denver team, and what you get is a Best Workplace Solution award from the CoreNet Mid-Atlantic chapter (in 2005).[23]

The intent of the Public Buildings Service (PBS) project in Denver, Colorado, was to use the workplace environment as a catalyst for social change (see Figure 5-21). With key goals centered on attracting and retaining high-caliber workers, the office was intended to serve as an environmental showcase that would provide optimal support for associates

Figure 1 This break room at Sprint Nextel is an inviting environment where employees can relax or engage in an impromptu meeting while enjoying a fabulous view of the Kansas sky. Image courtesy of Hillier Architecture; photography © 2002 Sam Fentress.

Figure 2 The dramatic S-shaped façade of the Alcoa Corporate Center, created by The Design Alliance Architects, makes a powerful statement about the company's commitment to the Pittsburgh business community. © 1999 Steve Hall, Hedrick Blessing.

Figure 3 Designed by STUDIOS Architecture, a series of different buildings, in rhythmic order, meet guests as they arrive at the Marconi Communications campus in Warrendale, Pennsylvania. © 1997 Richard Barnes.

Figure 4 Along the ridge of a Pennsylvania hilltop, STUDIOS Architecture created the Marconi Warrendale campus by knitting a diverse set of buildings together with a single main street. © 1997 Richard Barnes.

Figure 5 GSA's Public Buildings Service Rocky Mountain Regional Office in Denver, Colorado, designed by Gensler, was formerly a World War II munitions factory. The building's interior provided little access to windows or natural daylight. Today, the space is modern, efficient, and inviting. Shown here is a circular-shaped café, bathed in natural light coming through a large skylight. © 2007 Blake Mourer, Gensler.

Figure 6 In 1931, the Strawbridge Building in Philadelphia, Pennsylvania, was designed as a retail department store. Today, it stands as a proud example of a successful transformation project. It now serves as the GSA Mid-Atlantic Regional Office, completed using the WorkPlace 20\20 approach and principles, and designed against the U.S. General Services Administration's Hallmarks of the Productive Workplace. © 2006 Tom Crane

Figure 7 Meyer Design created this space for client Analytical Graphics Inc., to reflect the organization's commitment to communication. The "Water Cooler," a futurist-looking gathering place, symbolizes interaction and knowledge exchange, top priorities of the client firm. AGI has consistently been rated a Great Place to Work and was awarded the prestigious number-one position on the Best Medium Companies to Work for in America list, in 2006. © 2004 Don Pearse Photographers, Inc. (www.don-pearsephotographers.com).

Figure 8 The Pfizer Global Research & Development facility in Groton, Connecticut, is rich in detail, which has been incorporated into the space by CUH2A. © 2000 Tom Bernard.

Figure 9 Pfizer's Innovation Garden on the grounds of its Global Research & Development facility can be enjoyed during a brisk walk outdoors, or observed through numerous spaces within the building. Courtesy Rick Scanlan.

Figure 10 Gensler's headquarters is located in a wonderful old building on the San Francisco Bay. In renovating the space for the company's studio and offices, a commitment was made to honor the history of both the building and the firm. At the same time, the design reflects new organizational expectations for behaviors in the workplace. Courtesy Eric Laignel.

Figure 11 The reception area in Gensler's headquarters in San Francisco is elegant and inviting, to both visitors and staff. Courtesy Eric Laignel.

Figure 12 Clients visiting Gensler's headquarters in San Francisco can see directly from the reception area into the studios, where they can observe—and engage in—the creative process. The firm's attention to detail is evident in this conferencing space, visible upon entering the facility. Courtesy Eric Laignel.

Figure 13 Gensler's workspace is energized through splashes of vibrant color. Courtesy Eric Laignel.

Gensler's San Francisco work environment, formerly a GAP retail store. This comfortable setting takes advantage of natural light pouring through the large windows of this old building on the Bay. Courtesy Eric Laignel.

Figure 15 With two sides enclosed in glass, this small room provides a quiet place to meet in Gensler's San Francisco office, but does not impose a sense of isolation. Courtesy Eric

Figure 16 To help De Lage Landen employees adjust to their new work environment created by Meyer Design—and meet expectations for new behaviors—each was given three different-colored tennis balls. The ball employees displayed on their work surfaces signaled availability—green, for "open to interaction"; yellow, for "proceed with caution"; and red, for "don't interrupt." © 2001 Don Pearse Photographers, Inc. (www.don-pearsephotographers.com).

Figure 17 The café designed for De Lage Landen by Meyer Design, Inc. is vibrant and inviting. Its bold color palette draws individuals in to socialize with colleagues or to discuss business issues in a casual environment. © 2001 Don Pearse Photographers, Inc.

...ovation of Procter & Gamble's Baby Toddler ...uarters transformed a 1950's campus—consisting ...buildings, a connector building, a pedestrian ...standing, high bay facility—into the Envision ...nvironment colocates all functional business ...es offices, laboratories, pilot labs, customer ...nd prototype development spaces. With a focus ...:e, the space also includes a fitness center and ... Photographer: Ryan Kurtz.

Figure 19 The renovation of Procter & Gamble's lobby in its global headquarters was an opportunity to visually depict its core values and corporate brand identity. The corporate message, "Touching Lives, Improving Life," is the theme of the glass mural. Photographer: Hedrick Blessing.

Figure 20 Goss/Pasma Architects incorporated panels of textured glass to create visual interest, as well as filtered privacy, for meetings taking place at Que Net Media in Schaumberg, Illinois. Goss/Pasma Architects; © 2005 Kevin Beswick, People Places & Things Photographics.

Figure 21 The law offices of Bleakley Cypher Parent Warren & Quinn, P.C., Cherry Street Landing, Grand Rapids, Michigan, were created by Progressive AE. The space exudes warmth through the surface materials, yet conveys a clean, professional aesthetic. Progressive AE; © 2005 Kevin Beswick, People Places & Things Photographics.

Figure 22 A large island and stools at the top of a spiral staircase at Bleakley Cypher Parent Warren & Quinn's offices can serve a number of purposes, from a gathering place for lunch to a convenient spot to call an impromptu meeting. Progressive AE; © 2005 Kevin Beswick, People Places & Things Photographics.

Figure 23 The offices of Hanon McKendry, a public relations and advertising firm, located in the renovated Arena Station in Grand Rapids, Michigan, blend old and the new in a progressive work environment, resulting in a warm and inviting place to meet with clients. Rockford Construction Company; © 2005 Kevin Beswick, People Places & Things Photographics.

Figure 24 To test and evaluate strategies for the emerging workplace for its clients, Callison created the Future@Work laboratory. A rich mix of collaborative spaces, for group work at all scales, forms the heart of this installation. Copyright Callison/Chris Eden.

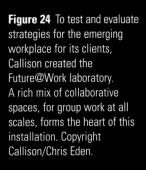

Figure 25 Elegant bench seating and wall treatments have been used by Eppstein Uhen Architects to enhance the guest experience for business groups at Hotel Metro Zen on Seven in Milwaukee, Wisconsin. © 2006 Eppstein Uhen Architects.

Figure 26 To enable the free exchange of ideas, openness is emphasized throughout this R&D facility's "room without walls" concept, developed by Hixson. Instead of predefined boundaries made of drywall, staff members can establish team centers and create a sense of place using flexible components. © 2006 Hixson Architecture, Engineering, Interiors.

Figure 27 Creativity is apparent throughout this workplace designed by Hixson, even in the stairwell. Kites hung from the ceiling symbolize soaring ideas and limitless discovery at this advanced R&D center. © 2006 Hixson Architecture, Engineering, Interiors.

Figure 28 To support its R&D client's desire for a space that fosters free thinking, creativity, and team collaboration, Hixson utilized existing garage door openings on exterior walls, then incorporated similar doors in the conference room. © 2006 Hixson Architecture, Engineering, Interiors.

Figure 29 The Guildford Textiles Design Studio was designed by Robert Luchetti Associates of Cambridge, Massachusetts. On the right are individual workstations, which also encourage team interaction; an inviting visitor's core extends to the end of the workspace. To the left, the team's shared studio features mobile displays and stand-up-height work surfaces. Planning and Design: Robert Luchetti Associates. Photographer and photo copyright 1997, Bill Kontzias.

Figure 30 Robert Luchetti Associates worked with client Cap Gemini Ernst and Young on its Center for Business Innovation project. Shown here, a small team room is energized by the color palette, glass walls, and reflective ceilings. Planning and Design: Robert Luchetti Associates. Photographer and photo copyright 2002, Greg Premru.

Figure 31 The Fitch Inc. Boston Studio, housed in a large, concrete building, which was formerly a warehouse, was transformed by Robert Luchetti Associates into a design studio and offices for 60 design professionals. Planning and Design: Robert Luchetti Associates. Photographer and photo copyright 1999, Richard Barnes.

Figure 32 Robert Luchetti Associates developed the International Business Services Headquarters for the Boston Consulting Group using a post-and-beam kit of parts to create both open and enclosed spaces. Featured here is a view from the reception area into the meeting and presentation room. Planning and Design: Robert Luchetti Associates. Photographer and photo copyright 1998, Paul Warchol.

Figure 33 Whitney, Inc. developed a sleek, sophisticated design for Synovate's Chicago office. This striking café area serves as both a cafeteria and touchdown space, where employees can grab a bite to eat, have a quick chat, or plug in a laptop. © 2007 Whitney, Inc.

Figure 34 Synovate's highly energized atmosphere includes vibrantly colored workstations that enable a constant flow of communication and stimulate collaboration while maintaining a sense of privacy. © 2007 Whitney, Inc.

Figure 35 Natural light streams in through the expansive windows of Synovate's New York office, designed by Whitney, Inc. The lunch room is a bright, airy environment where employees can both relax and collaborate while enjoying their midday meals. © 2007 Whitney, Inc.

PUBLIC BUILDINGS SERVICE

Figure 5-21: The Public Buildings Service has established itself as a leader, rather than a follower, in workplace design. The principles of the GSA WorkPlace 20\20 approach were applied to a former World War II munitions factory, which today is a collaborative work environment for the PBS Rocky Mountain Regional Office in Denver, Colorado.

© 2007 Blake Mourer, Gensler.

in their day-to-day work, enable better internal working relationships, and result in an improvement in services to external clients. In addition, the aim was to use the workspace as a way to show that PBS is a thought leader, rather than a follower, in workplace design.[24]

The PBS workplace solution created by Gensler was centered on improving the quality of work life for its associates. Bringing natural light into the former factory building was critical. Today, daylight illuminates common areas throughout the facility, as evidenced in skylights that brighten workplace entrances (Figure 5-22) and renovated stairways (Figure 5-23).

Prior to the renovation of the munitions factory-turned-office environment, interfacing with colleagues was a challenge. Conference rooms were in short supply, and often too large for the number of individuals gathered for a meeting. And because these rooms were "owned" by specific groups, they were generally unavailable to others in the building. In the new workplace design, priority was placed on interaction; to meet that requirement, it incorporates a wide variety of spaces to gather. Large conference rooms, clustered, are available to all staff members, and managed through electronic scheduling. The environment offers open space at central nodes for spontaneous interactions, workplace breakout areas, and numerous small, enclosed meeting spaces (see Figure 5-24).

With a focus on improving morale and strengthening internal relationships, Blake Mourer, senior associate/lead designer on Gensler's Denver team, incorporated a centrally located café, circular in shape and filled with

Figure 5-22: The interior of the former munitions factory in Denver once lacked daylight. Through the design work of Gensler, the workplace brings the outdoors in; now daylight streams in through skylights.

© 2007 Blake Mourer, Gensler.

Figure 5-23: The PBS Denver facility brings natural light into renovated stairways through the addition of skylights.

© 2007 Blake Mourer, Gensler.

Figure 5-24: The new workplace design created by Gensler for the GSA facility in Denver offers a variety of meeting spaces. Shown here is a workplace breakout area that can easily accommodate several small group interactions simultaneously.

© 2007 Blake Mourer, Gensler.

daylight (Figure 5-25 and Figure 5 in the color insert) and the P.I.T. (People Interacting Together), an area outfitted with lounge furniture, a pool table, a Ping-Pong table, and exercise room (Figure 5-26).

As mentioned earlier, the Denver WorkPlace 20\20 project was an opportunity to create a workplace environment that would function as a catalyst for social change. The project employed social network analysis to explore the level of connectivity—between groups, face to face, and virtual—and the potential of distance to cause isolation. The preliminary results gathered from the analysis, as well as an electronic survey, revealed that the renovated Denver work environment enables greater knowledge exchange, an improved sense of community, and enhanced opportunities to develop cross-functional

relationships. A surprising finding of the social network analysis indicated face-to-face conversations have increased substantially, prevailing over phone or e-mail interactions. In the words of Judith Heerwagen, "It is evident that spatial layout, visibility, and circulation can certainly influence interaction and communication—but it does not do so always and, in fact, may not work to improve communications between groups when there are cultural barriers."[25] Her comment reinforces the importance of addressing factors within the Critical Influence System that may negatively impact the success of the workplace strategy. Leadership behavior must support the changes being driven; the organizational culture must be in alignment; and, of course, there must be a perceived need for improved communication.

Figure 5-25: A highlight of the GSA Denver space is a circular-shaped café, which draws staff members in to enjoy the natural light and the opportunity to interface casually with colleagues.

© 2007 Blake Mourer, Gensler.

Figure 5-26: The P.I.T.— People Interacting Together— provides an area for GSA staff members to relax and strengthen social ties with their Denver peers.

© 2007 Blake Mourer, Gensler.

Public Buildings Service Great Lakes Regional Office, Chicago, Illinois

The renovation of the GSA Public Buildings Service's Great Lakes Regional Office in Chicago tells a story of preserving the past while transitioning to the future. The past, in this case, refers to the historic John C. Kluczynski Federal Building designed by German architect Ludwig Mies van der Rohe, widely recognized as a pioneer in modern architecture. For the federal staff members who work in this PBS office, the future necessitated a number of changes, including undergoing a major reorganization under a new executive leader, supplanting a "command and control" method of operation with one that emphasized collaborative results, and shifting from a culture perceived as reactionary to a learning organization that understands and anticipates client needs.

An organizational analysis was conducted to ensure the workplace strategy being developed would support the necessary work process changes. The strategy for the physical space also needed to align with the regional office's goals to better understand the customer and anticipate their needs and, through knowledge sharing, collaborate to optimize the team's performance. The matrix showing the alignment between the critical factors is featured in Table 5-5.[26]

The goal to open up the workplace using natural light drove changes in the physical space plan. Full and partial walls of glass allow daylight to peek through areas that were once solid drywall (see Figure 5-27). Managers, previously working in private offices on the windowed perimeter of the building, were relocated to the core of the building where their new offices are appointed in wood and glass. The offices at the building's

---

TABLE 5-5 Linking Work Process Change to Measures of Success

Work Process Change	Workplace Strategy and Solutions	Measures of Success
Better project integration and coordination across groups	Improve awareness and informal communication by reducing internal barriers	Improvements in communication and interaction within and across groups
	Support group work by providing a greater variety of shared meeting spaces	Improved customer satisfaction
More sharing of customer knowledge	Encourage information sharing and integration of information about project status by providing centralized project files	Timeliness of project progress and completion
		Improved customer satisfaction
	Support internal work flexibility and mobility with wireless technology	Improved knowledge of customer

Workplace Matters, U.S. General Services Administration, © 2006.

Figure 5-27: One of the goals of the renovation of the GSA Public Buildings Service's Great Lakes Regional Office, located in Chicago's historic John C. Kluczynski Federal Building, designed by Mies van der Rohe, was to open up the space with natural light. Full and partial glass walls supplanted solid drywall.

perimeter were converted into functional areas to support the entire office population. The corner offices were transformed into spacious conference rooms and smaller offices now available for uses ranging from structured project meetings (Figure 5-28) to impromptu team strategy sessions (Figure 5-29). Glass was employed to divide space while maintaining a sense of transparency, creating semiprivate work areas an employee can use when he or she wants to concentrate on individual tasks yet remain accessible to colleagues (Figure 5-30).

Feedback from staff members working in the new space has been very positive. In particular, the willingness of managers to move from the windowed perimeter of the building to internal offices has emphasized the importance of engaging each individual in changes crucial to organizational effectiveness.

GSA WorkPlace 20\20: Lessons Learned

The GSA WorkPlace 20\20 initiative has produced positive results and drawn attention to its aggressive attempts to improve the federal workplace. But the GSA team is not resting on its laurels. Kevin Kampschroer and numerous others committed to the long-term success of the concept continue to rigorously analyze quantifiable and qualifiable data from each project. Key findings are evaluated and applied as appropriate to subsequent workplace projects. Says Kampschroer, "There are so many influences on organizational effectiveness; we're still searching and seeking. We are affecting human behavior and this is a building block for organizational performance."

Lessons learned from GSA WorkPlace 20\20 projects include:

- It may take more time to adapt to a new way of working than an

Figure 5-28: The windowed offices at the building's perimeter—previously private offices for GSA Chicago's managers—were converted into functional areas to support activities such as project meetings.

Figure 5-29: In the GSA Public Buildings Service's Chicago facility, teams can gather in one of the windowed spaces that were previously assigned to managers as private offices.

organization is willing to invest. Where organizational and change management support were not included in the project, transitioning to the new space was difficult, especially for those who did not embrace the goals and objectives of the new environment.

- There is an increase in concern about loss of privacy and increased distraction. Workplace strategies centered on improving collaboration

Figure 5-30: In the GSA Chicago office, semiprivate work spaces available to all make it possible to balance between accessibility and the need to concentrate on work.

HALLMARKS OF THE PRODUCTIVE WORKPLACE

- *Spatial equity.* The workplace is designed to meet the functional needs of the users by accommodating the tasks to be undertaken without compromising individual access to privacy, daylight, outside views, and aesthetics.
- *Healthfulness.* The workplace is housed in a healthy environment with access to air, light, and water, and is free of harmful contaminants and excessive noise.
- *Flexibility.* The workplace configuration adapts to typical organizational and work process changes but can also be readily restructured to accommodate major functional changes.
- *Comfort.* The workplace allows workers to adjust thermal, lighting, acoustic, and furniture systems to meet personal and team comfort levels.
- *Technological connectivity.* Workplaces on-site (e.g., team space, conference/multimedia space, hoteling space) and off-site (e.g., telecommute center, home office) allow easy communication among distributed coworkers while allowing simultaneous access to data.
- *Reliability.* The workplace is supported by state-of-the-art HVAC, lighting, power, security, and telecommunication systems/equipment that require minimal maintenance downtime and are designed with back-up capabilities to ensure minimal loss of service.
- *Sense of place.* The workplace has a unique character, with an appropriate image and identity, enabling a sense of pride, purpose, and dedication for both the individual and the workplace community.

GSA WORKPLACE 20\20, OFFICE OF REAL PROPERTY,
OFFICE OF GOVERNMENTWIDE POLICY,
U.S. GENERAL SERVICES ADMINISTRATION.

and interaction are at odds with workers' needs for focused individual attention and confidentiality.

- Moving to a system of allocating space based on functional need is often met with resistance from those who support an entitlement-based approach.
- Cultural constraints may discourage use of informal collaborative spaces if there is a perception associates are "not working."

Is the WorkPlace 20\20 approach appropriate for every federal organization? That's what Kevin Kelly, AIA, director of Workplace Programs, is charged with answering. He oversees the entire initiative to determine how applicable the concept is, and the predicted demand for his team's direct involvement in the government's portfolio of 364 million square feet of leased space (and in light of the nearly 6 million square feet of government-occupied space that will expire each year over the next four years).[27] As in the private sector, there are federal government clients that just want a new workspace. These agencies are, essentially, asking for the end result; they do not want to engage in consulting activities, even though solutions have been proven more effective when they incorporate the WorkPlace 20\20 concepts. The perception of a lengthier process—despite the fast-track approach of the 20\20 methodology—or the interpretation that the workgroup is already functioning at its optimal level of performance, has at times led GSA's customers to want a bit of expertise; they are unwilling to participate in a full-blown process.

The next step for Kelly's team is to develop, then launch, the Program of Requirements (POR) Plus. This level of support will improve and expand upon the typical reporting of basic needs to help the customer make better decisions. With POR Plus, GSA clients can, on their own, use a standardized method founded on GSA WorkPlace 20\20 principles.[28]

As the WorkPlace 20\20 initiative continues to evolve, which key concepts can you apply to your workplace strategies today? My suggestion is to emphasize GSA's Hallmarks of the Productive Workplace (see the sidebar).[29] Change is constant in the office environment, yet principles like these hallmarks remain valid over time.

CASE STUDY: ANALYTICAL GRAPHICS, INC.

Analytical Graphics Inc. (AGI) in Exton, Pennsylvania, produces commercial off-the-shelf analysis software for land, sea, air, and space applications, including battle space management, geospatial intelligence initiatives, space systems, and national defense programs. The company's products are used by aerospace, defense, and intelligence professionals throughout the world.

AGI is, literally, a great place to work. According to the Great Places to Work Institute, of 250 organizations it evaluated, AGI was ranked number one on the Best Medium Companies to Work for in America list, in 2006, and number one of the Best Small Companies in 2004 and 2005.[30] Testimony to its ability to retain talented employees is that AGI's turnover rate is 3 percent, compared to the industry average of 20.5 percent. And there's more: Analytical Graphics has been ranked as one of five top aerospace/military work environments in North America by *Aviation Week* and *Space Technology*. In September 2005,

Leadership Excellence magazine selected AGI as the number-one small-to midsized firm in North America for leadership development programs. It has been named to a number of other prestigious lists, as well, including the *Inc.* 500, Technology Fast 50, Technology Fast 500, Philly 100, and *Softletter* Top 100. And its CEO, Paul Graziani, has been nominated for, and received, a number of entrepreneurial excellence awards at both local and national levels. Not bad for a company Graziani founded, with two partners, in 1989 in Graziani's living room.

Today at AGI, protecting the friendly, collegial culture, sharing ideas, and treating employees well are top priorities, even during periods of significant growth. To reinforce the corporate culture, the company offers numerous perks to its 195 headquarters employees, a partial list of which includes: three free meals a day for employees and their families; an on-site gym, with a free personal trainer and Pilates classes; free laundry facilities (AGI supplies the detergent); flex time; shipping of personal packages at cost through the firm's shipping department; oil changes conducted in the company parking lot; and weekly pickup and delivery of dry cleaning and shoe repair. But employees know where the true value lies. According to the article "AGI Rises to the Top—Again," in the July 2006 issue of *HR Magazine*, "all of the employees we asked said if they had to choose between the perks and the culture, they would choose the culture."[31] The pride the company takes in the AGI team is evident when you speak to Lisa Velte, director of Human Resources. The company is passionate about celebrating team success, evidenced by a long-standing tradition that takes place on the last workday of the year, when employees and their families gather to design, build, and launch model rockets. Rocket Day celebrates the conclusion of another great year, when more that 200 rockets lift off from AGI headquarters (see Figure 5-31).[32, 33, 34]

Does a successful workplace solution that enables collaborative behavior

Figure 5-31: Analytical Graphics Inc. was ranked number one on the Best Medium Companies to Work for in America list, in 2006. Employee engagement is a top priority at the organization. Shown here is AGI's Annual Rocket Day, a celebration for employees and their families to conclude another year of success for the entire team.

Courtesy Analytical Graphics, Inc.

contribute to innovative results? Let's take a look at some facts as they relate to this workplace project, completed in 2004. Analytical Graphics had been in a one-floor, contiguous space where its management occupied private offices located on the perimeter of the building. The decision was made to relocate to a four-story building, where AGI would initially occupy the first three floors, with the option of taking over the fourth floor as the company grew. The workplace solution designed by Meyer Design focused on cultural reinforcement.[35] AGI's emphasis on open communication is reflected both symbolically and functionally—for example, the CEO's office has no door—and is carried out throughout the facility (with the exception of sensitive areas that house the company's finance and human resource functions).

Meyer Design used such features as curved walls to create an appropriate sense of enclosure, enable interaction, and articulate the company's culture that interruptions are acceptable and, in fact, welcome (see Figures 5.32 and 5.33). AGI's lunch room is a primary gathering place, fostering unity and a sense of common purpose. It's in this room that the weekly Story Time is held each Friday, where department members can share new or updated information with colleagues. This room also serves as a forum in which to recognize team members for special efforts.

Along with recognizing communications as a Critical Influence on behavior in this workplace, employee compensation is strategically designed to promote collaboration: each individual gets the same quarterly bonus based on the overall performance results of the company.

To reflect AGI's involvement in the aerospace industry, the reception

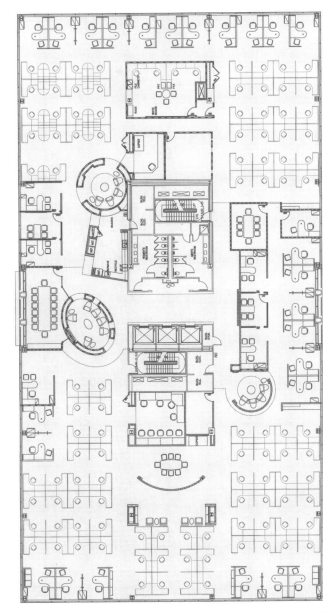

Figure 5-32: Meyer Design's layout for Analytical Graphics Inc. is an excellent example of how to achieve an appropriate sense of enclosure yet encourage interaction. Curved walls and other architectural elements support the company's priorities.

© 2004 Meyer Design, Inc. (www.meyerdesigninc.com).

area has a space-age feel, as shown in Figure 5-34. Meyer Design continued the innovative approach by incorporating the theme into the paths of circulation throughout the building. Mike Stanczak and the Meyer team took

Figure 5-33: Individual workspaces at AGI reflect the importance of remaining accessible to others in the company, and support the organizational culture, where interruptions are welcomed.

© 2004 Don Pearse Photographers, Inc. (www.donpearsephotographers.com).

Figure 5-34: Meyer Design's conceptual drawing for Analytical Graphic Inc.'s reception area reflects the company's industry focus.

© 2004 Meyer Design, Inc. (www.meyerdesigninc.com).

constellation photographs and laid out the circulation plan by connecting the celestial dots in interesting ways, as illustrated in Figure 5-35. On any given path of circulation, "travelers" pass through public nodes to inspire interaction. There are also brainstorming stations, complete with whiteboards, where occasionally an employee will be seen snapping a photo to capture

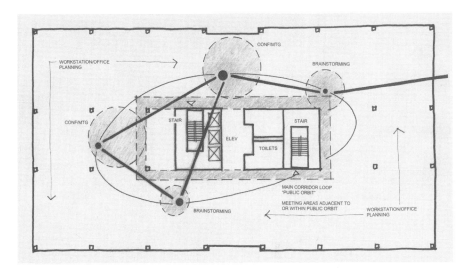

Figure 5-35: The development of the circulation paths for the Analytical Graphics workplace environment was the result of first taking constellation photographs and defining celestial patterns.

© 2004 Meyer Design, Inc. (www.meyerdesigninc.com).

the ideas written on one of them, to save for further discussion with peers. Applications support engineers will even share ideas by writing on the windows (see Figure 5-36).

Another creative approach from Meyer Design for the AGI workplace is evident in the company's large boardroom (able to accommodate 22 to 50 people), which serves double duty as a demonstration room for customer presentations and as a corporate theater (see Figure 5-37). Mike Stanczak comments that the furnishings reflect "a throwback to aviation," in that they use materials that make it clear to visitors what the company is all about. The cool, hard surface of

Figure 5-36: Visually capturing ideas contributes to innovative outputs at Analytical Graphics Inc. The company provides white boards and other tools for employee use. Individuals are also given the freedom to use the workplace creatively, as in the example here, where two Applications Support Engineers brainstorm a solution for a customer.

Courtesy Analytical Graphics, Inc.

Figure 5-37: AGI's large boardroom serves multiple purposes: as a space for internal meetings, as a demonstration room for customer presentations, and as a corporate theater, accommodating as many as 50 people.

© 2004 Don Pearse Photographers, Inc. (www.donpearsephotographers.com).

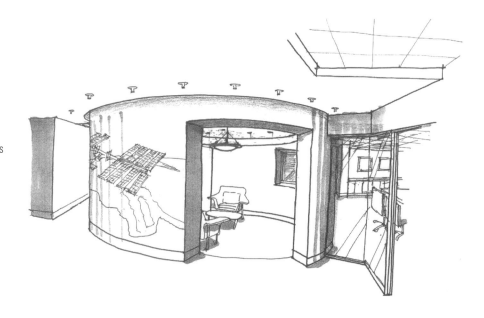

Figure 5-38: Meyer Design's conceptual drawing of the Water Cooler, a progressive gathering place, reflects Analytical Graphics' commitment to maintaining communication with both external and internal customers.

© 2004 Meyer Design, Inc. (www.meyerdesigninc.com).

structural aluminum, with rivets and bolts, was balanced by using soft, billowy cloth.

Symbolism of Analytical Graphics' commitment to communication is also reflected in Meyer Design's creation of a space called the Water Cooler, a futurist-looking gathering place that stimulates interaction and knowledge exchange (see Figure 5-38 and Figure 7 in the color insert).

Needless to say, I am not advocating that every workplace solution include on-site laundry facilities, or offer three free meals each day. I am, however, endorsing AGI's determination to reinforce its culture through the behaviors of its leaders and the design of its physical work environment. Thus, it's essential to understand the reason behind the many perks offered by the company. Says CEO Graziani,

as quoted in *HR Magazine*, "We don't serve dinner to get people to stay late. We serve dinner because people are staying late. It's a very critical distinction."

CASE STUDY: PFIZER GLOBAL RESEARCH & DEVELOPMENT

A major shift in the approach to drug research was the impetus for the development of a new workplace strategy for pharmaceutical leader Pfizer. Increasing market share and speed to market in this highly competitive industry is essential, and architectural firm CUH2A's client was focused not only on improving innovative outputs (drug discovery), but also on how the discovery process could be changed to become more innovative than in the past.

Figure 5-39: Pfizer Global Research & Development, Groton, Connecticut.

Courtesy Tom Bernard.

At the time, Pfizer was realizing tremendous growth, with approximately two new scientists coming onboard each week, and its research and development facilities were scattered among nine locations. Brian Kowalchuk, director of design for Princeton, New Jersey-headquartered CUH2A, worked closely with Pfizer as it reshaped its business organization and developed a plan to consolidate its R&D people and processes into one location.[36]

In the past, therapeutic team members worked in their respective departments, and earlier Pfizer buildings were designed to accommodate this setup. Chemists worked on the top floor, in fume-hood laboratories, which needed a great deal of ventilation; below them, on the lower floors, worked the biologists. This arrangement ensured that each department was efficient, but the physical separation between biologists and chemists impeded the day-to-day informal interaction that generates momentum for exchange and discovery. As many organizations across industries have been learning, a linear business process can increase the time it takes to bring a new product to market. In addition, when one department passes on its information to the next, to apply its area of expertise, the outcome is rarely as rich as when cross-functional teams work together to find a solution or develop a new product.

By conducting interviews with 800 scientists at the Groton, Connecticut, campus, and gathering feedback from Pfizer staff from around the globe, Pfizer and CUH2A gained a great deal of insight as to how the staff worked. Under the direction of Pfizer's Dr. George Milne, a thematic approach was established whereby therapeutic staff members became part of cross-functional teams who were colocated in the same physical space (see Figures 5-40, 5-41 and 5-42). Developing the various spaces to support the diverse types of work being carried out in chemistry and biology labs proved to be complex. Typically, a chemistry lab is staffed by one senior scientist, two associates, and a group of six other scientists; biology labs typically house 9 to 18 team members. In combining these two disciplines into one cross-functional project team, the physical space—therapeutic zones, or "research villages"—had to be able to support from 45 to 65 professionals. In the end, a total of 12 research villages on three lab floors were constructed to foster collaboration and increase innovative outputs.

Figure 5-40: A thematic approach changed the linear business process Pfizer employed to bring new products to market. Based on CUH2A's extensive interviews with Pfizer staff from around the globe, it was decided to put therapeutic staff members on cross-functional teams and colocate them in the same physical space.

Courtesy CUH2A.

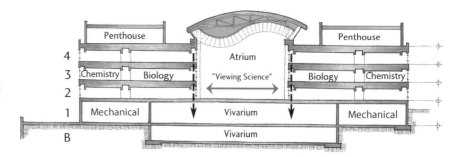

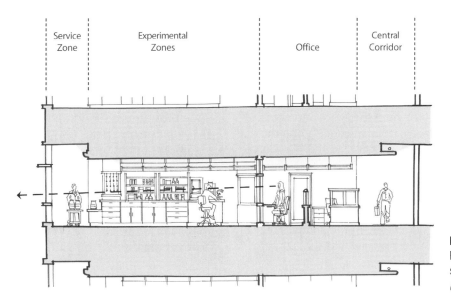

Service Zone | Experimental Zones | Office | Central Corridor

Figure 5-41: Pfizer Global Research & Development lab section created by CUH2A.

Courtesy CUH2A.

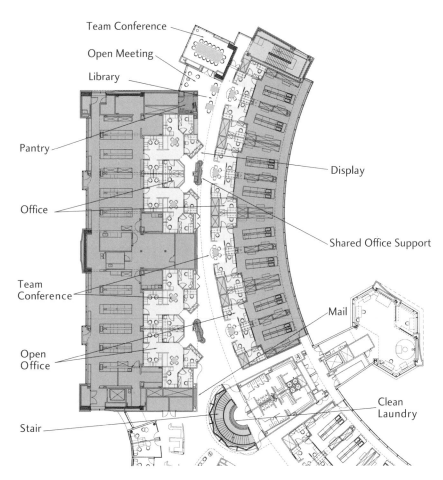

Team Conference

Open Meeting

Library

Pantry

Office

Team Conference

Open Office

Stair

Display

Shared Office Support

Mail

Clean Laundry

Figure 5-42: CUH2A's office layout developed for Pfizer.

Courtesy CUH2A.

Throughout the facility, CUH2A incorporated functionality, comfort, and a sophisticated, professional aesthetic. The firm also developed a concept called the "front porch," a circulation path that eases travel throughout the space and encourages staff interaction during the day (see Figures 5-43 and 5-44). Curved staircases ensure that individuals walking from floor to floor will cross paths with colleagues, encouraging spontaneous conversations (see Figure 5-45). In the library, staff can conduct research, as well confer quietly with others (see Figure 5-46). The atrium serves as a social hub as well as a team meeting location (see Figure 5-47).

Combining chemistry and biology laboratories on such a large scale proved to be an innovative solution, one that has garnered significant attention in the highly competitive pharmaceutical industry. As well, the Pfizer Global R&D project earned a High Honors award for overall excellence in *R&D Magazine*'s 2001 Laboratory of the Year competition.[37, 38, 39, 40]

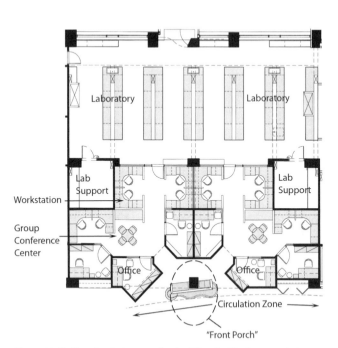

Figure 5-43: The circulation zone for the Pfizer facility incorporated a "front porch" concept to promote interaction among colleagues.

Courtesy CUH2A.

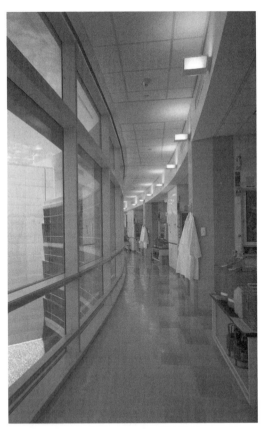

Figure 5-44: This corridor in Pfizer's chemical services area integrates "front porches" along a busy circulation path.

Courtesy Tom Bernard.

Figure 5-45: This curved staircase in Pfizer Global R&D facility encourages spontaneous conversation.
Courtesy Scott McDonald.

Figure 5-46: CUH2A designed this elegant library in the Pfizer Global Research & Development facility.
Courtesy Scott McDonald.

Figure 5-47: The Pfizer atrium, with its soaring height and view of the upper floors, draws in staff members for meals, conversations, and informal meetings.

Courtesy Tom Bernard.

CASE STUDY: CISCO—THE CONNECTED WORKPLACE

By the early 2000s, Cisco's headquarters in San Jose, California, needed a more effective workplace for its employees. The company's utilization statistics revealed an environment that was "broken." Meeting rooms were in short supply, while private offices and cubicles were vacant an average of 65 percent of the time. Changes in the nature of work and globalization meant that employees had to be more mobile and work more collaboratively. Offices and cubicles were poorly utilized because many employees were no longer involved in extended periods of "individual contributor" work. Instead, they were spending their time in various types of meetings and interactions. Also, some employees were working nontraditional hours to accommodate external and internal demands, which meant they were often working off-site. In addressing these issues, Cisco's Workplace Resources team focused on three goals: raise productivity, increase employee satisfaction, and reduce overall real estate expense.

Mark Golan, vice president of the Connected Real Estate Practice in Cisco's Internet Business Solutions Group, and former VP of Workplace Resources, compares the utilization of office space to that used in a manufacturing facility:[41] "Nobody would consider building a manufacturing facility that they intended to use just one-third of the time. And yet that's what we routinely do with work space." Golan, who is also chairman of CoreNet Global, said that the company wanted to tailor environments that were specific to the challenges of any given work location, avoiding a one-size-fits-all approach.[42]

Cisco has a facilities portfolio of 17 million square feet, which includes 400 buildings in 90 countries, supporting more than 48,000 employees. Cisco's objective was to strike a balance between a portfolio of proven, effective choices and customizable elements that would meet the needs of individual workgroups. To achieve that objective, Cisco's real estate department created a Workplace Effectiveness team staffed with information technology experts,

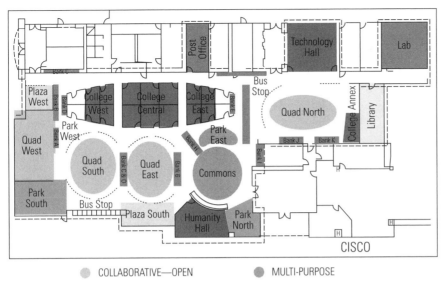

Figure 5-48: Cisco Connected Workplace concepts were applied to a project adopting a university theme. The layout for this space in its San Jose headquarters blends open, semienclosed, and enclosed spaces to support the various tasks being performed by staff.

human resources specialists, cultural anthropologists, architects, designers, psychologists, and sociologists.

One of the solutions developed by the cross-functional team was an environment based on a university theme, complete with quads, plazas, commons, and enclosed spaces called colleges (see Figure 5-48). Throughout the campus, various spaces were designed to support collaboration, including open, semienclosed, and enclosed collaborative areas. The configuration of a collaborative area would often morph several times throughout the day based on the preferences of the various teams using the space, as with the example shown in Figures 5-49 and 50.[43, 44]

What were the critical technologies Cisco needed to support its employees in its Connected Workplace? The company employed a number of its own technology tools in the new environment, including a docking station in each workstation, Cisco IP 7960 phones, and the Cisco IP Communicator, which allows telephony from laptops. Lab areas accommodate IP communications and data networking. Extension Mobility allows employees to configure an IP phone to their phone number and settings simply by logging in. VT Advantage (for video telephony) and MeetingPlace (for audio and Web conferencing) enable workers to conference with coworkers and customers around the globe. And, because the Connected Workplace accommodates almost twice as many individuals in the same space, the company established a WLAN solution, which comprises 10 wireless access points, instead of two to three, and placed a limit of six to eight devices for each access point.

As an executive of Cisco, a company that manufactures these technology solutions, Mark Golan takes a holistic view of the role technology plays in the workplace. He says, "Worker productivity is the biggest issue. Even though

Figure 5-49: Flexibility is designed into the Cisco work environment, with few hard walls that can often create barriers. Mobile furniture can be easily reconfigured by end users, to adapt to their work styles and preferences.

Figure 5-50: This same collaborative area takes on a different configuration to suit the preference of the current team using the space.

real estate and information technology make up the second and third largest components of OPEX (operational expenditures), even a small drop in worker productivity will eliminate the infrastructure savings. It's critical to drive productivity. Technology, in combination with the work environment, can definitely accomplish this."[45]

Cisco is, understandably, proud that its emphasis on improving the workplace to enable greater productivity, collaboration, and employee satisfaction has contributed to the company's success. For nine consecutive years (1998-2007), the company has made *Fortune Magazine's* 100 Best Companies for Work For list, as well as related lists in Denmark, France, Italy, Mexico, and the United Kingdom.[46] According to Golan, physical space can create a significant competitive advantage by helping a company to attract and retain talented college graduates. The Connected Workplace strategy used by Cisco Systems has also resulted in some compelling cost benefits, guaranteed to impress the most skeptical of finance executives (see Table 5-6).[47]

TABLE 5-6 Cisco: The Connected Workplace Cost Savings

Cost Category	Savings
Real estate rent: Accommodate more people in the same amount of space.	37%
Construction: Build a smaller space than typically required for 140 employees.	42%
Workplace services: Reduce utilities and maintenance costs, and nearly eliminate the costs of moves, adds, and changes for workspaces through the use of flexible furniture settings.	37%
Furniture: Purchase less, and less expensive, furniture than typically used in cubicles.	50%
IT capital spending: Spend less on switches and switch ports.	40%
Cabling: Reduce the number of wired IP cables required per workspace.	60%
Equipment room space: Rack fewer switches using wireless infrastructure.	50%

For example, the company saved $1 million in corporate real estate costs over a period of three years when Connected Workplace principles were applied to its Sao Paulo, Brazil, field office.[48] With success like that, it's no surprise that Cisco is proceeding with the introduction of the Connected Workplace to its facilities throughout the world, including the United States, Bangkok, Taipei, and Bangalore.[49, 50] Impressive? Very. And I've been known to be skeptical.

CASE STUDY: GENSLER HEADQUARTERS

Gensler Architecture's San Francisco headquarters was not keeping pace with the firm's changing business. With the entire team dispersed among three floors, individuals felt disconnected from one another. Because this location supports more than 2,000 Gensler staff employees in 28 cities around the globe, there was significant emphasis on meshing the firmwide resources to ensure an efficient and effective delivery model.

Gensler's business issues were not dramatically different from those of its clients. Flattening the organizational hierarchy, which had expanded over the years, would support the objectives of transferring knowledge more quickly and improving collaboration to achieve more innovative results. Another high priority was the desire to better articulate to clients who they are, and engage them more fully in the Gensler process. Also, attracting and retaining talented employees was a growing requirement.

According to principal Collin Burry, the firm was fortunate in securing a space right on the Bay that would become their new home (see Figure 10 in the color insert).[51] When

Figure 5-51: Gensler Headquarters, San Francisco, California.

Courtesy Eric Laignel.

they started demolishing what once had been a Gap store, the skeleton of a beautiful old building began to emerge. The rich character of the building and the Gensler legacy were perfect for each other. Thus, the commitment was made to preserve both in the new space, using them as the foundation from which to move forward. To maintain the character of the physical space, yet enable the workplace to support evolving work processes, it was decided that they needed to "design for change." To that end, the space had to be as flexible as possible, which would necessitate behavioral changes among staff. Employees would be expected to go to the workplace setting appropriate for the type of activity they would be doing. With the goal of improving interaction, the design intentionally avoided duplication of areas such as mailrooms and break rooms in order to increase employee circulation throughout the space.[52]

The solution works. Upon entering the space, visitors become enveloped by the fluid space. To support the goal of better engaging clients in Gensler's design process, the facility has few walls, and visitors can see from the reception area (see Figure 11 in the color insert) directly into the studios, to watch creativity in progress (see Figures 5-52 and 5-53). To enable the café to serve as a center of energy, it is in the open, rather than being tucked away to avoid social chatter creating a distraction. Like the café, most of the spaces have been designed for multiple uses for optimal adaptability.

A variety of conference and team rooms give staff members a range of places to meet, from the open conference room seen in Figure 5-54, where only an architectural column establishes a boundary, to spaces enveloped in glass where team members passing by can join in and contribute (see Figure 5-55 and Figure 15 in the color insert). Gathering spaces close to work areas encourage spontaneous idea generation among peers (see Figure 5-56 and Figure 14 in the color insert), while the differing heights of workstation components create an interesting skyline effect (see Figure 5-57).

On April 5, 2006, Gensler was named one of the Best Places to Work in the Greater Bay Area in the category of medium-sized

Figure 5-52: Entering Gensler headquarters in San Francisco, visitors are drawn into a fluid space. Guests can observe creative activities taking place in the studios as a result of the workplace having been designed with few walls.

Courtesy Sherman Takata, Gensler.

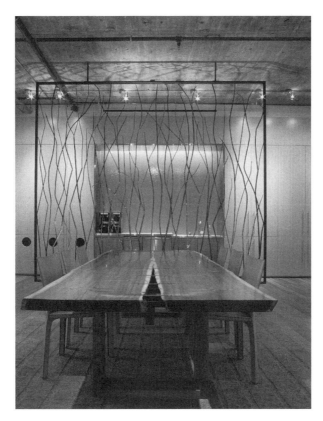

Figure 5-53: To better articulate to clients who they are, Gensler seeks to engage them in the firm's design process. The space shown here achieves both by providing a place to interact with clients where a fresh aesthetic conveys the firm's image.

Courtesy Eric Laignel.

Figure 5-54: The column in this Gensler conference room defines the space. The openness of this space encourages staff members to walk in and contribute knowledge to better serve the firm's clients.

Courtesy Eric Laignel.

Figure 5-55: Gensler's headquarters building features a variety of spaces. Glass-front project rooms, open team spaces, and semienclosed rooms (where privacy is controlled by the participants) all are available to staff.

Courtesy Eric Laignel.

Figure 5-56: Collaboration among peers occurs more easily when a small gathering space is set adjacent to workstations, such as here in the Gensler office in San Francisco. This arrangement often reduces the demand for the use of conference rooms.

Courtesy Sherman Takata, Gensler.

Figure 5-57: Work areas in the Gensler space combine functionality with stimulating design.

Courtesy Eric Laignel.

companies employing 101 to 500 local workers in the San Francisco region. Competing with approximately 400 other organizations, Gensler employees participated in an anonymous survey conducted by an independent research company. They were asked 38 questions about the work culture, team collaboration, management practices, and other key factors of their workplace.[53] The award does much more than support the firm's goal of attracting new talent and retaining the highest-caliber staff members. It also provides a great opportunity to draw clients into their studio to convey firsthand their ability to create a collaborative workplace that works.[54]

CASE STUDY: DE LAGE LANDEN

In 1998, Meyer Design began working with Tokai Financial Services, a Japanese company providing leasing and financing programs to manufacturers, vendors, and banks. Tokai was growing quickly, anticipating its staff of 468 would soon number 582. The firm was already out of space in its 110,000-square-foot facility located in King of Prussia, Pennsylvania.[55]

A major concern for Tokai was how to compete for talented employees. At the time, there was a hiring boom within a 20-mile radius of its facility, and Tokai was facing strong competition from other financial institutions, as well as many

Figure 5-58: The De Lage Landen reception area, created by Meyer Design, has sophisticated, sleek lines and elegant aesthetics.

© 2001 Don Pearse Photographers, Inc. (www.donpearsephotographers.com).

windows, isolated from lower-level employees. Everyone understood their "place" in the firm, and followed precise protocols regarding use of the work environment.

Then, in spring of 1999, midway through the workplace project, Tokai was acquired by De Lage Landen, a Dutch company with a dramatically different culture and management style. Not only were there were no Soji screens in the executive offices at De Lage Landen, its CEO had no office at all. This was a culture where everyone was considered an equal contributor, and where information was readily shared with all employees.

Suzanne Nicholson and Mike Stanczak of Meyer Design were given a very specific edict from their new clients. They were not to use drywall, or build enclosed rooms that had no visual connections. They were told that De Lage Landen managers were expected to support their employees throughout the day, meaning that interruptions were not only acceptable, but welcome. Thus, the architectural firm understood they would have to include a symbolic connection to this policy in the workplace design.

This new culture was reinforced in the design of the conference rooms, where glass walls conveyed openness and information exchange (see Figure 5-59).

The company's high churn rate (each employee moved an average of 2.3 times a year) set the direction for exploring movable, demountable systems to allow flexibility from a facilities standpoint. An added benefit of this approach was to make the visual connection the client desired. The selection of flexible components upfront

local employers representing other industries.

In hiring Meyer Design, Tokai Financial Services challenged the firm to design a workplace that would support its strategy to attract and retain the top talent in the area.

The Tokai operation in the United States had a strong Japanese influence. It was a traditional, suit-and-tie environment, and the physical workplace—complete with Asian artwork and Soji screens—reflected the formality of the organizational culture to both employees and visitors. Managers and executives worked in private offices with would prove to be a wise investment in adaptability in the future.

De Lage Landen is an excellent example of a company that leveraged elements of the Critical Influence System to hold its managers accountable for the effectiveness of the physical work environment. According to Mike Stanczak, the company made sure managers and department heads understood the link between their physical space requirements and the financial impact on the company. Each department was considered a cost center, including the furniture in the space. The churn cost was linked to the cost center as well. The managers and department heads, who were motivated to ensure their departments worked productively, gave a great deal of thought to what would keep employees productive and the workplace cost-efficient.

Leveraging the physical workplace to support the attraction and retention of talented associates was as important to De Lage Landen as it was to Tokai Financial. DLL wanted each individual, team, group and department to have a sense of place, a sense of community. To meet that requirement the Meyer team designed a vibrant cafeteria and a café, welcome venues for employee interaction throughout the day (see Figure 5-60 and Figure 17 in the color insert). Executives wanted each staff member to feel as good about his or her own department as about the company overall. To support one of the company's business goals of increasing the quality of its customer service, the workplace was intended to become a tool for improving collaboration between different departments or business groups serving the same customers.

Figure 5-59: De Lage Landen's workplace reflects its culture of openness and accessibility. The conference room shown here incorporates glass walls to provide visual access into the space.

© 2001 Don Pearse Photographers, Inc. (www.donpearsephotographers.com).

To ensure the new workplace environment was optimized, the Meyer Design professionals helped the staff from Tokai, who were used to following specific behavior protocols, become comfortable interacting in a very open, empowered way. It was decided to employ a "signal system." Following the move into the new facility, each person received a tennis ball sleeve containing one green, one yellow, and one red tennis ball. The color of the ball an employee chose to display on his or her work surface signaled to other people their availability to interact throughout the

Figure 5-60: Meyer Design created a vibrant cafeteria for the De Lage Landen facility, supporting the client's goal to provide a gathering place and a sense of community for all employees.

© 2001 Don Pearse Photographers, Inc. (www.donpearsephotographers.com).

day. If the green tennis ball was out, the employee was open to interruptions. If the yellow ball was displayed, it signaled the individual was trying to concentrate. If the red ball was out, it meant "don't interrupt," due to a deadline or critical issue being addressed (see Figure 16 in the color insert).

According to Mike Parker, De Lage Landen's director of facilities, since moving into the new space in November 2000, the facility continues to receive attention.[56] The company's fitness center was featured in 2001 in *Onsite Fitness* magazine. In addition, De Lage Landen's workplace earned the 2005 BOMA Office of the Year award for the Philadelphia region, in the Corporate Facility category.

The transformation from the formal Tokai Financial Services environment was indeed radical. Today, at

De Lage Landen, casual attire is the norm in an open office environment, where everyone is considered an equal contributor to the organization. The absence of private offices allows natural sunlight to be enjoyed by the entire workforce, and sends a message to employees that the spotlight shines on a team of equals.

NOTES

[1] Powell, Martin, AIA, NCARB, Principal, LEED™ AP, the Design Alliance Architects, interview with the author, September 26, 2006, www.tda-architects.com.
[2] The Design Alliance Architects, *Alcoa Corporate Center Visitors' Guide*, August 1998.
[3] *Open for Business*, Corporate Design Foundation, Volume 5, Number 2. http://www .cdf.org/journal/0502_alcoa.php (accessed July 25, 2006).
[4] Gannon, Joyce, "Firms Betting Open-Office Design, Amenities Lead to Happier, More Productive Workers," *Pittsburgh Post-Gazette*,

February 9, 2003. http://www.post-gazette.com/businessnews/20030209offices0209bnp3.asp (accessed August 30, 2006).

[5] McQuillen, Daniel, "3 Case Studies for Improved IAQ," *Environmental Design & Construction Magazine*, January 24, 2001, http://www.edcmag.com/copyright/4d3e11c097697010VgnCM100000f932a8c0_?vie (accessed August 30, 2006).

[6] "The Alcoa Story," American Institute of Architects, 2005. http://www.aia.org/ca_alcoa (accessed August 30, 2006).

[7] Marconi Corporation plc. http://www.marconi.com/Home/about_us/Our%20History/Marconi%20Heritage/Marconi (accessed September 19, 2006).

[8] Marconi Corporation plc. http://www.marconi.com/Home/about_us/Our%20History/Marconi%20Heritage/Titanic% (accessed September 19, 2006).

[9] Sueberkrop, Erik, FAIA Architect, Principal, STUDIOS Architecture, ongoing communications with the author.

[10] SEI Investments, Oaks, Pennsylvania, site visit, May 15, 2006.

[11] West, Al, CEO, SEI Investments, communications with the author, August 8, 2006.

[12] SEI Investments, *The Financial Strength of an Industry Leader*, Oaks, Pennsylvania. http://www.seic.com/global/aboutsei/finstren.asp (accessed July 4, 2006).

[13] West, Alfred P. Jr., and Yoram (Jerry) Wind, "Putting the Organization on Wheels: Workplace Design at SEI," *California Management Review*, December 13, 2005, pp. 138–153.

[14] West, Alfred P., Jr., and Yoram (Jerry) Wind, "Putting the Organization on Wheels: Workplace Design at SEI," *California Management Review*, Winter 2007, pp. 138–153.

[15] Kampschroer, Kevin, Research & Expert Services, Office of Applied Science—Public Buildings Service, U.S. General Services Administration, interview with the author, September 8, 2006, and ongoing communications.

[16] Powell, Kevin M., Director of Research, Office of Applied Science, GSA, Public Buildings Service, ongoing communications with the author.

[17] Heerwagen, J., K. Kelly, and K. Kampschroer, "Workplace Research: Changing Nature of Organizations," *Work & Workplace—GSA*, 2005. http://www.gsa.gov (accessed August 1, 2006).

[18] "What Is WorkPlace 20\20?" GSA, 2003. http://www.gsa.gov (accessed August 1, 2006).

[19] Kaplan, Robert and David Norton, *Balanced Scorecard*, Cambridge, MA: Harvard Business School Press, 1996.

[20] Senior Leadership Space, GSA Regional Office, Auburn, Washington, site visit, February 2, 2007.

[21] Heerwagen, Judith H., Ph.D., J.H. Heerwagen & Associates, Inc., "Workplace Projects: Senior Leadership Space, GSA Regional Office, Auburn, Washington," www.gsa.gov (accessed September 12, 2006), and communications with the author, October 6, 2006.

[22] "Adaptable Workplace Lab," Washington, DC, http://www.gsa.gov (accessed August 15, 2006).

[23] Mourer, Blake, AIA, LEED AP, Senior Associate, Gensler, communications with the author, January 23, 2007.

[24] "The Workplace Environment as a Catalyst for Social Change," PBS, Denver, Colorado. http://www.gsa.gov (accessed January 6, 2007).

[25] Heerwagen, Judith H., Ph.D., J.H. Heerwagen & Associates, Inc., communications with the author, October 6, 2006.

[26] *Workplace Matters*, U.S. General Services Administration, Washington, D.C.: GSA, 2006.

[27] Natarajan, Prabha, "GSA on Track to Renew," *Washington Business Journal*, September 22, 2006. http://www.bizjournals.com/washington/stories/2006/09/25/story6.html (accessed October 1, 2006).

[28] Kelly, Kevin, AIA, Director, Workplace Programs, Office of Applied Science—Public Buildings Service, U.S. General Services Administration, ongoing communications with the author.

[29] "New Adventures in Office Space: The Integrated Workplace," Office of Real Property, Office of Governmentwide Policy, U.S. General Services Administration, February 2002.

[30] Great Place to Work Institute, http://www.greatplacetowork.com (accessed November 25, 2006).

[31] Mirza, Patrick, "AGI Rises to the Top–Again," *HR Magazine*, July 2006. http://www.shrm.org/hrmagazine/articles/0706/0706gptw_agi.asp (accessed July 14, 2006).

[32] Velte, Lisa, Director of Human Resources, Analytical Graphics Inc., ongoing communications with the author.

33 Rubis, Leon, "Cultural Consistency Amid Change at Analytical Graphics," *HR Magazine*, July 2005. http://www.shrm.org/hrmagazine/articles/0705/0705GPTWNum1Small.asp (accessed July 14, 2006).

34 Von Bergen, Jane M., "Happiness Equals Productivity," *Philadelphia Inquirer*, July 7, 2001. http://www.shrm.org/hrmagazine/articles/0705/0705GPTWNum1Small.asp (accessed July 14, 2006).

35 Stanczak, Mike, AIA, Studio Manager, Meyer Design, Inc., interview with the author, August 4, 2006, www.meyerdesigninc.com.

36 Kowalchuk, Brian, Director of Design, CUH2A, interview with the author, August 9, 2006, www.cuh2a.com.

37 Higginbotham, Julie S., "Synergy Breeds Fertile Environment at Pharma Facility," *Research & Development*, May 2001. http://www.cuh2a.com/company/inthenews.asp (accessed July 17, 2006).

38 Ibid., "Interactivity Spurs Productivity," *Drug Discovery & Development*, April 2001. http:www.dddmag.com (accessed July 17, 2006).

39 Hawkins, Beth Leibson, "Idealism with a Business Edge," *Facilities Design & Management*, May 2002, pp. 32–36.

40 Alati, Danine, "Pharm House, CUH2A Crafts Its Own High-Design Remedy for Global Pharmaceutical Giant Pfizer with a Striking New R&D Executive Headquarters," *Contract Magazine*, May 2002, pp. 122–126.

41 Golan, Mark, Vice President, Worldwide Real Estate and Workplace Resources, Cisco Systems, Inc., interview with the author, October 5, 2006.

42 CoreNet Global, http://www.corenetglobal.org (accessed September 8, 2006).

43 "Cisco Connected Workplace: Cisco IT at Work," Case Study, December 13, 2004. http://www.cisco.com/go/ciscoitatwork (accessed October 5, 2006).

44 "Cisco Connected Workplace Enhances Work Experience and Cuts Costs," Case Study, 2003. http://www.cisco.com/en/US/about/ciscoitatwork/case_studies (accessed October 5, 2006).

45 Golan, Mark, Vice President, Worldwide Real Estate and Workplace Resources, Cisco Systems, Inc., interview with author, October 5, 2006.

46 Great Place to Work Institute, http://www.greatplacetowork.com (accessed October 19, 2006).

47 "Cisco 'Connected Workplace' Slashes Real Estate Costs and Enhances Employee Work Experience," 2004. http://www.cisco.com/en/US/about/ciscoitatwork/case_studies (accessed October 5, 2006).

48 "Cisco Sao Paulo Office Saves One Million Dollars in Corporate Real Estate Costs Over Three Years," Case Study, 2003. http://www.cisco.com/en/US/about/ciscoitatwork/case_studies/wireless_dl3 (accessed October 5, 2006).

49 Foresight 2020, Economic, Industry, and Corporate Trends, *The Economist Intelligence Unit*, 2006.

50 "Innovation Most Critical Factor to Success Say U.S. Business Leaders," Cisco Innovation Study 2005, News Release, August 10, 2005, Cisco Systems, Inc.

51 Burry, Collin, Principal, Gensler Architecture, Design & Planning Worldwide, interview with the author, September 6, 2006, www.gensler.com.

52 Weiss, Tara, "Creating Offices with Ambiance," August 8, 2006. http://www.forbes.com/2006/08/07/leadership_biz_basics (accessed October 2, 2006).

53 Huss, Mary et al, "Best Places to Work in the Bay Area 2006," *San Francisco Business Times*, April 7–13, 2006. http://www.bizjournals.com (accessed December 9, 2006).

54 "Well-Designed Office Key to Improving Employee Performance: New Survey," News Release. http://www.gensler.com (accessed October 2, 2006).

55 Nicholson, Suzanne, ASID NCIDQ, Executive Vice President, and Mike Stanczak, AIA, Studio Manager, Meyer Design, Inc. interview with the author, September 15, 2006, www.meyerdesigninc.com.

56 Parker, Mike, Director of Facilities, De Lage Landen, ongoing communications with the author. www.delagelanden.com.

CHAPTER 6
COLLABORATIVE WORKPLACE PRINCIPLES

Organizations that have identified innovation as a key business goal must create appropriate physical work environments to achieve it. As pointed out repeatedly in this book, providing a more stimulating work environment can help a company attract, inspire, and retain the "best minds" critical to the achievement of desired business results. Not doing so can stifle innovative output for the organization, as well as possibly cause the loss of key talent to competitors whose environments are considered more intellectually appealing.

Over the years, I've facilitated meetings and brainstorming sessions with numerous groups of interior designers, architects, and end users, whose purpose was to identify and analyze factors that can enable or, conversely, raise barriers to innovation in the workplace. A number of common threads have become clear. The objective of some of these meetings was to guide the clients to ways to improve collaboration in the workplace, to produce richer innovative results for the enterprise. In other cases, a knowledge-exchange workshop was convened, in which architects, designers, and industry peers from a variety of firms participated. Whatever the venue, however, always the ideas generated were captured for further analysis. The elements found to foster collaboration, enable innovative behavior, and contribute positively to an innovation-friendly workplace can be divided into three broad classifications: cultural, operational, and environmental. Together, they comprise what I call the Collaborative Workplace Principles.

Designing an innovation-friendly office—one that reinforces sustainable, collaborative behaviors leading to innovation—is the result of multiple, interdependent factors. It is essential that the cultural, operational, and environmental elements that enable this behavior be considered throughout the office design process. Interior design alone cannot produce fertile conditions for optimal performance. Other key factors, especially those that business leaders define, influence, and control, must also be part of the process if the workplace design is to guide the desired employee behaviors.

Let's take a closer look at the cultural, operational, and environmental elements in turn, to establish a common foundation of understanding.

CULTURAL ELEMENTS FOSTERING INNOVATIVE BEHAVIOR

As discussed in Chapter 2, the culture of an organization is often an illusive image, hard to describe accurately. This is particularly true for those at the top of the firm—a sort of "you can't see the forest for the trees" phenomenon. Ironically, often it is the first impressions of individuals external to the company, such as new hires and job candidates, vendors, and customers, that can produce the most on-target cultural definition.

In comparing organizational cultures, it's important to recognize the varying degrees of influence specific elements have on a corporate culture. In analyzing a single enterprise, you may even find variations of a particular cultural factor among different business units, departments, or workgroups. Which cultural elements contribute positively to an innovation-friendly workplace by fostering collaborative behavior? An organizational culture that not only treats people as equal contributors, and welcomes ideas from all levels of the enterprise, but also consciously works to leverage this diversity when forming ad hoc task forces and work teams, will have positive results.

Organizations successful at introducing innovations often share common cultural factors, such as encouraging honesty and respect, valuing curiosity and restlessness, and welcoming staff to challenge the status quo. Organizations where strong, collaborative cultures drive innovative behavior are often described as casual, informal, and collegial. Spontaneous interaction at all levels of the enterprise is the norm, and group problem solving is encouraged.

The design work of Hixson Inc., shown in Figure 6-1 and Figure 27 and 28 in the color insert, illustrates how this firm incorporated many of these cultural elements into an advanced research and development center for one of its clients, emphasizing the importance of the exchange of new ideas.

Another common element of successful collaborative organizations is a heavy emphasis on learning. In enterprises such as this, formal learning is more than encouraged; typically, it is required of employees at all levels. Equally valued is informal discovery as a means of increasing the intellectual capital of the firm. This is accomplished when employees "shadow" their teammates to experience new situations, or volunteer to support initiatives outside their realm of knowledge and experience.

Cultures that foster innovative business results also commonly encourage employees to take educated risks, and to accept the occasional failure. Obviously, not every innovative concept developed within the enterprise will be successful. It's not about the ratio of wins to losses; more important is the attitude toward risk and failure. A culture of "failing forward" ensures that the emphasis is

Figure 6-1: Throughout this advanced R&D center, Hixson's workplace design fosters innovation with multipurpose areas where employees can gather to exchange ideas.

© 2006 Hixson Architecture, Engineering, Interiors.

on understanding the process that led to the failed concept, not on whom to blame for the failure. Anything that can be learned from an unsuccessful attempt at innovation brings the organization closer to success.

Finally, celebrating success is an essential cultural element to fostering innovative behavior. When positive results are attributed to the joint efforts of cross-functional groups and team contributions, rather than to an individual or team leader, typically this leads to further innovative outputs in the future.

OPERATIONAL ELEMENTS FOSTERING INNOVATIVE BEHAVIOR

Operational elements are generally more easily recognized and understood by senior management than those categorized as cultural or environmental. The reason is that these factors are related to issues such

as technology, compensation, performance measurement, and facilities maintenance, which are within the direct purview of managers.

In the typical organization, there are guidelines, policies, and procedures related to such operational elements. In contrast, typically there are no formal rules in place that say to value curiosity and creativity; in fact, many office facilities policies clearly state the opposite—that end users are not permitted to make changes to their workspaces. But giving end users the freedom to make adaptations to their work environment, rather than adapting themselves to the work setting, reflects one of the Collaborative Workplace Principles: "changes made quickly by end-users."

Hixson Inc.'s advanced research and development center project, described in the previous section, is an exemplar of the focus on operational elements that foster innovative behavior. Figure 6-2 and Figure 26

Figure 6-2: Hixson's "room without walls" concept provides an abundance of work tools to support innovative output. The design firm also hung whiteboards on perimeter walls where employees can capture their ideas anywhere, anytime.

© 2006 Hixson Architecture, Engineering, Interiors.

in the color insert feature the firm's "room without walls" concept, which supported the client's goals for flexibility and collaboration. This workplace allows end users to create team centers and a sense of place without raising territorial barriers.

When asked, business leaders almost always will say that effective communication is critical to future organizational success. Yet time and again, they will admit there is much room for improvement and will target the area as one that is necessary to address in order to produce significant innovative results. The days of dictating, typing, and distributing hard-copy, internal memos are long gone in most companies today. The speed of communication necessary in today's fast-paced business environments, coupled with reduced administrative staff in most enterprises, precludes the time-consuming linear process of old.

Enabling free-flowing communication and multiple ways of connecting people in an organization can be accomplished by offering diverse

methods of transferring knowledge. Eppstein Uhen Architects designed a circulation core for its client, GE Healthcare in Waukesha, Wisconsin. Figure 6-3 spotlights the core, rich in natural light and featuring an open view of colleagues passing by, to encourage connectivity among workforce members. Office amenities have been strategically aligned with these paths for circulation, resulting in both convenience and greater opportunities for interaction.

Technology, obviously, is vital for connecting employees. But plug-and-play capability and networked computer systems that let staff exchange e-mail messages are not nearly enough to satisfy the demand for immediate access to coworkers and virtually instantaneous responses to requests. As the internal reshuffling of employees increases, and the roles they play expand in response to shifting organizational requirements, employers need to determine how to give employees access to specialized knowledge when operating in these flattened reporting structures. Technology becomes the communication vehicle. Basic in most companies today is giving staff the ability to post questions and answers to electronic bulletin boards or internal blogs. A robust database accessible to employees via a structured system may also be essential to expedite the transfer of knowledge in today's fast-paced enterprises. Recall from Chapter 1 how Sprint Nextel's workplace evolved. Eileen Forbes described the need for universal access to voice and data everywhere on the organization's campus. She also stressed the growing importance of geolocation indicators and presence-based applications to facilitate impromptu collaboration in both virtual and physical environments.

To ensure the speed of communication is adequate to support business operations, the wise human resources executive will ensure that the information technology department conducts ongoing training for its employees, so that they may continue to leverage the firm's technological resources to the maximum possible. Further, the IT team must understand that not all employees share the same level of knowledge and comfort with the technology in place at the company, due to the mixed-generation makeup of most workforces today. IT personnel also must be aware of, and know how to address, the needs of staff members who travel and, thus, require reliable remote connections to the Internet and company network from other corporate facilities, hotel rooms, airports, and so on.

An important operational element that encourages collaboration, and can lead to richer, innovative output, is a mentor program that offers

Figure 6-3: The circulation core at GE Healthcare in Waukesha, Wisconsin, suffused with daylight, enables connectivity, and is surrounded by office amenity areas.

© 2004 Eppstein Uhen Architects.

opportunities for informal learning. The enterprise may have a structured mentoring initiative whereby new hires or those on a management track are assigned to a more senior individual from whom they can glean insight and learn new approaches. Some progressive organizations also institute initiatives to "mentor up," whereby individuals in senior positions or with more tenure are aligned with newer employees, in particular with Gen Xers or members of the millennial generation. A very different type of knowledge exchange occurs in mentoring up. Learning the perspectives and approaches of those in the younger generations can bring new insight to company executives, and potentially result in new product or service developments geared toward the younger demographic.

Performance management mechanisms established within an organization also are considered operational elements that can foster innovative behavior. There's a big difference between an organization in which the employer provides safe and easy-to-achieve annual goals to each employee, and one in which employees sit down with their managers to codevelop more far-reaching goals. Which process is in place can greatly impact the degree to which the workforce achieves innovative results. Some progressive organizations, in driving performance, are shifting to the use of metrics centered on measuring team results, with less emphasis on individual outcomes.

Closely related to performance management targeting the attainment of team objectives, the enterprise must address both team and individual compensation, as well as rewards and recognition for both individual and team successes. John E. Tropman, in his book *The Compensation Solution: How to Develop an Employee-Driven Rewards System*, warns of a structural lag found in many organizations.[1] The phrase "structural lag" refers to new values put in place while the organizational practices lag behind. Many employers attempt to shift their focus from individual results to team-based performance outcomes, recognizing the efforts achieved by formal and informal groups within the entire employee population. The practice

that has not changed in many of these firms is the compensation structure. Individuals are still paid only for their own efforts. By refining the total compensation equation to ensure alignment with the innovative outputs desired by the firm, the organization will also benefit from attracting and retaining talented professionals. According to Tropman, effective compensation structures include more variables now than have typically been incorporated in the past. New approaches to paying employees for their contributions to their companies are changing the fundamental assumption that compensation is employer-driven, shifting to an employee-driven concept. The most exciting physical spaces designed to inspire teamwork and collaboration can fall short of achieving optimal results when outdated compensation structures erect barriers to the open exchange of ideas among peers.

In this category of the Collaborative Workplace Principles, organizational leaders also need to reduce what is referred to as "operational punishment," which sometimes results when an employee proposes a new idea that could reap significant rewards for the firm. Companies do not generally relieve a staff member from his or her day-to-day duties immediately to devote time to, for example, exploring the feasibility of a new competitive advantage. More often than not, the employee is expected to carry the same workload while investigating what could be a frame-breaking concept. Even well-meaning organizations that acknowledge the value of such activities can slow down the process of discovery due to existing policies and procedures ("red tape"), which require the employee to develop a formal business plan for the initiative, submitted in triplicate for approval by management. Needless to say, the lead time for writing the business plan that complies with corporate guidelines, followed by an approval process, can reduce the window of opportunity to take advantage of a potentially rewarding idea. Why not give the employee the necessary flexibility for an agreed-upon time period to determine whether the concept is worthy of further development? Ultimately, in this way, the organization could review a greater number of new ideas, weeding out those that are not good investments of time or money.

ENVIRONMENTAL ELEMENTS FOSTERING INNOVATIVE BEHAVIOR

Serving as an advisor to clients on the environmental elements that foster innovative behavior is a natural role for an architect or interior designer. The importance that physical space plays in guiding behavior in the workplace cannot be overemphasized. Yet the architect or interior designer should at all times keep the interrelatedness of environmental factors with both cultural and operational elements in the forefront of dialogue with the client. By taking this holistic approach, architects and designers will more readily earn the client's trust, and build a reputation for understanding clients' big-picture business issues. This can result in their being brought into projects earlier in the process, potentially improving their competitive advantage.

An important environmental element fostering innovative behavior is that of visual openness. Using glass to divide space, yet establish a boundary where needed, can go a long way toward maintaining a fresh, open feel in the office environment. Strategically designing conference rooms, team huddle rooms, and gathering spaces with glass walls, rather than drywall, also can signal colleagues walking by a space where peers have spontaneously gathered, to join the group and contribute to the discussion regarding a potential innovative concept. Physical proximity of team members has been identified in brainstorming sessions as an environmental element to include in office design. However, opinions differ as to whether it is best to provide employees private offices, dedicated workstations, free addresses, or totally unassigned spaces. What is not in dispute is that people should have easy access to each other but, at the same time, be given space for privacy and personal interaction, in a variety of workplace settings.

To meet increasing organizational emphasis on attracting and retaining talented employees, as well as on helping employees balance their work and personal lives, interior designers also are applying the concept of bringing the "comforts of home" to the office. The opinion of those in support of this concept is that, by doing so, employees will spend more time on campus. Remember the environmental element "social heartbeat" introduced in Chapter 5? In the Marconi case study, it was essential to the client that energy and excitement be extended throughout the physical office environment.

Another environmental element seen to foster innovative behavior is exposure to the work in progress of colleagues. When one employee displays drawings and notes of a project he or she is working on, a colleague casually viewing these ideas may discover something to help solve a challenging component of his or her own project. Or after reviewing individual research on the same project, two colleagues may test the feasibility of combining their different approaches, rather than assuming an either/or choice is necessary. Together, rather than separately, they may find the next breakthrough product that creates a competitive advantage for their enterprise.

Team members often comment that they are much more productive as a group when they have control over a dedicated team space. Not having to find an available first-come, first-served area to meet, or to set up and tear down materials, increase the time devoted to team interaction itself. Figure 6-4 and Figure 29 in the color insert show excellent examples of how to incorporate environmental elements that foster innovative behavior, such as control over team space and the physical proximity of team members. Robert Luchetti Associates created this team area for Guildford Textiles Design Studio, complete with sliding displays and storage towers.

Providing dedicated team space, regardless how small, is an approach being used more often. Doing so does not, however, mean permanently allocating real estate. If, say, the organization has established a six-month deadline for a workgroup to complete a set of objectives, giving them their own area only for the duration of that project can accelerate the attainment of their goals by greatly reducing time spent negotiating and juggling shared resources.

Another element, "rubbing elbows in close quarters," was a phrase used in one brainstorming session to describe the increased productivity that can result from high-energy team sessions where people work closely together, literally, to achieve a common goal.

Thomas Edison said, "Surround people with every tool imaginable." This philosophy has been incorporated into the environmental elements fostering innovative behavior. Likewise, displayed thinking, cognitive artifacts, and disparate visual reminders are known to stimulate the generation of new ideas. Some of the best illustrations of energizing spaces can be found in the studios architectural and design

Figure 6-4: The Guildford Textiles Design Studio was created by Robert Luchetti Associates. Housed in a nineteenth-century brick-and-beam mill building, the dedicated team area is spacious, functional, and well organized, featuring sliding displays, storage towers, and generous horizontal work surfaces.

Planning and Design: Robert Luchetti Associates; photographer and photo copyright 1997, Bill Kontzias.

firms have created for themselves. Figures 6-5 and 6-6 show the partially enclosed project rooms where BHDP Architecture engages in brainstorming sessions and charrettes. Figures 6-7 and 6-8 convey the environmental elements of visual openness, cognitive artifacts, and physical proximity of team members in the Robert Luchetti Associates design studio.

Figure 6-5: The space BHDP Architecture created for its own team was designed to be flexible, changing with evolving work processes and styles. Project rooms are scattered throughout the workspace, providing areas for brainstorming sessions and charrettes. The openness of these spaces, such as the one featured here, encourages greater team interaction.

Photograph courtesy Michael Houghton, Studiohio, Inc. (614-224-4885).

Figure 6-6: To support its collaborative culture, BHDP Architecture's various project rooms are only partially enclosed. The result is an environment that encourages collaboration and knowledge sharing, helping the firm to offer more innovative solutions to its clients.

Photograph courtesy Michael Houghton, Studiohio, Inc. (614-224-4885).

Figure 6-7: The Robert Luchetti Associates Design Studio is a great example of how cognitive artifacts can contribute to innovative thinking. The skeletal chair frames hung on the wall and suspended from the soaring ceiling animate the space.

Planning and Design: Robert Luchetti Associates; photographer and photo copyright 2001, Paul Warchol.

Figure 6-8: The openness of the Robert Luchetti Associates Design Studio creates a feeling of "one firm," rather than of individuals working on separate projects. Visual access to colleagues fosters interaction and the exchange of ideas.

Planning and Design: Robert Luchetti Associates; photographer and photo copyright 2001, Paul Warchol.

During a visit to IDEO in Palo Alto, California, I witnessed firsthand the powerful impact an emphasis on visual stimulation can have on innovative outputs. The IDEO Tech Box, described in Chapter 3, is a colorful example of a robust collection of visual inspirations, tactile objects, and cognitive artifacts that can ignite creative thought. IDEO's studio reflects these important environmental elements, and the firm's business success is a testimony to the effectiveness of its workplace to support collaborative behavior and innovative outputs.

COLLABORATIVE WORKPLACE PRINCIPLES

As noted at the beginning of the chapter, the cultural, operational, and environmental elements fostering innovative behavior comprise the Collaborative Workplace Principles. They are delineated here in Table 6-1 for easy reference for architects and interior designers when developing collaborative workplaces to support an increase in innovative organizational results. Note, however, that the list cannot be considered complete, for with every interaction with

TABLE 6-1 Collaborative Workplace Principles

Cultural Elements Fostering Innovative Behavior	Operational Elements Fostering Innovative Behavior	Environmental Elements Fostering Innovative Behavior
Consider people equal contributors	Free-flowing communication	Balance of space for privacy and interaction
Welcome all ideas	Multiple ways of connecting people quickly	Visual openness
Look to unlikely people; form unlikely teams	Changes made quickly by end users	Variety and character of workplace settings
"Fail forward" by encouraging risk and accepting occasional failure	Plug-and-play capability	Physical proximity of team members
Casual, informal, and collegial relationships	Access to knowledge via structured system	Control over dedicated team space
Encourage honesty and respect	Opportunities for informal learning through mentor program	"Rub elbows" in close quarters
Spontaneous interaction and group problem solving	Include "stretch goals" in performance management	Surround people with every tool imaginable
Value curiosity and restlessness	Address team and individual compensation elements	Exposure to others' ideas in progress
Encourage formal learning as well as informal discovery	Address team as well as individual rewards and recognition	Cognitive artifacts, displayed thinking, and visual reminders to stimulate idea generation
Challenge the status quo	Reduction of "operational punishment" to investigate new ideas	Comforts of home
Celebrate success	Reduction of red tape in exploring new concepts	"Social heartbeat"

architectural and design professionals, and on every workplace project, the list of Collaborative Workplace Principles morphs somewhat. The contents of this table should be regarded only as a snapshot taken at one point in time of the cultural, operational, and environmental elements that foster innovative behavior.

In conclusion, it is not just environmental elements alone that will produce innovative behavior in the workplace. Likewise, cultural and operational elements cannot optimize innovative outputs without the strong influence of environmental factors. Effectiveness comes from the interrelatedness of the three categories—cultural, operational, and environmental—in conjunction with a conscious effort to understand the impact each of these elements on innovative behavior in the workplace. All three are critical to creating physical work environments that support innovation as a key business goal.

NOTES

[1] Tropman, John E., *The Compensation Solution: How to Develop an Employee-Driven Rewards System*, San Francisco: Jossey-Bass, 2001.

CHAPTER 7
COLLABORATIVE
PRINCIPLE INDEX

Expanding on the Collaborative Workplace Principles introduced in the last chapter, this chapter describes the Collaborative Principle Index, developed to measure how well organizations are integrating the cultural, operational, and environmental principles into their work. For architectural and design firms engaged by clients that want to improve the innovative outputs of the enterprise, these principles become points of dialogue to ensure the business leaders are realistic about just how much change the physical space can drive, given other constraints. Executive sponsorship to support a cultural transformation and ensure barriers are identified and addressed is essential to the successful implementation of any workplace strategy.

But, first, some background. In 2003, I coauthored a white paper entitled "From Competitive Office to Collaborative Workplace" with architect Paul Rosenblatt.[1] Subsequently, we were invited to be guest speakers at NeoCon in Chicago and IIDEX in Toronto, to share our research findings on how the existing, competitive workplace model can be transformed into a new, more collaborative environment where the desired employee behaviors are enabled—and sustained.

The Competitive Office model is characterized by many factors:

- People working against each other, rather than together
- Individuals visually isolated in cubicles, rather than colocated in team spaces
- Information-hoarding, rather than knowledge sharing

People who work in a Competitive Office are rewarded for individual accomplishments rather than for group productivity and creative growth. In contrast, the Collaborative Workplace model is an environment in which:

- Visual connections and interactions foster trust and creativity

- Information is shared
- Teams are rewarded for productivity and growth

Studies indicate that competition and collaboration are complementary forces. Competition—"rivalry for supremacy"—can, in fact, stimulate creativity and inspire goals. However, too much competition results in a divisive organization where rival individuals work at cross purposes. Resources are not put to most effective use, resulting in damage to social capital. In contrast, collaboration can be a good strategy for maximizing resource utilization by creating a culture of information sharing, resulting in outputs not possible if each person were working in isolation. A key emphasis in transforming the Competitive Office into the Collaborative Workplace is the facilitation of relationship-building as a basis for fostering the appropriate employee behaviors.

While conducting our research on shifting a competitive work environment to one that is collaborative, Paul and I came up with what we call the "Eight Myths of Workplace Collaboration,"[2] a humorous way of describing the tendency of many organizations to expect designers of new office environments to perform miracles. More seriously, we captured lessons learned from a number of organizations that have struggled with changing behaviors when challenging these myths. We then tied each myth to specific Collaborative Workplace Principles as a means of guiding the correct use of these concepts in workplace design projects.

EIGHT MYTHS OF WORKPLACE COLLABORATION

Myth 1: "Teaming is the answer to all our problems."

Lessons Learned

Moving employees from private offices to an open plan will not automatically result in team spirit or in a collaborative workplace. Dividing the employee population into various workgroups and calling each one a "team" is not an effective way of educating or preparing the workforce to operate as a high-performance team. In fact, many organizational tasks are still best left to individuals, so employees and their managers need to learn to balance interactive time with individual time for concentrated activities. The point is, companies are advised to invest time in better understanding when an individual approach is better than a team approach, and vice versa, and plan accordingly for the necessary physical space requirements.

Issues surrounding myth 1 include the perceived loss of power by managers who once had private offices and are expected to "live" among their direct reports in the open work environment. Often the need to "save face" results in managers taking such counterproductive actions as intentionally withholding information. Their former workspace—a private, enclosed office—was, to them, a currency of power. In a culture that produces this type of behavior, physical space has become a reward based on individual status in the organization. The size and amenities of the space symbolize the person's power and value to the enterprise. In organizations where the person's ranking in the company hierarchy dictates the size and appearance of their workspace, there is too little emphasis on the design of the space being driven by the tasks performed by the user.

Collaborative Workplace Principles
- Challenge of the status quo
- Balance of space for privacy and interaction
- Variety and character of workplace settings
- Physical proximity of team members

Myth 2: "Adopt a free-address policy for teams to use conference rooms on a first-come, first-served basis."

Lessons Learned

As stated in Chapter 4, one of the four primary sources of conflict in the workplace is the use, or more precisely, limited use, of any given resource. Organizations typically focus narrowly on improving collaboration among members of a team, often overlooking the competition that may exist *between* teams. Much organizational conflict lies in interteam competition for resources, such as conference rooms, mobile whiteboards, and other work tools.

A false assumption that may be associated with myth 2 is that moving to an open, team-oriented environment will automatically decrease the total square footage of real estate needed, as well as reduce the overall costs of the facilities project. If individual teams are provided what they actually require to produce the results expected by the enterprise, it may in fact necessitate more, rather than less, space.

I had been called in to consult at the corporate headquarters location of a large services organization that wanted to create a true spirit of teamwork between the numerous departments that served the 80 field offices and their employees. The business leaders were confident that better teamwork between the corporate office and the field locations would result in improved treatment of external customers. This is turn would lead to raising the retention rate of customers and generating more referrals from satisfied customers. If properly executed, the company would enjoy significant business growth.

Interviews revealed that common goals and a strong sense of teamwork already existed between most individual departments at headquarters and the field offices. Teamwork was, however, found to be lacking between the corporate departments themselves. The constant struggle for scarce resources such as conference rooms, whiteboards, and other team tools resulted in a spirit of competition—an unfriendly one at that—which, naturally, impeded giving support to those working from the field offices.

Collaborative Workplace Principles
- Casual, informal, and collegial relationships
- Spontaneous interaction and problem solving
- Address team and individual compensation elements
- Dedicated team spaces and productivity tools

Myth 3: "Flexibility and mobility breed collaboration and innovation."

Lessons Learned

The process of having to reorganize project rooms and team spaces for each new initiative can be time-consuming and disruptive. Furthermore, creativity and innovation are facilitated by access to a variety of materials, sources, images, and personal tools that may or may not be incorporated into temporary project rooms. Many elements introduced as contributors to successful collaboration have very little to do with specific products designed and marketed as productivity tools.

Architectural and design firms should encourage their clients who are planning new workplaces to consider the words *flexibility* and *mobility* beyond tangible products. Adopting an organizational attitude of flexibility may be more appropriate to evaluating the unique needs of each work group. A team may be highly dependent on ideas captured in earlier meetings and documented on dozens of flipchart sheets, large work process flowcharts, or semi-permanent notes made on portable whiteboards. This material becomes the starting point for the next meeting and is, therefore, essential to the team advancing their project. One could argue that those items enable flexibility and can be transported to wherever that team will convene. The problem is often that *finding* a place to meet is only the first challenge. Productivity can be lost even after a suitable meeting place has been secured, because the team wastes precious time transporting their reference materials to the space and setting them up in the proper sequence so that the team members can pick up where they left off in the last meeting. Additional time is wasted in packing up the same items after each session concludes, or when another team interrupts them because they themselves have an urgent reason to use that same room.

And consider when a team member misses a meeting due to travel, vacation, or illness: How does that person get up to speed so that he or she can contribute at an optimal level to the work group's overall goals? Certainly asking a peer is an option; however, that takes the peer away from his or her other important duties. When teams have dedicated spaces where project materials can be displayed, the team member who missed a session can quickly see what progress has been made in his or her absence, and even discover what next steps he or she is responsible for, and their associated deadlines, simply by spending a few minutes in the project room reviewing the latest additions to the posted materials.

Collaborative Workplace Principles
- Balance of space for privacy and interaction
- Control over dedicated team space
- Exposure to others' ideas in progress
- Displayed thinking

Myth 4: "The physical spaces we created to encourage collaboration are not being used, ergo our employees do not like cappuccino!"

Lessons Learned

Organizations are investing in cyber-cafés, themed employee lounges, and other casual physical spaces to foster spontaneous interaction, then often wonder why these areas are not fully utilized. What those charged with implementing the new workplace strategy often fail to realize is that leadership behavior is a critical influence on employee behavior. If executives are not using these collaborative spaces, neither will the rest of the personnel.

While the intent of these collaborative spaces is spontaneity, the "cure" for the problem of underutilization by employees is highly structured. When clients request casual meeting places be included in a new workplace design, with the intent of encouraging productive interaction, it is critical that executives be educated on the impact their own behavior will have on the use of those spaces. Top managers must commit to practicing what the organization preaches. A cultural shift—which is necessary more often than not—has to be driven from the highest level that it's perfectly acceptable to be seen working in an environment where it looks as if the space has been provided only for socialization, not for conducting business.

Following the move into a new office, which includes, for example, a cappuccino bar, it's a good idea to ask senior executives to "schedule" spontaneous meetings for the next 21 business days. These interactions should be between "C-team" members (i.e., CEO, CFO, COO), as well as between these executives and their direct reports (vice presidents, directors, etc.). Why 21 days? This is the length of time psychologists have learned it takes for new habits to form. And if individuals throughout the organization have not seen executives, managers, supervisors, and front-line staff using the collaborative area within

21 business days, they will have heard about it at the water cooler. Those front-line staff with aspirations to move up in the company will quickly learn that the collaborative space is an ideal place to "be seen" by those influential to their career growth.

Collaborative Workplace Principles
- Casual, informal, and collegial relationships
- Spontaneous interaction and problem solving
- Challenge the status quo
- Visual openness
- Variety of workplace settings
- Comforts of home
- Social heartbeat

Myth 5: "Clutter in the workplace should be avoided at all costs (a.k.a. cleanliness is next to godliness)."

Lessons Learned
In an attempt to control the business environment, historically, many organizations have established facilities standards and policies on what employees may leave or display in workstations or teaming areas—confusing clutter in the workplace with lack of cleanliness. Now, however, organizations serious about producing innovative outputs through employee collaboration are learning to ease up on controlling the appearance of the workplace. Many architects and interior designers have noticed a correlation between their own creativity and how they organize materials and sources of inspiration. Employees exposed to the work in progress of others, it turns out, are more apt to contribute to the success of team members' projects, as well as discover new ideas of their own.

Three rules of work:

1. *Out of clutter, find simplicity.*
2. *From discord, find harmony.*
3. *In the middle of difficulty lies opportunity.*

—ALBERT EINSTEIN

That's not to say that protocols should not be put in place to ensure the appropriate level of professionalism in the workplace. For example, most organizations have set guidelines to mitigate the risks of lawsuits by individuals who may be offended by personal materials posted in other employees' workstations. Types of items managers should monitor closely are comic strips or derogatory statements that clearly clash with organizational values. To understand how damaging such behavior can be, consider this experience of a consultant-colleague of mine. His client, a small organization, was struggling with low employee morale, both before and after moving into their fabulous new workplace. Through focus groups he held, he was able to quickly identify the source of the problem: one individual who hated her job so much she was having a negative influence on everyone in the company with whom she came in contact. On further investigation, he found clearly displayed on the tackboard of her workstation the following quotation: "If we stop answering the phone, perhaps the customers will stop calling." My colleague spoke with the employee's supervisor, who agreed that this woman's attitude had to be addressed. The supervisor admitted she had heard comments made by the employee's peers that the young woman was affecting morale, but because no customers had complained, she didn't think it was worth complaining to the company's owners. That employee's role at the company? Key account representative! Need I say more?

The "clutter" that is beneficial to producing innovative results in the workplace includes inspirational written and visual reminders that stimulate idea generation. Sketches and notes related to a tough challenge an employee may be working on are examples of items that can lead more quickly to creative solutions if others are given the opportunity to contribute their ideas.

Information persistence—for example, displaying work in progress—has been shown to enable the environment where an individual can get assistance in producing a better result through the input of others. Moreover, visual reminders can also inspire the imagination of peers from the same or other departments, which in turn can produce better results for *their* projects as well.

Collaborative Workplace Principles

- Encourage honesty and respect
- Spontaneous interaction and group problem solving
- Exposure to others' ideas in progress
- Cognitive artifacts, displayed thinking, and visual reminders to stimulate idea generation

Myth 6: "Klogs are clunky wooden shoes from Holland."

Lessons Learned

Klogs, knowledge logs, weblogs, or blogs: Call them what you will, these technologically savvy methods of fostering collaboration on a virtual basis are important for individuals to exchange information at different points in space and time. To optimize collaboration, organizations need to look at both the physical and the virtual workplace. Increasingly, companies are allowing the use of blogs launched specifically for small workgroups who need to collaborate in a private forum. Employees need access to knowledge through both formal systems and informal sharing, both virtually and face to face.

Many organizations have reduced the footprint of individual workstations in an attempt to cut costs. While myth 5 focuses on the benefits of allowing displayed thinking and visual reminders in individuals' workspaces and team areas, the truth is that, often, there just is not enough physical space to make this possible. In cases such as this, it becomes even more important that the enterprise leverage its technology to enable information sharing and collaboration.

Organizations with a highly mobile workforce, or that offer flexible work arrangements, often transition to free-address, or "hoteling," to better utilize their overall real estate. Even when employees do not travel as part of their job responsibilities, as noted previously, many firms find they have an increasing number of empty office and workstations throughout the workday. Staff members may spend the majority of their day in structured meetings and informal interactions with others, using their dedicated workspace as merely a touchdown spot, where they quickly prepare for the next event. It's becoming more difficult to justify providing a dedicated workspace for each full-time employee in the workplace. As a result, the concept of the unassigned workplace will be increasingly put into effect in the business world.

Sophisticated technology already exists to manage the complexity of checking workspace availability, reserving rooms when necessary, and accounting for cancellations and "no shows." The scheduling process can incorporate audiovisual equipment requests, specific room setups, and catering requirements. The only challenge left to tackle is human resistance to change.

Collaborative Workplace Principles
- Spontaneous interaction and group problem solving
- Access to knowledge via structured system
- Informal knowledge discovery
- Multiple ways of connecting people quickly
- Surround people with every tool imaginable

Myth 7: "Employees will recognize all that they're gaining in the new collaborative environment, and thank us."

Lessons Learned

In the new collaborative environment, what employees generally notice first is that private offices are taken away, workspaces shrink, and individual resources have to be shared. Successful business communication focuses first on the positive outcomes being planned, followed by how the advancements will be achieved (often, by compromise). Announcing physical workplace changes is no different. Those charged with introducing new workplace strategies need to proactively sell the positive, while being honest about how it will be accomplished.

The importance of developing a strong workplace communication strategy—and implementing it earlier rather than later—cannot be overemphasized. While many employees are not given the opportunity to make decisions related to workplace changes, they do need to feel as though they have a voice. One key difference between successful workplace change initiatives and those that fail is the emphasis on employee involvement. In failed workplace change initiatives, employees often are heard to say they feel that change has "been done to them." Note that employee involvement does not equate to handing power to the front-line workforce. Asking for feedback and ideas from staff members should be positioned appropriately so as not to set false expectations. A request for employee feedback could include verbiage such as: "The organization values your opinions regarding the new workplace being planned. While we cannot implement every suggestion for safety, security, financial, logistical, or other reasons, we do guarantee that each comment submitted will be read and discussed by the workplace planning team."

The findings of my 10-year workplace research study reinforce the power of communication to drive physical space change. A strong communication strategy is proactive, anticipating specific areas of resistance. In many failed workplace change initiatives, the lack of communication is a key contributor to unsuccessful results. Table 7-1 itemizes a number of fundamental differences between failed and successful workplace change initiatives.

Collaborative Workplace Principles
- Free-flowing communication
- Multiple ways of connecting people quickly
- Encourage honesty and respect
- Value curiosity and restlessness

Myth 8: "Do not rock the organizational boat! Don't try to drive other changes while moving employees from private offices to the open plan."

Lessons Learned

Organizations can—and should—plan holistically and lead changes simultaneously as appropriate. Planning physical space changes in isolation, without understanding other influences on employee behavior, can result in workplace strategy failure. Many organizations make the mistake of moving personnel from private offices to the open plan to achieve collaboration before they understand the impact of the compensation system. How people are paid may escalate internal competition when employees are compensated as individuals and in the absence of a bonus for team performance. It is much easier to overcome employee resistance to change when a comprehensive plan is introduced, one that outlines all of the changes to be made, the reasons for the transformation, and how the changes are aligned with organizational, departmental, and individual goals.

TABLE 7-1 Communication Impacts Workplace Change Success

Failed Workplace Change Initiatives	Successful Workplace Change Initiatives
Employees perceive that change is "done *to* them."	Employees believe they are given a voice to influence change.
Communication occurs much too late and in response to damage already done.	Communication is planned strategically and begins early in the change process.
Communication focuses on justification of what employees are giving up in the new work environment.	Communication focuses on what employees will gain in the new environment and how it will be achieved.
Eventually, employees will be told what changes they will have to make.	Employees are educated on the business reasons the changes are being made.

The burden of successful workplace change often falls 100 percent on the shoulders of the firm's corporate real estate and facilities professionals, along with their architectural and interior design partners. When edicts are passed down from the senior executives to reduce costs through physical space changes that are not planned holistically with other organizational changes, the real estate or facility manager is forced to operate on a reactionary basis. Becoming educated on the potential risks and rewards of workplace change, and focusing on change management early in the process, positions the real estate or facilities professional to serve a consultative role, which eventually can lead to a seat at the executive table. Likewise, for architects and interior designers, a heightened awareness of the numerous barriers to workplace strategy success can elevate the role they play in influencing change at the client organization.

Collaborative Workplace Principles
- Encourage honesty and respect
- Challenge the status quo
- Free-flowing communication
- Address team and individual compensation elements

And those are the Eight Myths of Workplace Collaboration. Chances are, there are a few other myths floating around your own organization right now.

COLLABORATIVE PRINCIPLE INDEX

As mentioned at the beginning of the chapter, Paul Rosenblatt and I developed a tool called the Collaborative Principle Index to measure how well organizations are integrating the Collaborative Workplace Principles into their work environments.[3] At the end of our speaking engagements at NeoCon in Chicago and IIDEX in Toronto in 2003, we invited members of the audience to take our index survey. The results were entered into a database, which since has grown as a result of the participation of others in the survey.

Collaborative Principle Index
You are invited to participate in a brief survey on how well organizations today are integrating collaborative principles into their workplaces. Please answer each question as it relates to your organization on a scale of 1–5.

1 = Strongly Disagree
2 = Disagree
3 = Neither Agree nor Disagree
4 = Agree
5 = Strongly Agree
N/A = Not Applicable

"Don't be afraid to take a big step if one is indicated. You can't cross a chasm in two small jumps."
—DAVID LLOYD GEORGE

	1	2	3	4	5	N/A
1. Our organization does a good job of meeting the physical space requirements for both the individual and teamwork being conducted.						
2. A lack of sufficient shared resources (conference/project rooms, team spaces, whiteboards, and other work tools, etc.) creates a source of conflict in our workplace.						
3. The process of reorganizing project rooms, team spaces, equipment, and work tools reduces productivity in our workplace.						

	1	2	3	4	5	N/A

4. Our organization's leaders utilize the physical spaces created to encourage collaboration and knowledge sharing on a day-to-day basis.

5. Our current facilities standards and policies allow employees freedom to display cognitive artifacts and visual reminders, supporting information persistence.

6. Our organization has and uses technology that enables employees to share knowledge as well as work in virtual teams.

7. Employees have accepted workplace transformation (moving from private offices to open plan, smaller workstations, shared workspaces, etc.) with little resistance.

8. In our organization, workplace change is proactively managed as part of holistic organizational change, articulating to employees how the two are linked.

It's a good idea to take the Collaborative Principle Index while reflecting on the eight myths and the Collaborative Workplace Principles. It's also recommended that you distribute the survey in your own organization as a way of taking its pulse—how well is it currently integrating the Collaborative Workplace Principles? Doing so also can assist in helping your organization prioritize areas for improvement moving forward. Finally, the Collaborative Principle Index can be administered for the purpose of generating a baseline metric prior to developing a workplace strategy. Increasingly, executive leaders are requiring measurement of improvements and quantifiable evidence on the return on investment for office design projects. In conjunction with workforce productivity studies conducted prior to, and following, the implementation of the workplace strategy, the Collaborative Principle Index not only documents the success of the workplace transformation, but also identifies areas for continued improvement.

Prior to updating the results to include in the book, I made a promise to the International Facility Management Association members and their guests who participated in the IFMA LIVE Webinar entitled "Critical Influence Design: Preventing Workplace Strategy Failure."[4] IFMA hosted the forum to introduce findings from my 10-year workplace research study and to preview highlights of this book. The session was moderated by Greg Bendis, managing director, Brokerage Services, Charles Dunn Company Advisory Services. Participants were invited to take the Collaborative Principle Index online. Those who completed the survey by a designated date had the option to have their feedback included anonymously in this book. The results of the Collaborative Principle Index can be seen in Table 7-2.

Interestingly, from the time the survey was introduced, the biggest change in the results of the Collaborative Principle Index reflects a downward trend in the average response to question 4: Our organization's leaders utilize the physical spaces created to encourage collaboration and knowledge sharing on a day-to-day basis. At the time of the completion of this book, the average response to this question, as indicated in Table 7-2, was 3.348 on a five-point scale. When the survey was conducted in 2003 at NeoCon in Chicago and at IIDEX in Toronto, the average response for this same question was 3.53. We had expected to find steady improvement in executives using spaces designed to foster interaction and knowledge exchange.

The importance of business leaders modeling the behaviors expected of the entire workforce cannot be overstated. Employees at lower levels within the organization will mirror the actions of those higher up in the chain of command. If direct reports observe managers working in isolation by choice, rather than interfacing with others, they will follow suit. Do not think they are avoiding the corporate café because they are trying to reduce their intake of caffeine!

TABLE 7-2 Collaborative Principle Index Results

Question Number	Range of Responses	Average Response
1	2 to 5	3.416
2	1 to 4	3.000
3	2 to 5	3.021
4	1 to 5	3.348
5	1 to 5	3.875
6	2 to 5	3.583
7	2 to 4	3.136
8	1 to 4	2.390

NOTES

[1] Rosenblatt, Paul, and Diane Stegmeier, "From Competitive Office to Collaborative Workplace," white paper presented at NeoCon, Chicago, June 18, 2003, and at IIDEX, Toronto, September 19, 2003. Chicago: Merchandise Mart Properties, Inc., www.merchandisemart.com.

[2] Ibid. The 8 Myths of Workplace Collaboration. Presented as part of "From Competitive Office to Collaborative Workplace," white paper presented at NeoCon, Chicago, June 18, 2003, and at IIDEX, Toronto, September 19, 2003. Chicago: Merchandise Mart Properties, Inc., www.merchandisemart.com.

[3] Ibid. The Collaborative Principle Index. Presented as part of "From Competitive Office to Collaborative Workplace," white paper presented at NeoCon, Chicago, June 18, 2003, and at IIDEX, Toronto, September 19, 2003. Chicago: Merchandise Mart Properties, Inc., www.merchandisemart.com.

[4] Stegmeier, Diane, "Critical Influence Design: Preventing Workplace Strategy Failure," IFMA LIVE Webinar, February 13, 2007, www.ifma.org.

CHAPTER 8
CRITICAL INFLUENCE
DESIGN MODEL

INCORPORATING DISTINCT AREAS OF FUNCTIONAL EXPERTISE

Throughout this book, I have stressed the importance of collaboration in achieving greater innovative results for the organization. Case studies have been presented to illustrate the unending quest of business leaders to maximize organizational effectiveness. Some pursued improvements in the interaction between staff members to create competitive advantage; others, to provide excellence in customer service. Many of these executives were passionate about increasing knowledge exchange and fostering collaboration in order to leverage intellectual capital and generate a larger number of innovative ideas that had potential for the commercialization of new products or services. In nearly every circumstance, these executives felt it imperative to create a flexible infrastructure capable of adapting to future challenges, which they could not imagine at the

time they sat down with their architect and interior designer to begin discussing a workplace transformation project.

The recurring theme of interdependency has been woven throughout the book, highlighting the Critical Influences that can either enable or hinder the organization's expectations for the behaviors of its workforce, and thus the attainment of the goals established for the workplace strategy and the physical workplace solution. Elements of the Critical Influence System affecting the optimal utilization of the office environment as intended by the designer can surface regardless of the client's industry. Examples of this fact were strategically selected from organizations operating in the fields of telecommunications, government, health care, manufacturing, high technology, financial, pharmaceutical, entertainment, and professional services—including architectural and design firms, themselves—to convey the universal nature of influences on workplace behavior, and highlight factors that can positively or negatively impact the success of a physical workplace design.

In case after case, you saw the intense focus of business executives to drive interdisciplinary collaboration within the enterprise. These leaders realize strong communication is essential to collaboration and that there is significant room for improvement in their firms. Certainly, better communication between the company and its customers will enhance business-to-business relationships. However, often it is the weak internal communication links between departments, divisions, and business units—even among the functional leaders of the executive team—that raise the highest, hence most frustrating, barriers to the desired organizational results. Suboptimal performance in the company can cause customers to take their business to the competition, motivate talented employees to resign from its workforce, drive stockholders to invest their money elsewhere, and ultimately, result in the enterprise lacking sufficient human and capital resources to support the development of innovations to ensure future success.

THE CRITICAL INFLUENCE DESIGN MODEL

The Sprint Nextel operational headquarters project, the largest office campus endeavor in the United States, was intentionally spotlighted in the first chapter of this book to encourage architects and interior designers to adopt an interdisciplinary approach, when appropriate, to

produce superior results for the client organization. Here, in contrast, we'll begin building the Critical Influence Design Model on a much smaller scale than that of the 125 team members engaged in the Sprint Nextel office design. As we progress in this chapter, you'll observe how the model can grow easily based on the complexity of the client's requirements. We'll then apply the model to business issues of increasing importance to executive leaders, and take a peek at how the Critical Influence Design Model may evolve over time in response to these and emerging organizational challenges.

The Critical Influence Design Model featured in Figure 8-1 represents a simplified view of an interdisciplinary approach involving the architectural and design firm, commercial real estate advisors, and the change management consultancy. [1] In this graphic depiction, it's important to note that the architectural and design partners own the development of the workplace strategy. The real estate and change management partners contribute to the development, actively supporting the architect and designer based on their experiences with other client organizations. As often is the case in a structured collaboration of interdisciplinary specialists, the terms of engagement may be widely different between the client and each individual external partner. In addition, the entrance points on a project, as well as the levels of involvement in various phases, vary for the partners, as seen in Figure 8-2. [2]

While forging new and nurturing ongoing relationships with prospective clients is an important function of each of the three professions

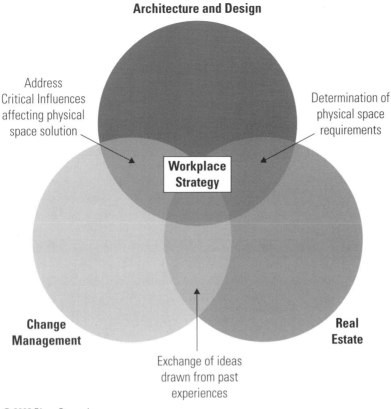

Architecture and Design

Address Critical Influences affecting physical space solution

Determination of physical space requirements

Workplace Strategy

Change Management

Real Estate

Exchange of ideas drawn from past experiences

© 2006 Diane Stegmeier

Figure 8-1: The Critical Influence Design Model illustrates a simplified view of an interdisciplinary approach involving the architectural and design firm and other key specialists supporting a workplace project (in this example, a commercial real estate advisor and a change management consultant). The architectural and design partners own the development of the workplace strategy, with the real estate and change management specialists actively supporting the architect and designer based on their experiences with other client organizations.

© 2006 Diane Stegmeier.

depicted in this version of the model, the real estate specialist is often the first of the three partners awarded a contract by the client for a workplace project. This would be the case whether or not a tactical real estate agent was signaled by an upcoming lease expiration, or a real estate advisor had an established relationship with the client, due to previous work together. In either case, a number of the real estate specialist's primary tasks may be completed early in the process, before the other two partners are engaged by the client. Increasingly, however, the change management consultancy is brought in to educate business leaders as to the impact the Critical Influences can have on the success of the workplace project at the same time the real estate advisor is preparing the statement of criteria and space program for the client. Once selected and under contract, the A&D firm becomes immersed and is highly visible during subsequent phases of the workplace project, in contrast to a tactical real estate agent whose job is complete once the real estate transaction is complete, or the real estate advisor whose role is secondary during the implementation of design and construction activities.

This advance insight of change management advisors into the

Integrated Project Timeline™

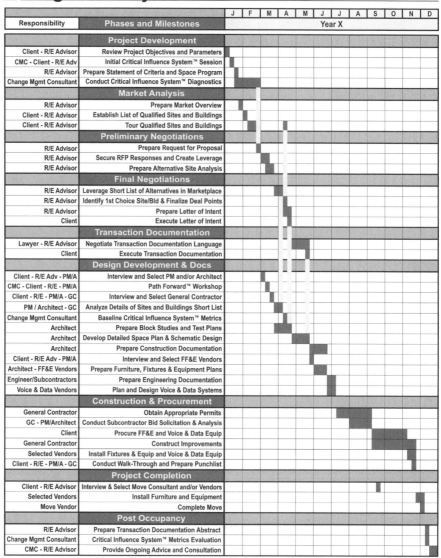

Integrated Project Timeline, © 2006 Greg Bendis.

specific Critical Influences that can create obstacles to the implementation of the workplace strategy benefit the client and the architectural and design firm in two ways:

- First, the earlier barriers impacting the success of the physical space design are identified, the greater the degree of flexibility the designer will have to make adaptations to the office concept.

- Second, the sooner the identified impediments are addressed, the lower the cost of change will be for the client on those elements of the physical space plan that the client and designer determine must be resolved with an alternative design solution.

THOUGHT LEADERSHIP OF GREG BENDIS

Greg Bendis graduated from the University of Florida with honors and a Bachelor of Arts degree in Architecture, and also completed the MBA curriculum in finance and economics at Pepperdine University. Early in his career, he was director of Real Estate for Ford Aerospace, TRW Information Services, and Latham & Watkins, and later, a commercial real estate consultant and broker. Over nearly 25 years, he has developed and implemented trend-setting real estate programs, and has completed projects in 160 cities throughout the United States and abroad.

I was honored to have Greg Bendis serve as moderator in 2007 for my IFMA LIVE Webinar, *Critical Influence Design: Preventing Workplace Strategy Failure,* during which he contributed his insight on internally positioning the facilities of the organization as a strategic asset, and building the credibility of real estate and facilities professionals as business partners to the enterprise.[3] Bendis was a client of mine beginning in the 1980s; our strong business relationship—and friendship—continue today.

"As a real estate advisor, I embrace the Critical Influence Design Model. In fact, in my own practice, I developed the Integrated Project Timeline, which also depicts the integration of architecture and design, change management, and real estate. It is true that, as a real estate professional, I often have the opportunity to involve a variety of outside resources as I serve my clients throughout the Real Estate Cycle. A case in point was when, after having developed a relationship with Latham & Watkins that transcended a number of workplace projects, I was able to introduce Callison Architecture whose work also continued on a multiproject, multiyear basis. My firm and Callison Architecture both had the consultative approach that was needed to guide Latham & Watkins to maximum organizational effectiveness in their workplace. Today, this approach continues to provide our clients a higher level of value as compared to real estate agents responding to lease expiration dates and architects responding to RFPs. The former is holistic and proactive; the latter is tactical and reactive."

—GREG BENDIS

In comparing and contrasting the roles of the three partners highlighted in this example, both the work of the architectural and design firm and of the change management consultancy will typically involve interfacing with each level of the hierarchy of the client organization. In contrast, the real estate partner's activities may be exclusively with the C-level of the enterprise.

GROWING THE MODEL TO SUPPORT COMPLEX CLIENT REQUIREMENTS

It's important to mention that in the Critical Influence Design Model, Figure 8-1, the circles representing three distinct areas of functional expertise may be expanded for a large, complex project. The interlocking circles may grow to four, five, or more spheres, representing diverse knowledge domains critical to the outcome of the project. The circle corresponding to the architect and designer may represent a number of individuals employed by several firms working together as the A&D team, as was the case on the Sprint Nextel campus in Overland Park, Kansas. The model could also illustrate the same combination of firms, with one circle representing each separate firm.

The second version of the model, seen in Figure 8-3, conveys the beginning of growth of the interdisciplinary team based on a bit more complexity in the client's business issues. In this example, an ergonomics consultant

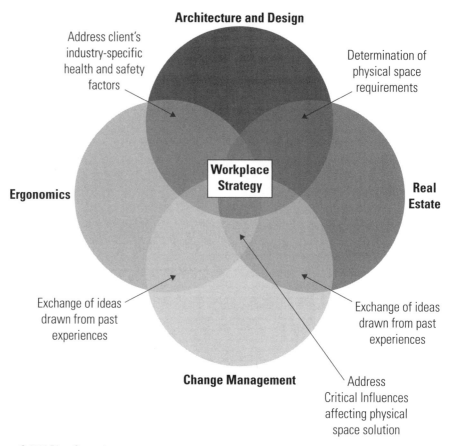

Architecture and Design

Address client's industry-specific health and safety factors

Determination of physical space requirements

Ergonomics

Workplace Strategy

Real Estate

Exchange of ideas drawn from past experiences

Exchange of ideas drawn from past experiences

Change Management

Address Critical Influences affecting physical space solution

Figure 8-3: The Critical Influence Design Model is capable of expanding as a function of the complexity of the client's business issues. In the example depicted here, the client requested the involvement of an ergonomics consultant to address the organization's unique challenges.

© 2006 Diane Stegmeier.

© 2006 Diane Stegmeier

has been brought in by the client to address the organization's unique challenges. Certainly the architectural and design firm, the real estate advisor, and the change management consultancy are well versed on the topic of ergonomics, yet the business leaders in the client company do not expect any one of these partners to be an authority on every facet of the project—just their own area of specialization. In the situation here, the enterprise was involved in a lawsuit centered on a safety issue; management was also concerned about how evolving OSHA legislation would

impact their industry. That ergonomics expert is a very important member of the interdisciplinary team, yet is not taking work from the other firms contracted by the client.

DISTINGUISHING CRITICAL INFLUENCE DESIGN FROM OTHER APPROACHES

The Critical Influence Design Model is characterized by a number of factors that distinguish it from previous office design methodologies. Although Critical Influence Design has a strong foundation in change management, it is very different from other techniques deployed to drive behavioral change in the workplace. Definitions of change management are as varied as the challenges clients face due to the ever-accelerating rate of change in today's business environment. There are change management consultants whose work is centered exclusively on the integration of new computer systems. In the workplace interiors field, there are change management specialists whose focus is limited to team-building in the workplace or to work culture change. Critical Influence Design is a multidisciplinary approach to change management and is far more holistic in nature. While culture is an important element of the Critical Influence System, Critical Influence Design goes beyond culture change. It identifies and addresses barriers to sustainable change, whether in the culture, compensation system, organizational structure, or any other factors of the Critical Influence System impacting behavior in the enterprise. But for the purpose of this discussion, I define the Critical Influence approach to change management as follows:

"Change Management is the practice of strategically guiding organizational transformation while maintaining human psychological stability and minimizing business process disruption."

When applied to workplace transformation projects, this philosophy—and the resulting approach to change management—ensures the inclusion of the elements essential to drive sustainable change. The findings of research conducted on the Critical

Influence System impacting behavior in the workplace, integrated with strategic, business management principles, and combined with sound workplace design techniques, establish the foundation for Critical Influence Design's interdisciplinary approach (see the sidebar, "The Critical Influence Design Equation").[4]

The comprehensive methodology balances the cultural, environmental, and operational elements impacting employee behavior. In contrast with other design processes, the results of Critical Influence Diagnostics can be analyzed together with the data gathered by the designer during programming to identify incongruence—for example, to compare self-reported behaviors or employee estimates of how they spend their time against findings of an exploration of the Critical Influence System—so can provide much greater insight on the effectiveness of the current workplace. The outcome of this interdisciplinary collaboration is a physical space solution that is aligned with other Critical Influences that enable, rather than erect barriers to, the achievement of the client's evolving organizational goals.

A SUSTAINABLE PLATFORM FOR CHANGE

In March 2004, I was invited to speak at the Futures in Property and Facilities Management II Conference in London, England, cosponsored by University College London, the University of Reading, and the College of Estate Management, and attended by delegates from around the globe. The topic was my work, "Critical Influence Systems: Understanding the Key Factors Enabling a Sustainable Platform for Change."[5] Perhaps the greatest benefit of participating in such an event was the opportunity to connect with those engaging in diverse research, but all centered on the physical work environment, and in particular to listen to the findings of my peers.

Common imperatives that surfaced in the three-day event were: the importance of designing flexibility, adaptability, and elasticity into the workplace; and how to meet the challenges of designing work environments today for the not-too-distant future, given the accelerating speed of change.

I left the conference imagining the current typical organization as having its workforce situated in a square box called the office environment. This physical container is intended to shelter and hold employees while they do their work. But I wondered: perhaps that box is simply a constrained space composed of four inflexible walls and stagnant, recycled air that stifles performance.

I concluded: Designers need to turn that physical container upside down, and use it as a platform that can change as quickly as the business itself changes. This horizontal plane would feel open—like a breath of fresh air—and be capable of rapidly altering its configurations based on the work being performed by its occupants. The sturdy platform—let's call it a stage—would inspire movement, collaboration, and innovation.

Continuing with the image of the workplace as a stage, on it, the "actors" (staff members) can manipulate "props" (work tools, mobile/reconfigurable furniture, portable technology, etc.) based on the changing "script" (rapidly changing organizational direction in response to the competitive business landscape, new government regulations, etc.) they are handed each day and expected to perform. In this theatrical metaphor, the executive leaders no longer direct and dictate from "off-stage" (behind the closed doors of private offices), where they are close enough to monitor and direct the every movement of individual cast members, who are reciting the same script over and over. The expectations of the audience (the organization's stakeholders) have changed. They no longer value seeing the same performance night after night; they now want to see a cast that can improvise, responding with spontaneity and creativity to unpredictable cues thrown at them. The "director" (business leader) would also perform on stage (the open office environment), perhaps assuming a number of roles, including stage hand, set designer, and coach.

How can workplace design be made as flexible as a stage set? Which "set design" is the appropriate one to guide the desired employee behaviors necessary to lead business organizations successfully into the future? What are some of the emerging characteristics of work environments designed to function as a sustainable platform for change? Here are some answers to these questions:

- *The space is branded as a tool for serving internal and external clients.* Stegmeier Consulting

> "It's not just setting the stage . . . it's how you use the stage."
> ——BRIAN FERGUSON, GENSLER

Group's Customer Centricity Workshop[6] was developed to support behavioral change in client service excellence. Following waves of downsizing, companies are often reluctant to hire additional employees when the business climate begins to improve. As a result, departments are left short-handed and the remaining staff are spread too thin. A competitive culture existing between internal functional groups due to limited resources often causes staff members to assign a low priority to (or ignore) other departmental requests for information or assistance, even though they are serving the same customers. It is in recognizing and serving customers within the organization, while balancing direct client demands, that customer centricity is achieved. The workplace must reflect and support this behavioral change as well.

- *Default behaviors are designed into the space*. According to STUDIOS Architecture's Christopher Budd, historically, the default behavior designed into workplaces in the United States is one that has the individual sitting alone in either a workstation or in a private office, with little or no interaction with others in the firm. Each person is responsible for locating the physical space necessary for one-on-one, team, or group interface. With the increasing emphasis on collaborative behavior as a means to achieve more innovative outputs for the organization, this approach is no longer effective. Budd suggests taking the reverse approach, whereby the default behavior designed into the physical environment is group-focused, and

individuals actively work to find the private space they need, when they need it. In Budd's words, the goal is to "make users active negotiators and manipulators of space to meet whatever process requirement they need at the time."

- *"Deferred customization" is applied to the workplace*. This concept, shared by Brian Ferguson of Gensler, has its roots in the manufacture of automobiles. In assembling a basic car, as it moves toward the end of the process, a custom engine is added, and, finally, it is painted in the color requested by the customer. Taking this same approach in the design of the physical space for organizations that have real estate holdings in multiple regions throughout the nation or around the globe allows optimal customization. The company image can then be tailored on a location-by-location basis to suit local desires and needs. Importantly, this approach also enables relatively easy changes in the future, since the physical space is not rigid or fixed.

- *The workplace solution strikes a balance*. Client organizations will continue to challenge architectural and design firms to ensure company dollars budgeted for the workplace are spent wisely. Providing a higher quality of surface materials and/or furniture may be considered a sound financial decision, especially if the new workplace design will result in a reduction in the quantity of private offices, or no private offices at all, such as the Design Alliance Architects' solution for Alcoa (see Figure 8-4). In the past, has the enterprise invested more money than necessary into areas that

Figure 8-4: The Alcoa Corporate Center serves as an excellent example of providing a higher quality of surface materials and/or furniture to create upscale workstations when moving managers out of private offices into the open work environment.

© 1999 Steve Hall, Hedrick Blessing.

did not produce benefits, such as spaces designed for the occasional visit of clients? Could this square footage be better deployed if converted to team space, where everyone could enjoy a great view, as adopted by Alcoa (see Figure 8-5), small meeting spaces, as designed by Whitney, Inc. for Synovate Chicago (see Figure 8-6), or unassigned private offices to be used by any staff member requiring temporary solitude, such as developed for Synovate New York (see Figure 8-7)? In the case of Hanson Dodge Creative, an advertising and branding agency in Milwaukee, Wisconsin, Eppstein Uhen Architects translated the client's top priority of entertaining guests into a variety of flexible spaces for meetings, lounging, and casual encounters (see Figure 8-8).

- *Elasticity is designed into the workplace.* The work environment being planned as a platform for sustainable change must adapt to future needs, both those that can be anticipated and those that cannot. It must respond to changes in constraints and challenges, and be capable of morphing according to the shifts in both short-term objectives and long-term organizational goals. The use of movable walls constructed of metal, glass, or other materials, while more expensive up front than drywall, will enable the work environment to be reconfigured as often as needed to support shifting requirements. Similarly, raised flooring will optimize the firm's investment in technology, and free individuals from being tethered to dedicated workstations (see Figure 8-9).

Figure 8-5: Can prime real estate—such as corner offices—be better deployed in today's evolving workplace? Rather than using spaces such as this for dedicated offices, the Alcoa Corporate Center designated "best views" areas to be used by all employees, as shown in this photograph.

© 1999 Steve Hall, Hedrick Blessing.

Figure 8-6: Casual meeting areas throughout Synovate's Chicago office help create a collaborative yet relaxed environment, allowing employees to easily have impromptu discussions.

© 2007 Whitney, Inc.

Figure 8-7: Whitney distinguished the New York Synovate office by employing a motif that reflects the cultural diversity of Manhattan and the creativity encouraged by the client. Certain rooms were named after local landmarks, such as the Carnegie Hall conference room seen here.

© 2007 Whitney, Inc.

Figure 8-8: Employees and guests at Hanson Dodge Creative, an advertising and branding agency in Milwaukee, Wisconsin, can sit and page through a variety of design-related publications at one of the many "built-ins" that encourage casual encounters.

© 2005 Eppstein Uhen Architects.

Figure 8-9: Designing elasticity into the work environment is achieved by the use of furniture that is easily reconfigurable to meet the changing business requirements of the organization, as well as the shifting work styles of end users.

Focal Point Lights; © 2004 Kevin Beswick, People Places & Things Photographics.

Last, the physical environment will become much more agile by reducing the reliance on paper, which in turn will decrease the number of filing cabinets and other storage equipment required.

THE CRITICAL INFLUENCE DESIGN MODEL: ADDRESSING EMERGING BUSINESS ISSUES

As the competitive business landscape becomes increasingly complex, it's critical to determine which distinct specializations will be needed in the future to support client workplace strategies designed to achieve their organizational goals. As discussed earlier in this chapter, the Critical Influence Design Model is capable of growing with the complexity of client business requirements. Let's now translate business issues into emerging specializations that one day could appear in a future version of the model (see Figure 8-10)

Security and business continuity are growing as driving forces for change. Whether because of the fear of terrorist attacks or natural disasters, establishments are taking the necessary precautions to protect employees, buildings, equipment,

> *"As for the future, your task is not to foresee it, but to enable it."*
> —ANTOINE DE SAINT-EXUPERY, FRENCH AVIATOR, 1900–1944

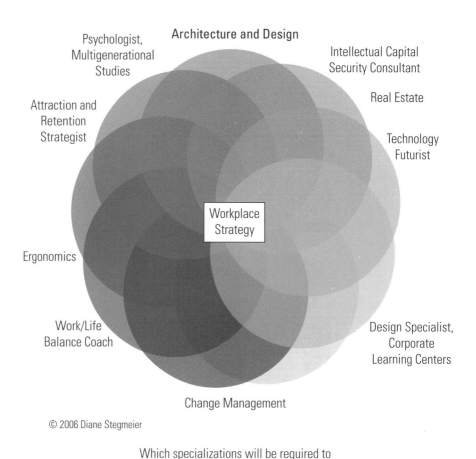

Psychologist, Multigenerational Studies

Architecture and Design

Intellectual Capital Security Consultant

Attraction and Retention Strategist

Real Estate

Technology Futurist

Ergonomics

Workplace Strategy

Work/Life Balance Coach

Design Specialist, Corporate Learning Centers

Change Management

© 2006 Diane Stegmeier

Which specializations will be required to support workplace design in the future?

Figure 8-10: The Critical Influence Design Model can easily expand to keep pace with the emerging business issues that will challenge clients in the future.

© 2006 Diane Stegmeier.

"Access to talented and creative people is to modern business what access to coal and iron ore was to steelmaking."

—RICHARD FLORIDA, SOCIAL THEORIST AND AUTHOR OF *THE RISE OF THE CREATIVE CLASS: AND HOW IT'S TRANSFORMING WORK, LEISURE, COMMUNITY, & EVERYDAY LIFE*

and paper and electronic documents. Companies are taking greater care to limit access to sensitive areas within their facilities. The wrong person gaining entry to a research and development laboratory could, for example, put intellectual capital at risk of "attack" prior to the launch of a new product. Businesses entrusted with consumers' confidential information, such as Social Security numbers, financial data, account numbers, and passwords, are increasingly challenged to find effective ways to protect that data from access by unauthorized individuals. In that effort executives will turn to experts

to determine the appropriate methods to reduce such business risks, whether the solutions come in the form of changes to the physical space, technology, or the processes used for conducting background searches on job candidates. Enter the new specialist, the intellectual capital security consultant.

Over time, issues surrounding the multigenerational workforce also will warrant increasing attention by business leaders. The lightning-speed introduction of new technologies— and obsolescence of old ones—will impact the next generation of entrants to the workforce differently from the one getting ready to retire, in terms of adoption speed and the learning curve. Does the enterprise invest in technology at the level of the least common denominator so that members of all generations employed can easily learn and utilize new tools in their work? Or does it continuously invest in the bleeding-edge technology—those electronic tools not yet fully lauched in the commercial market, when the prices are exorbitant and the "bugs" not yet worked out—in order to attract the next generation of candidates for employment—the future leaders of the company?

The business executives of the organizations will demand quantitative proof of those strategies centered on attraction and retention; they will want to know, for example: What percentage increase in job offers to candidates aged 22 to 26 are accepted? To what degree does advanced technology contribute to an individual's decision to accept an offer from the company? As the architect and interior designer begin to contemplate the appropriate workplace solution to support the client's attraction and retention strategy, to meet the organization's challenges regarding management of the multigenerational workforce, or to accommodate its decision on how quickly to adopt new technologies, they should not attempt to make the physical space solution the answer to all their client's issues. Instead, architects and designers should expect to need the support of other experts, such as a psychologist in multigenerational studies, a technology futurist, or an attraction and retention strategist. It is these specialists who will be able to identify and address barriers

to the optimal performance of the organization as it relates to specific areas of expertise—and, thus, support the success of the architectural and design firm's workplace strategy.

The workforce, too, will become more vocal in its demands in the future, especially during periods of talent shortages. Many members of the younger generations grew up as latchkey kids, watching their career-driven parents sacrifice personal relationships and experience divorce. As they begin their careers and start their own families, they will place growing emphasis on avoiding the one-track paths of their parents—that is, they will want to balance their professional and personal lives more effectively. Employers will have to support this demand through flexibility. Consequently, future workplace transformation projects may require the expertise of a professional trained to negotiate and craft customized work/life balance contracts for each employee; or perhaps develop the terms of an enterprisewide agreement, whereby the corporation provides child-care and elder-care facilities or a natural foods grocery store, or subsidizes the costs of physicians making "office calls." So, although the A&D firm will be called on to design physical space solutions for these and other emerging demands, a work/life balance coach may also be necessary to support the workplace strategy team by providing insight on factors that might hinder the workforce from performing well in the physical space.

Finally, architects and interior designers may be asked more frequently to collaborate with other members of the architectural and design community due to the need for unique skills required on a project not available within a single firm. The Sprint Nextel operational campus project described in Chapter 1 is an example of just such a complex collaboration. Its success is, in large part, due to the proper combination of talents called in to meet the organization's challenges, as well as the commitment by each team

COMMON THREADS FROM SUCCESSFUL WORKPLACE STRATEGY COLLABORATIONS

A number of common threads have surfaced from the successful collaborations of multidisciplinary team approaches to workplace design. Some emerged from clients that appointed independent experts to a workplace strategy team already in place; others from groups of experts of several firms who strategically aligned to provide the necessary combination of talents that enabled them to target a wider range of prospective clients.

- *Shared vision.* Each member of the workplace strategy team should be committed to contributing his or her expertise in the best interest of the client's vision for the project.
- *Different terms of engagement.* The contract between the client and each member of the workplace strategy team may vary greatly. Team members need to accept that each contract is dependent on the expertise the specialist is hired to contribute, the phase or phases in the project in which those skills will be utilized, and the amount of time necessary to perform the activities required.
- *Role clarity.* There will most likely be circumstances where two or more workplace strategy team members are capable of performing the same task. Thus, it is important

that roles be defined early, and put in writing. Team members need to be willing to hand over overlapping activities to an equally qualified associate, if appropriate, to achieve the client's vision.

- *Conceptual thinking.* Each workplace strategy team member needs the ability to visualize in the abstract and work in undefined, gray areas.
- *Strength and patience.* Each member of the workplace strategy team must be able to articulate new ideas clearly to others, and be willing to help others understand unfamiliar concepts.
- *Balance of approaches.* Each workplace strategy team member must be willing to balance his or her own approach with that of others.
- *Ability to compromise.* There is no one way to approach the client's project; nor is there one right workplace solution. Each workplace strategy team member must be prepared to make concessions at times.
- *Commitment to communication.* Lines of communication exist between the client and individual workplace strategy team members, as well as between workplace strategy team professionals themselves. Ideally, the client and the entire team should reach

consensus on who receives which communications, whether there should be one point of contact between the client and the team leader, or whether some other structure for sharing information throughout the project should be instituted.

- *Touchpoints.* The client and the workplace strategy team should schedule specific times to meet at critical junctures throughout the project, to share updates on individual and shared activities.
- *Realistic time frames.* Individual workplace strategy team members should estimate the amount of time needed only for their own activities, not for others. They should not commit to deadlines on behalf of other members, especially for tasks with which they have little experience.
- *Impact on others.* As workplace strategy team members make recommendations regarding actions within their areas of expertise, they must be able to recognize the implications of their actions on others on the team.
- *Shared spotlight.* Workplace strategy team members should accept the fact that they are working with the best of the best. Each individual needs to be willing to share the spotlight, and to focus on team performance.

member to contribute for the good of the workplace project. So, in the future, you may find yourself calling on an industry peer to assist in one small, yet significant, part of a project for which he or she has expertise. For example, your client, whose objective is to remain a world-class learning organization, may request that you work with a designer who specializes in corporate learning centers. By taking an interdisciplinary approach, and sharing a vision of the successful workplace solution, everyone wins.

SUMMARY

To close this chapter, I want to reinforce the importance of taking an interdisciplinary approach to designing the workplace environment. The most successful firms—and those most respected by their clients—are the ones willing to forge strategic alliances with independent experts in specific fields. Clients do not expect the architect and interior designer to be experts in everything. Nor do they expect the A&D firm to have such highly specialized individuals on its payroll full-time, for that would certainly translate into higher overall costs to the client. They would rather pay for service they need, when

they need it. Organizations across all industries have witnessed and/or experienced waves of downsizing over the past two and a half decades, and they are well aware how this has altered the way business is conducted. It's not uncommon, therefore, that some of their most highly regarded consultants are former employees who, after being right- or downsized, started their own firms and have become providers of outsourced services to the former employers.

The sidebar here summarizes lessons learned from multidisciplinary team experiences of various architectural and design firms.

NOTES

[1] Stegmeier, Diane, Critical Influence Design Model, 2006, www.stegmeierconsulting.com.
[2] Bendis, Greg, Integrated Project Timeline, 2006.
[3] Stegmeier, Diane, *Critical Influence Design: Preventing Workplace Strategy Failure*, IFMA LIVE 2007 Webinar series, February 14, 2007.
[4] Stegmeier Diane, Critical Influence Design Equation, 2007, www.stegmeierconsulting.com.
[5] Ibid., "Critical Influence Systems: Understanding the Key Factors Enabling a Sustainable Platform for Change," white paper presented at the Futures in Property and Facilities Management II Conference in London, England, March 26, 2004.
[6] Ibid., Customer Centricity Workshop, 2002, www.stegmeierconsulting.com.

CHAPTER 9
APPLYING THE MODEL

STILL NOT CONVINCED?

If you are still not convinced that the Critical Influence System—and the interdependency of its 15 elements—has significant impact on the successful implementation of a workplace strategy, the purpose of this chapter is to point out a number of reasons why office design needs to be elevated to a higher, more strategic level than in the past. A fresh approach is long overdue in the rapidly changing business environment, where organizational leaders set expectations for quantifiable, and sustainable, results.

Mergers, acquisitions, and restructuring will continue to be part of the business landscape, bringing workplace design opportunities to architectural and design firms. The diverse scope of projects will range from combining two business units from the same company following a restructuring to the complex merger of two Fortune 500 enterprises. The commonality of

the organizations going through a merger, acquisition, or restructuring is that there is no guarantee that this is the last significant upheaval the firm will go through. For the savvy architect or designer, understanding early the Critical Influence System impacting behavior in the workplace can help identify barriers that may negatively affect the success of the workplace strategy being developed to support the client's business changes. The importance of designing elasticity into the workplace is especially critical for those clients whose strategic plans for growth include acquisitions. For example, saving money using drywall to create inflexible divisions of space will cost the client more in the long run when compared to investing in reconfigurable components that can flex in response to shifting business objectives.

Leveraging the physical workplace to achieve the human resources goals of organizations will gain broader recognition for the "power of place."

And those architects and interior designers who understand the Critical Influences impacting behavior in the workplace will gain a competitive advantage in their pursuit of new business opportunities. According to the Bureau of Labor Statistics, by the year 2010, there will be 76 million baby boomers beginning to reach the age of retirement. In the United States, 10 million more job vacancies will exist than there are workers to fill them.[1] As these baby boomers begin to retire, there will be even greater need to promote knowledge transfer within the work environment. Thus, designing workplaces that foster interaction and the exchange of knowledge is critical to strengthening the intellectual capital of organizations. The heavy emphasis on attracting, enabling, and retaining talented employees will increase over time, with the anticipated shortage of candidates resulting from these retirements. Increasingly, organizations are embarking on branding initiatives tied to their attraction and retention strategies. In addition, companies that have won Great Place to Work awards are not only receiving a greater number of resumes from candidates interested in potential employment with the firm but also a higher quality of resumes, giving those enterprises a competitive advantage over other employers within their industry and/or within their geographic areas of operation.[2] Interestingly, a tremendous opportunity lies in this niche for architectural and design firms. Research results reveal that few organizations formally pursuing Great Place to Work status are leveraging the physical work environment in their business strategies.

Many attraction and retention strategies today center on recruiting younger generations, in order to begin to train the future leaders of the organization. But the expectations—and demands—of those younger workers are putting pressure on employers to help them achieve a work/life balance. This results in a number of workplace design challenges. For one, designing physical work spaces for individuals who are away from their desks the majority of the workday requires that designers accomplish seemingly conflicting goals of developing a cost-effective workplace solution that also will inspire recent college graduates to accept job offers extended by the client organization, as well as accommodate the complexities of a workplace environment that must be able to optimize the different work styles of four generations of workers. Regardless of how fluid or elastic the physical workplace is, there are limitations to what one work environment can provide at any given point in time. But by being able to articulate to your client how the Critical Influences affect employee behavior, you can help prevent causing additional incongruence and assist them to prioritize their most important needs in the office design.

There is one more reason the Critical Influence System is important to the future of office design: the emerging trend to employ real estate metrics centered on utilization, rather than on the traditional measure of building occupancy. As detailed earlier in the book, recent findings from a research study commissioned by CoreNet Global revealed that by the year 2010, 20 percent of large companies anticipate having 25 to 50 percent of their employees working in unassigned workspaces.

With the growing acceptance of this practice to cut costs and to use real estate holdings more effectively, it is anticipated that by the year 2020, the majority of large organizations will transition to the use of unassigned workspaces to some degree.[3] At minimum, a baseline knowledge of the Critical Influence System will aid architects and interior designers in acknowledging, and then addressing, so-called silent sabotage and other manifestations of resistance to change.

PRECONDITIONS FOR SUCCESS

What are the conditions necessary to ensure successful project results when employing Critical Influence Design? A well-informed, engaged, and supportive client who is enthusiastic about the power of the work environment in driving change is important. Recall Chairman Paul O'Neill's active involvement with Martin Powell and The Design Alliance team in the development of the Alcoa Corporate Center project? His decision to conduct business at a workstation in the open environment made a statement to the entire Alcoa workforce, one that could not be undermined by silent sabotage or open debate by other managers who were losing their private offices.

Another important element that greatly contributes to the success of a workplace design project is managing client expectations. As I have stressed throughout this book, do not allow the physical workplace to bear 100 percent of the burden of transforming the way people work. Along with making a commitment to your client to maintain a relationship based on mutual trust, it's important to communicate any barriers that are likely to surface, as a way to help that client define potential risks and develop an appropriate risk mitigation strategy.

Along a similar line, educating business leaders within the client organization is essential early in the project. Gather the leaders of the functional groups in the enterprise, and introduce them to the Critical Influence System; open the discussion to questions and concerns. In some cases, the session will become a lively forum for identifying areas for immediate improvement, with executives committing to activities within their areas of responsibility. If one or more Critical Influences are identified as potential or probable hindrances in advance of the development of the workplace strategy, and addressed, designers are given, essentially, a "blank canvas" on which to create the workplace solution, as opposed to being handed a paint-by-number kit with boundaries already in place, which stifle freedom of design. For the client, when barriers are revealed and resolved early in the project, while the design is still fluid, the cost of change is typically much lower. In addition, understanding the Critical Influences impacting the behavior of an organization's employees sheds light not just on environmental barriers, but also on misalignment with operational and cultural elements impacting the overall performance of the enterprise.

Unfortunately, addressing the Critical Influences causing barriers to the effective use of the work environment is not always initiated prior to the development of the workplace strategy. In fact, Stegmeier Consulting Group often is called in by the architect, designer, or client, who requests support only after the workforce has transitioned into the new environment and the space is not being used as the designer intended. Things just aren't "clicking" between the organization's expectations for the new workplace and employee behaviors. At this point, rather than revising the workplace strategy and making significant changes to the physical space, conducting an analysis of the Critical Influence System can identify areas of incongruence, which may reveal that only minor adaptations to the configuration of the space are needed.

The importance of the sponsorship and visibility of executives cannot be overstressed. The developers of the workplace strategy essentially have no power without the sanction from the highest level of the organization. In the words of Gensler's Brian Ferguson, "If you don't have the logic of muscle, you have to develop the muscle of logic to build a business case." I've seen this in practice. Vice presidents of facilities or corporate real estate may be convinced the workplace strategy can positively impact organizational change, yet they clearly lack the confidence to enroll the CEO in endorsing the physical space change throughout the project. What is missing is the ability to articulate to the CEO how the workplace is linked to the new company direction, and how, without transformation of the physical space, the merger, acquisition, or other large financial investment can fail. It's critical to encourage the CEO and his or her senior leadership team to invest their time in a Path Forward Workshop[4] to ensure alignment as they move ahead with the necessary

changes. Failure to do so raises a red flag that a rocky road lies ahead for the workplace professional, especially if he or she takes sole responsibility for driving change in the physical space.

APPLYING THE CRITICAL INFLUENCE DESIGN MODEL

Throughout this book, I've presented examples from organizations in various industries to illustrate the universal impact that certain barriers can have on the success of workplace transformation initiatives. No doubt at this point, you now have insight as to why some of the projects in which you were involved achieved less-than-optimal results for the client organization. Ideally, you have also discovered obstacles that you have not yet experienced, and that you will now be able to recognize and address before they grow to unmanageable proportions.

By way of review, in the following subsections, I highlight the key concepts spotlighted throughout the book, along with lessons learned and words from thought leaders on the "power of place."

Key Concepts: Introduction

- Critical Influence Design is the result of a 10-year exploration of why workplace strategies fail. The research was conducted to understand why appropriately designed workplace solutions failed in varying degrees, not to critique the competencies of the architectural and design firms or the design integrity of the failed workplace transformation projects.

- A key finding of the research is that innovation is increasingly an important area of focus for 89.3 percent of business leaders. These executives expressed concern with the lack of innovation in their enterprises, and recognized collaboration as a means to improving innovative outputs.
- With growing acknowledgment of the need for collaboration in the workplace, many workplace strategies have been focused on developing work environments intended to foster interaction, teamwork, and collaboration. Many attempts to drive change through workplace transformation have failed to live up to clients' expectations due to resistance to change. The effectiveness of the physical office is often analyzed after the fact, and in isolation from other influences. As a result, the workplace often is expected to bear 100 percent of the burden of transforming the way people work.

Key Concepts: Chapter 1, An Interdisciplinary Approach
- The 10-year study involving diverse organizations revealed the following:
  - The success of workplace transformation is impacted by other influences on the organization's workforce.
  - Workplace transformation presents an opportunity to drive other changes necessary for the organization's success in the future.
- Architectural and design firms are often asked by their clients to develop workplaces to encourage collaboration between functional departments and interdisciplinary groups. With clients' business requirements becoming more and more complex, they are beginning to expect architects and designers to take a more collaborative approach to their workplace projects, including calling on additional specialists to join their project teams, as appropriate.
- In the words of thought leader Ronald C. Weston, AIA, and principal, Hillier Architecture, "The success of the Sprint campus project was grounded in a commitment by all stakeholders to form a 'true design partnership.'"
- There is growing expectation among clients that architectural and design firms be able to leverage the expertise of other disciplines on workplace transformation projects. With the goal of better serving the client, professionals who are comfortable sharing their expertise with members of an interdisciplinary workplace team can realize time savings and, often, produce much more innovative design solutions.

Key Concepts: Chapter 2, The Critical Influence System
- The Critical Influence System theory formally positions the physical workplace as an influence on employee behavior, and introduces 14 other Critical Influences:
  - Vision and mission
  - Core values
  - Culture
  - Image
  - Leadership behavior
  - Compensation
  - Rewards and consequences
  - Technology
  - Knowledge management
  - Organizational structure
  - Autonomy and authority

- Business processes
- Communications
- Performance management
- Together, these tangible and intangible factors operate interdependently and can enable or hinder the achievement of organizational goals.
- With the increasing emphasis business leaders are placing on improving innovative organizational outputs, workplace professionals charged with developing environments meant to enable innovation would be wise to heed warnings of barriers that can undermine their office design solutions. The key learning is that the physical workplace needs to be considered simultaneously with the other elements. A change in one element often causes a disruption elsewhere in the system. All factors within the Critical Influence System need to be congruent, and working in harmony.

Key Concepts: Chapter 3, Creativity, Innovation, and the Innovation-Friendly Workplace
- As research results have revealed, providing the ideal office design does not guarantee that the physical space will be used as intended. Furthermore, even if the end users make their best effort to work in the space as the physical cues suggest, other Critical Influences may hinder the type of behaviors the organization requires to achieve its goals of innovative results.
- Organizational goals to bring new products, services, and approaches to market, resulting in profits for the firm, have been driving forces for business leaders as they strive to understand the dynamics of

creativity and innovation, and to develop strategies to leverage the workforce, intellectual capital, and the physical workplace to improve the quality of innovative outputs for the organization.
- In the words of thought leader Howard Gardner, "A master of change readily acquires new information, solves problems, forms 'weak ties' with mobile and highly dispersed people, and adjusts easily to changing circumstances."
- Both convergent and divergent thought processes must be supported in office design. In general, both divergent and convergent thinking can be supported by a variety of workplace settings. Common mistakes are made by assuming that because convergent thought is more analytical it is always conducted in a private space, or that work settings for divergent thinking should be designed with only groups in mind.
- The concepts of continuity and discontinuity can be applied to workplace design using flexible components (mobile furniture, technology, work tools, etc.). For example, a team forms and selects furniture components from a "kit of parts," configuring their ideal office environment suited to the tasks they will be performing, and making incremental changes to the space as necessary. At the end of a particular assignment, the collection of furniture components—and the people—scatter in different directions, each moving on to the next initiative.
- Be suspicious of workplace designs that only "look creative," but address creativity on a surface level only. When you can recognize a

mismatch with the culture, management style, level of autonomy, and processes for getting things done in the organization, these physical space solutions can quickly fail. Sound principles of behavioral psychology centered on driving change must be integrated into the workplace strategy.

- Lessons learned in developing an innovation-friendly workplace include:
  - Many workplace environments designed for innovation make the mistake of downplaying, or ignoring, the importance of performance maximization.
  - The innovation-friendly workplace must also be designed to support performance maximization through alternative choices of work settings, where an individual or groups of individuals can analyze and improve existing tasks and processes.
  - The physical workplace needs to be fluid, or elastic, to provide flexible work settings to accommodate both divergent and convergent thinking in a dynamic, ever-changing way.

Key Concepts: Chapter 4, Under the Influence

- It is beneficial to gain insight as to when workplace transformation projects are most susceptible to the Critical Influence System. Learning which circumstances produce the greatest resistance to change from the workforce will prepare the workplace strategy team in advance, enabling them to advise the client of risks to the success of the physical space design under consideration. At the same time, a heightened awareness of business

initiatives where the physical workplace is typically not being leveraged opens a new niche for the A&D firm's business development pursuits.

- Workplace strategy failure often occurs because of a failure to merge cultures following mergers and acquisitions.
- Without moving toward a more collaborative decision-making process, simply designing collaborative team spaces within the new workplace environment often proves futile.
- The most successful workplace transformation teams understand that the endeavor is not simply a facilities charge. The initiative needs to be well integrated with the expertise of human resources, information technology, and other functional areas of the company.
- The overall success of the workplace transformation is highly dependent on business leaders' commitments to model the behaviors desired of the entire staff.
- Clients may not know specifically where they should be headed in relation to the physical work environment. The challenge for the designer is the unknown—developing and designing for where the organization needs to be. Remember Brian Ferguson's football metaphor? "When you throw a pass to someone, you don't throw to where they are, but rather to where they're running."
- STUDIOS Architecture's Christopher Budd described broken aspects of the design process. More often than not, the questions asked of clients early in an office design project are not focused on how people should be working,

only on how they currently are working. This approach of self-reporting or self-perception looks at where they are today, rather than where they're headed. The architectural or design firm needs to propel the client leadership group into setting the direction and linking what the organization has to do in order to meet its goals.

- The emphasis on work/life balance and the increasingly complex multigenerational workforce will result in new challenges—and opportunities—for architects and designers. The culture of entitlement and the perception of physical space as a currency need to change in order for more progressive workplace strategies to gain acceptance. Many young people do not interpret a private office as a reward or as having much value.
- In the words of HOK Canada's Don Crichton, "Over the past three years, we have taken numerous clients through HOK's visioning process to identify their key issues and priorities. They have all indicated that attraction and retention is a major challenge."

Key Concepts: Chapter 5, Case Studies: Collaborative Workplaces That Work

- The Alcoa Corporate Center was designed by Martin Powell and The Design Alliance to offer numerous options from which a staff member can choose to work. Its design concept, that "a person's office is the entire facility," is a powerful statement to explain why this collaborative workplace works.
- Marconi Communications charged Erik Sueberkrop and the STUDIOS

Architecture team with establishing a common platform to be tested in a pilot program involving 10,050 people working in three sites within two countries, and eventually applied to multiple locations globally. Building an infrastructure that would provide sufficient variation in work settings, team organization, and work tools to fit the identified range of job profiles within the company required defining an entirely new spatial model in order to transform the old workplace attributes and culture. "Space as a right" became "space as a tool"; "information comes to me" was transformed to "I go to information"; "invisible architecture" became "messaging architecture"; and "management by control" was converted to "facilitated management."

- Goals were established for the SEI headquarters that the appropriate workplace design, developed by Meyer, Scherer & Rockcastle, Ltd., would foster a mind-set for transformation, enable the free flow of ideas, place emphasis on teams, spark creativity, and execute innovations. According to CEO Al West, "Values encapsulated in words are just not as clear and concrete as those embodied in the office itself." The work place environment would give "a physical presence to SEI values."
- The GSA WorkPlace 20\20 team engaged in projects involving dramatic shifts in both the allocation of space and expectations for leadership behavior. These professionals emphasized the importance of an organization taking a holistic approach to driving change by leveraging the workplace, yet not

setting false expectations that the physical space could take the place of other areas of expertise needed to develop a sustainable framework for behavioral change. According to Judith Heerwagen, "The physical environment alone cannot be expected to carry the burden of change. In projects such as this, experts in organizational effectiveness and change management should be engaged to help build internal support structures that reward, model, and encourage changes in behaviors, values, and relationships."

- In the words of GSA's Kevin Kampschroer, "We are affecting human behavior, and this is a building block for organizational performance. It can take a lot longer to adapt to a new way of working than an organization is willing to invest. Where organizational and change management support were not included in the project, transitioning to the new space was difficult, especially for those who did not embrace the goals and objectives for the new environment."

- In the Cisco case study, Mark Golan, vice president of the Connected Real Estate Practice and former VP of Workplace Resources, compared the utilization of office space to that used in a manufacturing facility. "Nobody would consider building a manufacturing facility that they intended to use just one-third of the time. And yet that's what we routinely do with work space."

- The Gensler case study pointed out the striking and symbolic connection between the rich character of the building the firm selected

as its headquarters and the legacy of the firm's past. A commitment was made to build on the past and move forward. To maintain the character of the physical space yet enable the workplace to support the way work needed to get done today, Collin Burry and the Gensler team designed the workplace for change. It was decided that behavioral change would need to take place as well. Employees would be expected to go to the workplace setting appropriate for the type of activity they would be doing.

Key Concepts: Chapter 6, Collaborative Workplace Principles

- It is essential that the cultural, operational, and environmental elements that enable collaborative behavior be considered throughout the office design process. Interior design alone will not generate fertile conditions for optimal performance. Other key factors, especially those that business leaders define, influence, and control, must also be considered in order for the workplace design to guide the desired employee behaviors.

- Operational elements are often more easily recognized and understood by senior management than those categorized as cultural or environmental. In general, these factors are related to issues such as technology, compensation, performance measurement, and facilities maintenance.

- Serving as an advisor to clients on the environmental elements that foster innovative behavior is a natural role for an architect or interior designer. The importance that physical space plays in guiding behavior in the workplace cannot be overemphasized. That said, it is recommended that the architect or interior designer keep the interrelatedness of environmental factors with both cultural and operational elements in the forefront of dialogue with the client. Taking a holistic approach will help to earn the client's trust much more quickly. Moreover, doing so will go a long way toward building the architectural and design firm's reputation for understanding clients' big-picture business issues, resulting in their being brought into projects earlier in the process.

Key Concepts: Chapter 7, Collaborative Principle Index

- Teaming is not the answer to all of an organization's problems; nor will moving employees from private offices to an open plan automatically result in a collaborative workplace. Many organizational tasks are still best left to individual work, and employees need to be able to balance interactive time with individual time for concentrated activities.

- Organizations typically focus narrowly on improving the collaboration of members of an individual team, yet often overlook the competition *between* the numerous teams. A great deal of organizational conflict lies in the interteam competition for limited resources, such as conference rooms, mobile whiteboards, and other work tools. The false assumption sometimes made is that moving to an open, team-oriented environment will automatically decrease the total square footage needed. If individual

teams are provided what they actually require to produce the results expected by the enterprise, it may in fact necessitate more, not less, space.

- When the physical spaces created to encourage collaboration are not being used, ask first whether business leaders are using those spaces. Leadership behavior is a Critical Influence on employee behavior. If executives are not using these collaborative spaces, it is likely that neither will the rest of the personnel.

- A key difference between successful workplace change initiatives and those that have failed is the strength of communications. In successful change initiatives, employees perceive they are given a voice to influence change; communication is planned strategically, and begins early in the change process; communication focuses on what employees will gain in the new environment and how it will be achieved; and employees are educated on the business reasons for the changes being implemented.

- A common mistake made is to assume workplace change must be driven separately from other organizational changes. Companies can—and should—plan holistically and lead changes simultaneously, as appropriate. It is much easier to overcome employee resistance to change when a comprehensive plan is introduced, outlining all of the changes to be made, identifying the reasons for the transformation, and explaining how the changes are linked to organizational, departmental, and individual goals.

Key Concepts: Chapter 8, The Critical Influence Design Model

- In the Critical Influence Design Model, the architectural and design firm owns the development of the workplace strategy. Partners in commercial real estate, change management, or any number of interdisciplinary specialties contribute to the development, actively supporting the architect and designer based on their experiences with other client organizations. In this structured collaboration, the terms of engagement, entrance points on a project, as well as the levels of involvement in various phases, vary for individual partners.

- Early analysis of the Critical Influence System results in benefits to both the client and the design firm. The sooner barriers impacting the success of the physical space design are identified, the greater the degree of flexibility the designer will have to make adaptations to the office concept. In addition, the earlier these impediments are addressed, the lower the cost of change for the client.

- To design the work environment to function as a sustainable platform for change, keep these characteristics in mind:
  - The space is branded as a tool for serving both internal and external clients.
  - Default behaviors are designed into the space.
  - "Deferred customization" is applied to the workplace.
  - The workplace solution strikes a balance.
  - Elasticity is designed into the workplace.

CONCLUSION

Recall from the Introduction that I mentioned a common complaint/concern of architects and interior designers: not being invited into the client's strategic planning early enough in the workplace design process, or at a high enough level. It's the same for facilities and corporate real estate professionals, as well as others whose work involves planning, providing, or managing physical space. Several problems arise when these professionals are brought into strategy formation late in the game. When decisions are made that will limit how the designer may develop a solution, the resulting workplace environment typically is less flexible in adapting to future changes. When architects and designers are called in to develop a workplace solution only *after* all the details of the business strategy have been put into place, the client cannot fully benefit from the knowledge and expertise of these individuals on how best to leverage the workplace in support of the attainment of other goals of the enterprise. Furthermore, if business leaders are convinced too late in the game to take a new direction with the office design, it can be much more costly to make changes than had the appropriate direction been established earlier.

The Introduction to this book also presented a personal challenge to architects and designers, in the form of three learning objectives. This was done so that you might arm yourself with the knowledge necessary to protect your workplace projects from unreasonable expectations of client organizations as they undertake to change behaviors in the workplace. To review, the objectives are:

- *Learning Objective 1:* Identify barriers to the successful implementation of workplace strategy, avoiding the common mistakes made in driving change.
- *Learning Objective 2:* Serve as a strategic business partner to the organization, and join in decision making earlier in the process.
- *Learning Objective 3:* Ensure the workplace solution does not bear 100 percent of the burden of transforming the way people work.

In closing, I remind you of my reason for writing *Innovations in Office Design: The Critical Influence Approach to Effective Work Environments*. My goal is to help you discover—at minimum—one important concept that will result in an "aha!" moment as it relates to your development of effective workplaces. Perhaps a new approach or an added insight will contribute to elevating your current level of success in your chosen field. I'd like to hear about your "ahas!" so please send me an e-mail message, at diane@stegmeierconsulting.com; that would be much less distracting to your coworkers than your shouting "Eureka" in the workplace. . . .

NOTES

[1] U.S. Bureau of Labor Statistics, http://www.bls.gov (accessed July 6, 2006).
[2] Great Place to Work Institute, http://www.greatplacetowork.com (accessed August 2, 2006).
[3] Durfee, Don, "Take My Desk—Please: By Rethinking Office Design, Companies Are Cutting Real-Estate Costs by Nearly Half," *CFO Magazine*, October 1, 2006, pp. 99–102.
[4] Stegmeier, Diane, Path Forward Workshop, 2002, www.stegmeierconsulting.com.

INDEX